# English Medical Terminology
# 医学英语词汇学
## 第2版

主　审　　白永权
主　编　　朱　元　李　莹
编　者　　朱　元　　李　莹　　白永权
　　　　　陈向京　　聂文信　　范晓晖
　　　　　晏国莉　　韦详刚　　米　乐
　　　　　詹菊红　　易　超

中国出版集团

西安　北京　广州　上海

## 图书在版编目(CIP)数据

医学英语词汇学/朱元,李莹主编.—2版.—西安:世界图书出版西安有限公司,2016.4(2025.2重印)
ISBN 978-7-5192-0595-9

Ⅰ.①医… Ⅱ.①朱… ②李… Ⅲ.①医学—英语—词汇—医学院校—自学参考资料 Ⅳ.①H313

中国版本图书馆CIP数据核字(2016)第012538号

### 医学英语词汇学(第2版)

| 主　　编 | 朱元　李莹 |
| --- | --- |
| 责任编辑 | 胡玉平 |

| 出版发行 | 世界图书出版西安有限公司 |
| --- | --- |
| 地　　址 | 西安市雁塔区曲江新区汇新路355号 |
| 邮　　编 | 710061 |
| 电　　话 | 029-87214941　87233647(市场营销部) |
| | 029-87235105(总编室) |
| 传　　真 | 029-87279675 |
| 经　　销 | 全国各地新华书店 |
| 印　　刷 | 西安真色彩设计印务有限公司 |
| 开　　本 | 889mm×1194mm　1/16 |
| 印　　张 | 20.25 |
| 字　　数 | 400千字 |
| 版　　次 | 2016年4月第2版 |
| 印　　次 | 2025年2月第2版第9次印刷 |
| 书　　号 | ISBN 978-7-5192-0595-9 |
| 定　　价 | 48.00元 |

☆如有印装错误,请寄回本公司更换☆

# Preface to the Second Edition

Two years after the publication of *English Medical Terminology* (first edition), we are glad to see that the book has served as a useful instrument for many students and instructors of medical English. This book is intended to provide medical students with an efficient and hand-on experience of medical terminology learning. For this purpose, we have selected 664 combining forms, prefixes and suffixes which are used at high frequency in composing English medical vocabulary. Also, over 1200 medical terms (anatomical, clinical and pharmaceutical) are presented in the order of body systems to illustrate the formation rule of medical terms and to cultivate a command of core medical terms among users. In addition, descriptions about each body system are provided in a plain and nontechnical manner to promote contextualized vocabulary learning. A variety of exercises are designed to keep our users active and alert when they use the book.

In the new edition, we have added a glossary of all the medical terms that are included in the book, together with their phonetic symbols and Chinese equivalents for our user's reference. To help students locate the word elements in each chapter, we added index to all prefixes, suffixes and combining forms at the back of the book. Also, Pinyin (which was designed in the first edition for the sake of overseas students studying medicine in China) has been removed since the book now enjoys wider readership among Chinese medical students.

We have made every effort to provide accurate information. However, there is no guarantee that the book will be free of errors. Hence, we are grateful for any feedback and suggestions for further improvement. Last but not least, we would like to extend our sincere gratitude to the editor Wang Menghua and all our users for their valuable suggestions and comments that have made this new edition possible.

Zhu Yuan

Li Ying

Feb. 20, 2016

# Preface to the First Edition

After thousands of years of development in medicine, a massive medical terminology system has been built up. The size of medical vocabulary is the biggest in all scientific fields which can be proven from the mere fact that a medium-sized medical dictionary would easily contain more than 100,000 terms. How to comprehend and use such terms is a gigantic problem facing the biomedical and health-related researchers and professionals.

It is never easy to understand and remember the massive medical terminology. Fortunately medical terms share some distinctive features that make these terms both comprehensible and expressive. Most terms are derived from ancient Greek and Latin, and can be divided into smaller word parts such as prefixes, suffixes, roots and combining vowels. Recognizing such word parts is key to understanding medical terminology.

This book is intended to help medical students to master medical terminology in a quick and easy way. The book explains and illustrates nearly 700 medical word parts which give rise to tens of thousands of medical terms. Through the explanation of the word parts and the exercises, readers can discover the features and rules of medical word formation and can both increase the size of their medical vocabulary and develop the ability to analyze the new terms they have never met before.

The book contains 15 chapters. The first three chapters introduce the general rules of medical word formation, pronunciation, prefixes and suffixes. The rest twelve chapters explain the word parts related to body structures and body systems. Each chapter begins with an introduction of general medical knowledge and is followed by the explanation of word parts. The word parts in each chapter are organized into different groups ranging from surgical procedures to pathological conditions. Following every group of word parts are exercises. When all the word parts of each chapter are explained, integrated exercises are provided to consolidate what readers have learnt. At the end of each chapter, we also provide the explanations for pathological conditions and diseases related to each chapter so that the readers could also gain some medical knowledge while studying this book.

This book is compiled for undergraduate and postgraduate students in medical schools and universities. Also the book could be helpful to health practitioners who want to increase their medical vocabulary. Meanwhile, to facilitate the oversea medical students learning Chinese, we added Chinese explanations and Pinyin to each word part.

We are grateful to many who assisted in the preparation of this book, particularly the support from Project 985. Without this precious knowledge, time and support, this book could not be published.

**Editors**
**Jun. 23, 2013**

# Contents

## Chapter 1   General Introduction

| | | |
|---|---|---|
| Part One | Overview of Medical Terminology | 2 |
| Part Two | Structure of a Medical Term | 2 |
| Part Three | Pronunciation of Medical Terms | 5 |
| Part Four | Spelling of Medical Terms | 7 |
| Part Five | Integrated Practice | 8 |

## Chapter 2   Suffixes

| | | |
|---|---|---|
| Part One | Introduction | 10 |
| Part Two | Combining Forms and Suffixes | 11 |
| Part Three | Integrated Practice | 21 |
| Part Four | Supplementary Readings | 22 |
| Part Five | Review Sheet | 24 |

## Chapter 3   Prefixes

| | | |
|---|---|---|
| Part One | Introduction | 26 |
| Part Two | Combining Forms and Prefixes | 27 |
| Part Three | Integrated Practice | 40 |
| Part Four | Supplementary Readings | 42 |
| Part Five | Review Sheet | 43 |

## Chapter 4   Body Structure & Directional Terms

| | | |
|---|---|---|
| Part One | Basic Body Structures & Directional Terms | 47 |
| Part Two | Combining Forms, Prefixes and Suffixes | 49 |
| Part Three | Integrated Practice | 56 |
| Part Four | Supplementary Readings | 57 |
| Part Five | Review Sheet | 58 |

## Chapter 5  Respiratory System

| | | |
|---|---|---|
| Part One | Overview of the System | 61 |
| Part Two | Combining Forms, Prefixes and Suffixes | 63 |
| Part Three | Integrated Practice | 72 |
| Part Four | Supplementary Readings | 74 |
| Part Five | Review Sheet | 76 |

## Chapter 6  Digestive System

| | | |
|---|---|---|
| Part One | Overview of the System | 79 |
| Part Two | Combining Forms, Prefixes and Suffixes | 81 |
| Part Three | Integrated Practice | 94 |
| Part Four | Supplementary Readings | 95 |
| Part Five | Review Sheet | 97 |

## Chapter 7  Cardiovascular System

| | | |
|---|---|---|
| Part One | Overview of the System | 100 |
| Part Two | Combining Forms, Prefixes and Suffixes | 102 |
| Part Three | Integrated Practice | 112 |
| Part Four | Supplementary Readings | 113 |
| Part Five | Review Sheet | 115 |

## Chapter 8  Lymphatic System and Immunity

| | | |
|---|---|---|
| Part One | Overview of the System | 118 |
| Part Two | Combining Forms, Prefixes and Suffixes | 119 |
| Part Three | Integrated Practice | 128 |
| Part Four | Supplementary Readings | 130 |
| Part Five | Review Sheet | 131 |

## Chapter 9  Nervous System

| | | |
|---|---|---|
| Part One | Overview of the System | 134 |

| Part Two | Combining Forms, Prefixes and Suffixes | 136 |
| Part Three | Integrated Practice | 145 |
| Part Four | Supplementary Readings | 148 |
| Part Five | Review Sheet | 150 |

## Chapter 10  Endocrine System

| Part One | Overview of the System | 153 |
| Part Two | Combining Forms, Prefixes and Suffixes | 155 |
| Part Three | Integrated Practice | 164 |
| Part Four | Supplementary Readings | 165 |
| Part Five | Review Sheet | 167 |

## Chapter 11  Urinary System

| Part One | Overview of the System | 170 |
| Part Two | Combining Forms, Prefixes and Suffixes | 171 |
| Part Three | Integrated Practice | 180 |
| Part Four | Supplementary Readings | 182 |
| Part Five | Review Sheet | 184 |

## Chapter 12  Reproductive System

| Part One | Overview of the System | 187 |
| Part Two | Combining Forms, Prefixes and Suffixes | 189 |
| Part Three | Integrated Practice | 201 |
| Part Four | Supplementary Readings | 201 |
| Part Five | Review Sheet | 204 |

## Chapter 13  Musculoskeletal System

| Part One | Overview of the System | 207 |
| Part Two | Combining Forms, Prefixes and Suffixes | 209 |
| Part Three | Integrated Practice | 222 |
| Part Four | Supplementary Readings | 223 |

| Part Five | Review Sheet | 226 |

## Chapter 14  Integumentary System

| Part One | Overview of the System | 229 |
| Part Two | Combining Forms, Prefixes and Suffixes | 230 |
| Part Three | Integrated Practice | 237 |
| Part Four | Supplementary Readings | 238 |
| Part Five | Review Sheet | 239 |

## Chapter 15  Special Senses: The Eye and The Ear

| Part One | Overview of the System | 242 |
| Part Two | Combining Forms, Prefixes and Suffixes | 244 |
| Part Three | Integrated Practice | 253 |
| Part Four | Supplementary Readings | 256 |
| Part Five | Review Sheet | 257 |

| Appendix 1 | Glossary | 259 |
| Appendix 2 | Medical Word Elements and Their Meanings | 300 |
| Appendix 3 | Keys to Exercises in Integrated Practice | 311 |

# Chapter 1  General Introduction

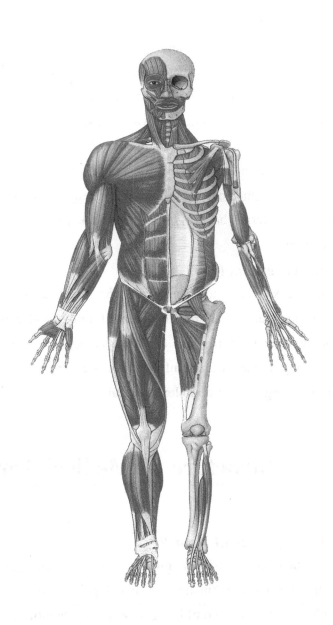

# Part One  Overview of Medical Terminology

## *What is medical terminology?*

Medical terminology is a special vocabulary used by health professionals for accurately describing the human body and its associated components, conditions (both healthy and diseased) and processes. Effective medical communication is only possible if the medical terms and their well-defined concepts are known and used correctly. The western medical knowledge originated from ancient Greek and Rome. As a result, words and word parts derived from Greek and Latin languages prevail in medical terminology. It is estimated that over seventy five percent of medical terms are based either on Greek or Latin, which explains why most medical terms have etymological background and can be divided into meaningful component parts.

## *How to study medical terminology?*

It is a daunting task trying to memorize tens of thousands of medical terms. Fortunately, most medical terms can be decomposed into smaller word parts, and the learning and memorization of the terms can easily be achieved through breaking them into component parts. As long as the meaningful word parts are properly understood, one can easily figure out the meanings of the complex medical terms.

# Part Two  Structure of Medical Term

## *What's the structure of medical terms?*

Medical terms contain high density of information and often squeeze an entire phrase into a single word through the combination of meaningful word parts. These word parts include: **roots**, **prefixes**, **suffixes**, **combining vowels** and **combining forms**. Familiarity with these word parts is essential in the understanding of medical terms. Take the word

## Chapter 1  General Introduction

"*polyneuritis*" for example. The word is composed of a prefix *poly-*, a root *neur/*, and a suffix-*itis*. To figure out what this word means, all one needs to do is to identify the meanings of these three word parts.

The **root** is the fundamental unit of each medical term and forms the primary meaning of the term. Unlike general English words in which roots can usually stand alone, most roots in medical terms need to be combined with other parts. A slash ( / ) is used to indicate the root, and in the above example, the root *neur/* means *nerve*.

The **suffix** is the word ending that follows a root. The suffix usually modifies the meaning of the root or indicates its grammatical function. In this book, suffixes are indicated by a hypen (-) in the front. The meaning of the suffix-*itis* is *inflammation*.

The **prefix** is the word part added before a root. The prefix can also modify the meaning of the root and is followed by a hyphen. The meaning of *poly-* is *many*.

The understanding of a medical term usually starts from the suffix. Once the suffix is identified, you can then move back to the beginning and finish the rest of the term. Hence, the explanation of polyneuritis is "the inflammation (*-itis*) of many (*poly-*) nerves (*neur/*).

### What's the combining form?

To make a medical term easier to pronounce, a **combining vowel** is often used to link the root and the suffix or to link the two roots. The letter *o* is the most commonly used combining vowel. Occasionally, *i* can also serve as the combining vowel, as in the word *centimeter*.

The **combining form** refers to the root joined with a combining vowel. The combining form for *nerve* is *neur/o*. The term *neurology* is composed of a combining form *neur/o* and a suffix-*logy* (meaning *the study of*).

The combining vowel is not always present in medical terms. It is omitted if the suffix itself begins with a vowel. In the term *neuritis*, the combining vowel is taken away because the suffix-*itis* (meaning *inflammation*) begins with a vowel.

The omitting of the combining vowel only applies when the combining form joins with a suffix. When two combining forms join together, however, the combining vowel shall be maintained even if the second one begins with a vowel. Look at *gastroenterology*, the term contains two combining forms *gastr/o* (meaning *stomach*) and *enter/o* (meaning *intestine*) and one suffix-*logy*. Notice how we retain the *o* in *gastr/o* when we join it with another combining form that also begins with a vowel. Also, based on what you have learned above, you can probably figure out that the meaning of *gastroenterology* is *the study of stomach and intestine*.

### Exercise 1

**Fill in the blanks with the terms you have learned in the above passage.**

1. The foundation of a term is called _____.
2. The _____ is the word ending that modifies the meaning of the term or indicates its grammatical function.
3. The _____ is the word element added to the beginning of a term.
4. The letter that links a suffix to a root, or a root to another root is called _____.
5. A combining form is a _____ with a/an _____ attached.

### Exercise 2

**Decide whether each of the following statements is true (T) or false (F).**

1. "O" is the only combining vowel used in medical terms. _____
2. Definition of medical terms usually begins with defining the suffix first, the prefix second, and the root(s) last. _____
3. When a suffix beginning with a vowel is attached to a combining form, both the combining vowel and the vowel in the suffix are omitted. _____
4. When two combining forms join together, the combining vowel of the first one is omitted if the second one begins with a vowel. _____

# Chapter 1  General Introduction

## Part Three  Pronunciation of Medical Terms

### Stress

Most medical terms contain many syllables (*multisyllabic*) and are, thus, quite long. Generally speaking, for multisyllabic vocabulary, the stress falls on either the second to the last syllable or the third to the last syllable.

The stress is placed on the second to the last syllable with words ending in "ic", "ia", "sion" or "tion".

e.g.

    sTAtic                Vision

    cePHAlic            inCIsion

    neuRALgia           soLUtion

    dysPLAsia           opeRAtion

The stress is placed on the third to the last syllable with words ending in "cy", "ty", "gy", "ous" or "al".

e.g.

    conSIstency          sponTAnious

    sensiBIlity           CORtical

    psyCHOlogy          CERvical

There are always exceptions to the above rules. However, when pronouncing medical terminology, you won't be wrong too far if you place the stress somewhere around the combining vowel, or, if the combining vowel is omitted, on the initial vowel of the suffix.

e.g.

    cardiOlogy           arthRItis

    encephaLOpathy     neuROma

    duodeNOstomy       aNEmia

    heMOlysis

## Sound omission

For certain letter combinations, when they appear at the beginning of a term, their first letter is not pronounced; when they appear in other positions, the first letter has the usual pronunciation. For example,

❖ Initial *gn* has the "n" sound as in *gnathitis* (næˈθaɪtɪs); elsewhere, it is pronounced as in *prognosis* (prɒgˈnoʊsɪs).

❖ Initial *mn* has the "n" sound as in *mnemonic* (nɪˈmɒnɪk); elsewhere, it is pronounced as in *insomnia* (ɪnˈsɒmnɪə).

❖ Initial *pt* has the "t" sound as in *ptosis* (ˈtoʊsɪs); elsewhere, it is pronounced as in *September* (sɛpˈtɛmbər).

❖ Initial *pn* has the "n" sound as in *pneumonia* (njuːˈmoʊnɪə); elsewhere, it is pronounced as in *hypnosis* (hɪpˈnoʊsɪs).

❖ Initial *ps* has the "s" sound as in *psychology* (saɪˈkɒlədʒɪ); elsewhere, it is pronounced as in *hips* (hɪps).

## Confusing sounds

Some consonants that might lead to confusion in pronunciation include:

❖ c before *a*, *o*, *u* and at the final position of a term has the "k" sound, as in *cardiac* (ˈkɑrdɪˌæk).

❖ c before *e* or *i* has the "s" sound, as in *thoracic* (θɒˈræsɪk).

❖ g before *a*, *o*, *u* has the "g" sound, as in *gonad* (ˈgɒnæd).

❖ g before *e* or *i* has the "j" sound, as in *gingivitis* (ˌdʒɪndʒəˈvaɪtɪs).

❖ Initial *x* has the "z" sound, as in *xerodermia* (ˌzɪərəˈdəmɪə); elsewhere, it sounds like *x* in *wax* (wæks).

❖ *ph* has the "f" sound, as in *phrenic* (ˈfrɛnɪk).

❖ *ch* has the "k" sound, as in *chronic* (ˈkrɒnɪk).

❖ The combination *rh* and *rrh* has the "r" sound, as *diarrhea* (ˌdaɪəˈrɪə), and *rhinitis* (raɪˈnaɪtɪs).

Chapter 1    General Introduction

*Pronounce the following terms. Pay attention to the underlined letter(s).*

1. chord
2. xenophobia
3. laryngeal
4. laryngotomy
5. thoracic

6. psychiatry
7. pharmacy
8. rheumatic
9. gnathic
10. gastralgia

## Part Four  Spelling of Medical Terms

### *Alternative spellings*

The spellings of diphthongs (double vowel) are often different in British and American English. In British English, the unpronounced vowel tends to be retained in spelling, whereas in American English, the word is recorded as it sounds. In this book, the American spelling system is adopted. Here is the list of the alternative spellings.

| Alternative spelling | British | American |
|---|---|---|
| *ae* for *e* | aetiology | etiology |
| | faeces | feces |
| | haematology | hematology |
| *oe* for *e* | oedema | edema |
| | diarrhoea | diarrhea |
| | coeliac | celiac |
| *our* for *or* | tumour | tumor |
| *re* for *er* | fibre | fiber |

### *Confusing spellings*

Be careful of the terms with confusing spellings. Some medical terms have similar pronunciation but different spellings. For example, *ileum*, meaning a part of the small intestine, is pronounced the same as the word *ilium*, which is a part of the hipbone. *Ile/o* is the combining form for small intestine while *ili/o* is the combining form for hipbone.

There are also a lot of words with similar spellings but different meanings, such as *abduction* and *adduction*, *artery* and *arteriole*, *faces* and *feces*, etc. Avoid misspellings resulting from carelessness or confusing sounds.

## Part Five  Integrated Practice

### Exercise 4

*Select the correct answer to complete each of the following statements. Note that there may be more than one correct answer to some questions.*

1. The root for nerve is _____.
   a. neur  b. neuro
   c. neural  d. neurology

2. A combining form is a word root plus a/an _____.
   a. prefix  b. suffix
   c. combining vowel  d. other root

3. An element at the end of a medical term is a _____.
   a. root  b. suffix
   c. prefix  d. combining form

4. The term "subhepatic" means pertaining to under the liver. In this word, *sub-* is a _____.
   a. root  b. suffix
   c. prefix  d. combining form

5. Interpretation of a medical term usually starts with defining the _____.
   a. suffix  b. prefix
   c. root  d. combining form

6. The foundamental unit of a medical term is called the _____.
   a. root  b. prefix
   c. suffix  d. combining vowel

7. The combination *ps* at the beginning of a term is usually pronounced _____.
   a. "s" as in *sad*          b. "p" as in *paper*
   c. "ps" as in *hips*        d. "f" as in *photo*
8. The letter *c* at the beginning of a term has the "s" sound when it is followed by _____.
   a. a            b. e
   c. e,i          d. a,o,u
9. The letter *g* at the beginning of a term has the "g" sound when it is followed by _____.
   a. a            b. e
   c. e,i          d. a,o,u
10. The alternative spelling of *etiology* is _____.
    a. itiology    b. aetiology
    c. eatiology   d. eetiology

# Chapter 2  Suffixes

## Part One  Introduction

The suffix is the element that is placed at the end of a word to modify its meaning or indicate its grammatical property, such as the part of speech or the singular or plural form. Suffixes indicating part of speech are frequently used in general English. However, there are a lot of word endings used specifically in medical science to denote certain changes, conditions or procedures.

Medical terminology contains both simple suffixes and compound suffixes. Simple suffixes refer to the word endings that have nothing else added to them, such as *-al* in *dental* (meaning *pertaining to teeth*), or *-itis* in *neuritis*. Compound suffixes are formed by adding one or more element to a simple suffix. The compound suffix *-logy* is made up of a root *log* and a simple suffix *-y*. There are many compound suffixes in medical terminology. Sometimes the suffix itself can have a complete structure. The compound suffix *-ectomy* is composed of a prefix *ec-* (out), a root *tom/* (to cut) and a suffix *-y* (the process), meaning *the process of cutting out* or *excision*.

In this chapter, we will study some commonly used medical suffixes sorted in different categories. But before that, we will first introduce some combining forms.

# Part Two  Combining Forms and Suffixes

**Common Combining Forms**

| Combining Forms | Meanings | Combining Forms | Meanings |
|---|---|---|---|
| aden/o | gland | gastr/o | stomach |
| angi/o | vessel | hemat/o, hem/o | blood |
| arthr/o | joints | hepat/o | liver |
| bi/o | life | iatr/o | treatment |
| cardi/o | heart | my/o | muscle |
| cephal/o | head | neur/o | nerve |
| cyt/o | cell | psych/o | mind |
| electr/o | electricity | path/o | disease |
| encephal/o | brain | oste/o | bone |
| enter/o | small intestine | rhin/o, nas/o | nose |

**Suffixes**

### Group 1  Suffixes for Pathological Conditions

❖ *-algia*, *-dynia*       *pain* 疼痛

gastralgia — pain of the stomach

myalgia — _____

neurodynia — _____

osteodynia — _____

❖ *-cele*       *hernia* 疝 ; *protrusion* 膨出

hepatocele — hernia of the liver

encephalocele — _____

❖ *-itis*　　　　　　　　***inflammation* 炎症**
arthritis　　　　　　　　inflammation of the joint
hepatitis

❖ *-lysis*　　　　　　　　***breaking down, separation* 溶解**
hemolysis　　　　　　　　breaking down of the blood cells
arthrolysis

❖ *-megaly*　　　　　　　***enlargement* 增大**
cardiomegaly　　　　　　enlargement of the heart
hepatomegaly

❖ *-oma*　　　　　　　　***tumor, mass or swelling* 肿瘤,肿胀**
myoma　　　　　　　　　tumor of the muscle
osteoma
hematoma　　　　　　　　a mass of blood

❖ *-osis*　　　　　　　　***abnormal condition* 病变**
psychosis　　　　　　　　abnormal condition of the mind
neurosis

❖ *-pathy*　　　　　　　　***disease* 疾病**
neuropathy　　　　　　　disease of the nerve
adenopathy

❖ *-plegia*　　　　　　　***paralysis* 麻痹,瘫痪**
cardioplegia　　　　　　　paralysis of the heart
myoplegia

❖ *-ptosis*　　　　　　　　***dropping, downward displacement* 下垂**
gastroptosis　　　　　　　downward displacement of the stomach
enteroptosis

## Chapter 2  Suffixes

❖ **-spasm**          *involuntary contraction* 痉挛
  myospasm        involuntary contraction of muscle
  enterospasm     _____

### Exercise 1

*Explain the meanings of the following suffixes.*

1. -spasm  _____
2. -itis    _____
3. -oma    _____
4. -algia  _____
5. -dynia  _____
6. -plegia _____
7. -osis   _____
8. -megaly _____
9. -cele   _____
10. -pathy _____
11. -ptosis _____

### Exercise 2

*Divide each of the following terms into its component parts with a slash (/) and explain its meaning.*

1. myopathy _____
2. neuralgia _____
3. neurosis _____
4. adenocele _____
5. cardiopathy _____
6. gastrospasm _____
7. hematoma _____
8. hemolysis _____
9. adenodynia _____
10. cardiomegaly _____

## Group 2  Suffixes for Surgical and Diagnostic Procedures

❖ **-centesis**            *surgical puncture* 穿刺
thoracocentesis            surgical puncture into the chest
(thorac/o = chest)
arthrocentesis             _____

❖ **-ectomy**              *surgical removal* 切除
hepatectomy                removal of the liver
neurectomy                 _____

❖ **-gram**                *record, image* 图像
electroencephalogram       record of the electric activity of the brain
angiogram                  _____

❖ **-graph**               *instrument to record* 仪器
electrocardiograph         instrument to record the electric activity of the heart
electromyograph            _____

❖ **-graphy**              *process of recording* 描计;记录
angiography                process of recording the (x-ray) image of the vessel
arthrography               _____

❖ **-meter**               *instrument to measure* 测量仪
cytometer                  instrument to measure cells
thermometer                _____
(therm/o = heat)

❖ **-metry**               *process of measuring* 测量术
pelvimetry                 process of measuring the pelvis
craniometry                _____
(crani/o = cranium)

## Chapter 2  Suffixes

❖ **-opsy**     *viewing* 观看
biopsy          viewing of the living tissue
necropsy        viewing of the dead body
( necr/o = dead )

❖ **-plasty**   *surgical repair* 修复,修复术
rhinoplasty     surgical repair of the nose
angioplasty     _____

❖ **-scope**    *instrument to view* 内镜
gastroscope     instrument to view into the stomach
enteroscope     _____

❖ **-scopy**    *process of viewing* 检查
abdominoscopy   process of viewing into the abdomen
arthroscopy     _____

❖ **-tomy**     *surgical incision* 切开术
osteotomy       surgical incision into the bones
myotomy         _____

### Exercise 3

*Explain the meanings of the following suffixes.*

1. -plasty   _____      7. -ectomy   _____
2. -graphy   _____      8. -scopy    _____
3. -scope    _____      9. -gram     _____
4. -meter    _____     10. -opsy     _____
5. -tomy     _____     11. -graph    _____
6. -centesis _____     12. -metry    _____

# *English Medical Terminology*

## Exercise 4

*Divide each of the following terms into its component parts with a slash (/) and explain its meaning.*

1. arthrotomy _____
2. angiography _____
3. gastrectomy _____
4. neuroplasty _____
5. arthrocentesis _____
6. electroencephalogram _____
7. rhinoscope _____
8. biopsy _____
9. electromyograph _____
10. enteroscopy _____

### Group 3  Noun Suffixes

❖ **-er**　　　　　　　　　　　*one who* 者
radiographer　　　　　　　　one who takes X-ray images
researcher　　　　　　　　　_____

❖ **-ia**　　　　　　　　　　　*condition* 状态
neuralgia　　　　　　　　　　painful conditions of nerves
megalocardia　　　　　　　　_____
(megal/o = large)

❖ **-iatry, -iatrics**　　　　　　*treatment* 治疗
psychiatry　　　　　　　　　treatment of mental illness
pediatrics　　　　　　　　　　_____
(ped/o = child)

# Chapter 2　Suffixes

| | | |
|---|---|---|
| ❖ *-ian , -cian* | *specialist* 专家 | |
| pediatrician | specialist in treating children's illness | |
| physician | | |
| ❖ *-ism* | *condition of* 状态 | |
| mutism | condition of being mute | |
| embolism | condition of the blockage of vessel | |
| ❖ *-ist* | *specialist* 专家 | |
| dentist | specialist in the study of teeth | |
| pharmacist | | |
| ❖ *-logy* | *study of* 学（科） | |
| psychology | study of the mind | |
| biology | | |
| ❖ *-sis* | *condition* 状态 | |
| centesis | condition of surgical puncture | |
| genesis | | |
| ❖ *-um* | *structure* 器官； *tissue* 组织 | |
| cardium | heart | |
| osteum | | |

**Exercise 5**

*Underline the suffixes in the following terms.*

1. gastrium
2. kinesis
3. amnesia
4. atrium
5. dentist
6. pathology
7. obstetrician
8. podiatry
9. abductor
10. alcoholism

## Group 4  Adjective Suffixes

| Suffixes | Examples |
|---|---|
| -ac | cardiac |
| -al | neural |
| -ar | muscular |
| -ary | biliary |
| -eal | laryngeal |
| -ial | medial |
| -ic | psychiatric |
| -ical | surgical |
| -ous | venous |
| -tic | hemolytic |

**Exercise 6**

***Explain the meanings of the following terms.***

1. cephalic _____
2. cardiac _____
3. pharyngeal ( pharyng/o = voice box ) _____
4. arterial ( arteri/o = artery ) _____
5. fibrous ( fibr/o = fiber ) _____
6. tonsillar ( tonsill/o = tonsil ) _____
7. maxillary ( maxill/o = upper jaw ) _____
8. metrical ( metr/i = measure ) _____
9. dietary _____
10. anatomical _____

Chapter 2  Suffixes

## Group 5  More Suffixes

❖ *-ad*                          *toward* 朝向
cephalad                         toward the head
caudad                           toward the tail
(caud/o = tail)

❖ *-cyte*                        *cell* 细胞
hematocyte                       blood cell
osteocyte                        _____

❖ *-form*                        *in the form of*, *resembling* 形状⋯样的
muciform                         resembling mucus
spongiform                       _____

> **Tips**: When *-form* is attached to a root, *i* is often used as the combining vowel. More examples include *oviform*, *papilliform*, etc.

❖ *-genic*                       *producing* 生成; *produced by* 源自⋯
carcinogenic                     pertaining to causing cancer
pathogenic                       _____
iatrogenic                       pertaining to being produced by treatment
(iatr/o = treatment)

❖ *-genesis*                     *formation* 生成
osteogenesis                     formation of the bones
carcinogenesis                   _____

❖ *-oid*                         *resembling* ⋯样的; *derived from* 源自⋯
ameboid                          resembling ameba

| | | |
|---|---|---|
| angioid | | |
| lymphoid | derived from lymph | |

❖ **-some**     ***body* 体**

chromosome     colored body

(chrom/o = color)

cytosome

❖ **-tome**     ***instrument to cut* 刀**

arthrotome     instrument to cut the joints

osteotome

### Exercise 7

*Explain the meanings of the following suffixes.*

1. -genic  _____
2. -oid  _____
3. -form  _____
4. -some  _____
5. -genesis  _____
6. -tome  _____
7. -ad  _____
8. -cyte  _____

### Exercise 8

*Match the terms in Column I with their meanings in Column II. Place the correct letter of the definition to the left of the term.*

| Column I | Column II |
|---|---|
| ____ 1. microtome | a. resembling a sphere or a ball |
| ____ 2. cytosome | b. formation of bones |
| ____ 3. diskiform | c. an instrument to cut something small |
| ____ 4. neurocyte | d. the cell body |
| ____ 5. spheroid | e. pertaining to causing disease |
| ____ 6. osteogenesis | f. pertaining to toward the head |
| ____ 7. pathogenic | g. a nerve cell |
| ____ 8. cephalad | h. resembling the form of a disk |

Chapter 2  Suffixes

# Part Three   Integrated Practice

**Exercise 11**

*Select the correct answer to complete each of the following statements.*

1. An abnormal mass, or tumor, is indicated by the suffix _____.
   a. -itis     b. -algia     c. -oma     d. -on
2. The suffix which means the study of is _____.
   a. -logy     b. -ist     c. -logist     d. -osis
3. The suffix which means surgical removal is _____.
   a. -tomy     b. -ectomy     c. -stomy     d. -tome
4. The suffix which means dropping is _____.
   a. -tome     b. -cide     c. -ptosis     d. -odynia
5. Which suffix does not indicate surgical procedure?
   a. -tomy     b. -ectomy     c. -plasty     d. -megaly
6. Which suffix does not indicate pathological condition?
   a. -oma     b. -ptosis     c. -pathy     d. -graphy
7. Which of the following suffix is not a noun suffix?
   a. -ism     b. -logy     c. -sis     d. -ous
8. Which suffix means pain?
   a. -algia     b. -dynia     c. -itis     d. both a and b
9. Which suffix is not an adjective suffix?
   a. -eal     b. -ous     c. -al     d. -sis
10. Which suffix does not indicate an instrument?
    a. -meter     b. -tome     c. -scope     d. -opsy

**Exercise 12**

*Explain the meanings of the following terms related to the liver.*

1. hepatology _____

2. hepatologist _____
3. hepatalgia _____
4. hepatodynia _____
5. hepatomegaly _____
6. hepatoma _____
7. hepatosis _____
8. hepatopathy _____
9. hepatotomy _____
10. hepatectomy _____
11. hepatogenesis _____
12. hepatogram _____
13. hepatography _____
14. hepatoplasty _____
15. hepatocyte _____
16. hepatocentesis _____
17. hepatocele _____
18. hepatitis _____
19. hepatolysis _____
20. hepatic _____

## Part Four   Supplementary Readings

**Anatomy** is the study of the physical structure of organisms. Anatomy is subdivided into gross anatomy (or macroscopic anatomy) and microscopic anatomy. *Gross anatomy* is the study of anatomical structures that can be seen by unaided eye, while *microscopic anatomy* is the study of minute anatomical structures assisted with microscopes.

**Biochemistry** is the study of the chemistry taking place in living organisms, especially the structure and function of their chemical components (bi/o = life).

**Cytology** is the microscopic study of individual cells in terms of structure, function and chemistry (cyt/o = cell).

**Epidemiology** is the study of the demographics of disease processes, and includes, but is not limited to, the study of epidemics (epi- = above, dem/o = land). It serves as the foundation and logic of interventions made in the interest of public health and preventive medicine. The work of epidemiologists ranges from outbreak investigation to study design, data collection and analysis.

**Histology** is the microscopic study of the structures of biological tissues (hist/o = tissue). It is performed by examining a thin slice of tissue under a light microscope. Histology is an essential tool of biology and medicine.

**Immunology** is the study of the immune system (immun/o = immune, protection). It deals with the physiological functioning of the immune system in states of both health and disease; malfunctions of the immune system in immunological disorders (autoimmune diseases, hypersensitivities, immune deficiency, transplant rejection); the physical, chemical and physiological characteristics of the components of the immune system.

**Oncology** is the study and treatment of tumor (onc/o = tumor). It involves the diagnosis of the tumor as well as the therapy (e.g. surgery, chemotherapy, radiotherapy) to deal with the tumor.

**Pathology** is the study and diagnosis of diseases through examination of organs, tissues, bodily fluids (biopsy) and whole bodies (autopsy). It tries to understand the nature of disease, including the structural and functional changes produced by the disorder.

**Pharmacology** is the study of drugs as well as their actions (pharmac/o = drugs). Pharmacology deals with how drugs interact within biological systems to affect function. It deals with drugs, the body's reaction to drugs, the sources of drugs, their nature, and their properties. The field includes drug composition and properties, interactions, toxicology, therapy, and medical applications and antipathogenic capabilities.

**Physiology** is the study of the normal mechanical, physical, and biochemical functions of the living cells, tissues, organs and system as well as their underlying regulatory mechanisms.

**Radiology** is the implementation of medical imaging technologies for the diagnosis and treatment of diseases. The imaging technologies include x-rays, magnetic resonance imaging (MRI), ultrasound waves, computed tomography (CT). There are two major subcategories to radiology: diagnostic radiology and therapeutic radiology.

**Surgery** is a medical specialty that uses operative techniques (both manual and instrumental) on a patient to investigate and/or treat a pathological condition such as disease or injury, to help improve bodily function or appearance, or sometimes for some other reasons. The person who performs the surgery or operation is a surgeon.

## Part Five　Review Sheet

Here is a collection of the word parts you have learned in this chapter. Write the meaning of each word part without referring to your previous work.

**Combining Forms**

| Combining Form | Meaning | Combining Form | Meaning |
|---|---|---|---|
| aden/o | _____ | hemat/o, hem/o | _____ |
| angi/o | _____ | hem/o | _____ |
| arthr/o | _____ | hepat/o | _____ |
| bi/o | _____ | iatr/o | _____ |
| cardi/o | _____ | my/o | _____ |
| cephal/o | _____ | nas/o | _____ |
| cyt/o | _____ | neur/o | _____ |
| electr/o | _____ | psych/o | _____ |
| encephal/o | _____ | path/o | _____ |
| enter/o | _____ | oste/o | _____ |
| gastr/o | _____ | rhin/o | _____ |

# Chapter 2  Suffixes

**Suffixes**

| Suffix | Meaning | Suffix | Meaning |
|---|---|---|---|
| -ac | | -cele | |
| -al | | -centesis | |
| -ar | | -cyte | |
| -ary | | -dynia | |
| -eal | | -ectomy | |
| -ad | | -er | |
| -algia | | -form | |
| -genic | | -oma | |
| -genesis | | -opsy | |
| -gram | | -osis | |
| -graph | | -ous | |
| -ia | | -pathy | |
| -ial | | -plasty | |
| -iatry, -iatrics | | -plegia | |
| -ian, -cian | | -ptosis | |
| -ic | | -scope | |
| -ism | | -scopy | |
| -ist | | -sis | |
| -itis | | -some | |
| -logy | | -spasm | |
| -lysis | | -tic | |
| -megaly | | -tome | |
| -meter | | -tomy | |
| -metry | | -um | |
| -oid | | | |

# Chapter 3 Prefixes

## Part One Introduction

Prefixes are placed at the beginning of a word to modify its meaning. Many prefixes can also be found in everyday English vocabulary. However, some prefixes are used specifically in medical terminology and studying them is an important step in learning medical terms and building up medical vocabulary.

Many prefixes end with a vowel, and if such a prefix is attached to a root beginning with a vowel, sometimes a dash is inserted between the prefix and root, as in *micro-organism*. Sometimes the vowel of the prefix could also be omitted as in *antacid*, which originally is *anti-acid*, but is later shortened to *antacid*, meaning the substance (usually alkaline) that can act against acid.

Sometimes, when a prefix ending with a consonant is affixed to a root beginning with a consonant, the consonant in the prefix may switch to the consonant in the root. This process is called **assimilation**. The following is a list of such assimilations:

*ad-* before *c* becomes *ac-*, as in *accelerate*
*ad-* before *f* becomes *af-*, as in *affinity*
*ad-* before *g* becomes *ag-*, as in *agglutination*
*ad-* before *p* becomes *ap-*, as in *appendix*
*ad-* before *s* becomes *as-*, as in *assimilate*
*ad-* before *t* becomes *at-*, as in *attrition*
*ex-* before *f* becomes *ef-*, as in *effusion*
*in-* before *l* becomes *il-*, as in *illumination*
*in-* before *m* becomes *im-*, as in *immersion*

*in-* before *r* becomes *ir-*, as in *irradiation*

*ob-* before *c* becomes *oc-*, as in *occlusion*

*sub-* before *f* becomes *suf-*, as in *suffocate*

*sub-* before *p* becomes *sup-*, as in *suppository*

*trans-* before *s* becomes *tran-*, as in *transpiration*

In this chapter, we will study most of the prefixes used in medical terminology. Some of them may already be familiar to you, even though you may not be aware of their exact meanings. You need to know that prefix is critical to the meaning of the term. For example, *hyper*glycemia (meaning high blood sugar) and *hypo*glycemia (meaning low blood sugar) describe two opposite conditions. Again, we will begin with some commonly used combining forms.

## Part Two  Combining Forms and Prefixes

**Common Combining Forms**

| Combining Forms | Meanings | Combining Forms | Meanings |
| --- | --- | --- | --- |
| cis/o | to cut | morph/o | shape, form |
| cost/o | rib | nat/o | born, birth |
| crin/o | secretion | odont/o | tooth |
| cusp/o | point | ophthalm/o | eye |
| duct/o | carry | ox/o | oxygen |
| flex/o | bend | plasi/o | formation |
| gn/o | knowledge | seps/o | decay |
| hydr/o | water | son/o | sound |
| later/o | side | top/o | position, place |
| lingu/o | tongue | troph/o | nourishment |

# Prefixes

## Group 1  Prefixes for Negation

❖ **a-**, **an-** (in front of vowel)     *not, without* 无
aseptic     free of infectious organisms
anoxia (ox/o = oxygen)

❖ **anti-**,
   **ant-** (in front of vowel)     *against* 抗，防
anticoagulant     substance that acts against clotting
antiseptic
antacid

❖ **contra-**     *against, opposite* 抗，反
contraception     prevention of conception (pregnancy)
(cept/o = receive, pregnant)
contralateral

❖ **counter-**     *against, opposite* 抗，反
counterextension     extension on the opposite direction
counterclockwise
counterirritant     substance that act against irritation
counteract

❖ **de-**     *down, from, lack of* 脱，去，除
dehydration     lack of water
decompose

❖ **dis-**     *free from, absence, separation* 脱，除
disinfection     free of infection
dislocation

## Chapter 3  Prefixes

❖ **in-,**
 **im-** (before b, m, p)                *not* 不,非

insomnia                                 sleeplessness
(somn/o = sleep)

infertile                                not fruitful, unable to have children

immobility
(mobil/o = movement)

❖ **non-**                                *not* 不,非
nonviable                                not able to survive

non-infectious

❖ **un-**                                 *not, without* 无,不
unconscious                              without consciousness

unbalance

### Exercise 1

**Draw a line between the terms and their corresponding meanings.**

1. amorphous            a. lack of fat
2. contrastimulant      b. without shape, shapeless
3. insane               c. the chemical that acts against toxin
4. countershock         d. the drug that acts against stimulation
5. dislocation          e. away from the normal location
6. antitoxin            f. the method to act against shock
7. defat                g. not specific
8. unspecific           h. not in a healthy mental state
9. nonviable            i. not able to survive
10. impotent            j. without sexual potency

· 29 ·

## Group 2  Prefixes for Size and Degree

| ❖ *hetero-* | *different* 异 |
|---|---|
| heterogeneous | consisting of different kinds |
| heterosexuality | |

| ❖ *homo-*, *homeo-* | *same* 同,相同 |
|---|---|
| homosexuality | sexually attracted to the same sex |
| homolateral (later/ = side) | |
| homeostasis (-stasis = maintaining) | |

| ❖ *hyper-* | *above*, *excessive*, *beyond* 超出,过度 |
|---|---|
| hypertrophy | excessive nourishment (cells increase in size) |
| hyperplasia | excessive formation (cells increase in number) |

| ❖ *hypo-* | *below* 低; *deficiency* 不足 |
|---|---|
| hypoxia | low levels of oxygen |
| hypotension | |

| ❖ *macro-* | *big*, *huge* 巨大 |
|---|---|
| macrocyte | big cell |
| macrodontia | |

| ❖ *mega-*, *megal(o)-* | *huge*, *great* 巨大; *million* 百万 |
|---|---|
| megacephaly | huge head |
| megalogastria | |
| megabyte | one million byte |
| megavolt | |

## Chapter 3  Prefixes

❖ *micro-*  small 小
microscope — instrument to view something small
microadenoma — _____

❖ *ultra-*  beyond, excessive 超出
ultrasonic — sound waves beyond limits of human hearing
ultrasonogram — _____

### Exercise 2

*Explain the meanings of the following combining forms.*

1. homo- _____
2. micro- _____
3. ultra- _____
4. megalo- _____
5. hypo- _____
6. hetero- _____
7. macro- _____
8. hyper- _____

### Exercise 3

*Build medical terms to complete the following statements.*

1. The term hyperglycemia means excessive sugar in the blood; the term for the deficiency of sugar in blood is _____.
2. The term _____ refers to the cells having abnormally large nucleus.
3. Macrocephaly refers to an abnormally large head, while _____ means an abnormally small head.
4. Homochromatic means pertaining to the same color, and _____ refers to pertaining to different colors.
5. _____ light refers to the invisible light that is beyond the violet end of the visible spectrum.

## Group 3  Prefixes for Time and Location

❖ *ante-*  before, forward 前
antenatal — before birth
anteflexion — _____

| | | |
|---|---|---|
| ❖ **circum-, peri-** | **around, about** 环,绕 | |
| circumflex | bending around | |
| circumoral | | |
| (or/o = mouth) | | |
| periosteum | structure around the bone | |
| periodontal | | |
| ❖ **en-, endo-,** | **inside** 内 | |
| encephalon | brain (in the head) | |
| endoscope | instrument to view inside the body | |
| endocrine | | |
| (-crine = secretion) | | |
| ❖ **epi-** | **on, above** 上 | |
| epidermis | outer layer of the skin | |
| epigastric | | |
| ❖ **ex-, exo-** | **out, outside** 外 | |
| excision | cutting out, removal | |
| exogenous | | |
| (gen/o = producing) | | |
| ❖ **infra-** | **downward, below** 下 | |
| infraduction | turning downward (of the eye) | |
| infracardiac | | |
| ❖ **inter-** | **between** 中间 | |
| intercostal | between the ribs | |
| interdental | | |
| ❖ **neo-** | **new** 新 | |
| neoplasm | new formation | |
| neonatal | | |

# Chapter 3  Prefixes

❖ **post-**          *after, behind* 后
postoperative      pertaining to after the operation
postnatal          _____

❖ **pre-**           *before* 前
prediction         telling in advance
premature          _____

❖ **pro-**           *before, in front* 前
prognosis          to know in advance (about the outcome of the illness)
prophylaxis        _____
(-phylaxia = prevention)

❖ **sub-**           *under, below* 下
sublingual         below the tongue
subhepatic         _____

❖ **supra-**         *above* 上
supraduction       turning upward (of the eye)
supranasal         _____

### Exercise 4

*Answer the following questions.*

1. Latin word *cibum* means meal. What is the meaning of *ante cibum*? What is the meaning of *post cibum*?
2. What is the meaning of *prenatal*, *postnatal*, and *neonatal*?

### Exercise 5

*Underline the prefixes in the following terms and explain the meanings of the whole terms.*

1. infracostal _____
2. subhepatic _____

· 33 ·

3. endoabdominal _____
4. circumcision _____
5. exocrine _____
6. perihepatic _____
7. supracostal _____
8. intercostal _____
9. endocrine _____
10. anterior _____

## Group 4   Prefixes for Directions

❖ *ab-*                 *away from* 离
abductor            muscle that leads the limb away from the body
abnormal            _____

❖ *ad-*                 *toward* 向
adneural            toward the nerve
adductor            _____

❖ *dia-*                *through* 穿过；*complete* 完整
diarrhea            frequent, watery feces discharge (the literal meaning
(-rrhea = flow)     is 'flow through')
diagonal            _____
(agon/o = angle)
dialysis            complete separation
diagnosis           complete knowledge of the disease

❖ *extra-*              *out, outside* 外
extracardiac        outside the heart
extracellular       _____

# Chapter 3  Prefixes

❖ *intra-*            *inside* 内
  intravenous        inside the vein
  intracardiac       _____

❖ *per-*             *through* 经,穿过
  peroral            through the mouth
  pernasal           _____
  (nas/o = nose)

❖ *trans-*           *across, through* 经,穿过
  transfer           to carry across
  (fer/o = carry)
  transdermal        _____
  (derm/o = skin)

### Exercise 6

*The term "articular" means pertaining to the joint. Explain the meanings of the following terms.*

1. epiarticular _____
2. interarticular _____
3. intra-articular _____
4. extra-articular _____
5. abarticular _____
6. circumarticular _____
7. transarticular _____

## Group 5   Prefixes for Numbers

❖ *hemi-, semi-*     *half, part* 半,偏
  hemisphere         half globe
  hemihepatectomy    _____
  semilunar          _____

(lun/o = moon)

| | | |
|---|---|---|
| ❖ **mono-**, **uni-** | **one**, **only** 单，一 | |
| monocellular | pertaining to having one cell | |
| monocular | | |
| (ocul/o = eye) | | |
| unilateral | | |

| | | |
|---|---|---|
| ❖ **bi-**, **di-** | **two**, **double** 二，双 | |
| bicuspid | (a tooth) having two points | |
| bilateral | | |
| dicentric | | |
| dioxide | | |

| | | |
|---|---|---|
| ❖ **tri-** | **three** 三 | |
| triad | a group of three | |
| triceps | (muscle) having three heads | |

| | | |
|---|---|---|
| ❖ **quadr-**, **tetra-** | **four** 四 | |
| quadrant | a quarter of an area | |
| quadriceps | | |
| tetrahedron | a figure with four surfaces | |
| tetradactyl | | |

| | | |
|---|---|---|
| ❖ **deca-**, **deci-** | **ten** 十; **one tenth** 十分之一 | |
| decapoda | (the insects that have) ten feet | |
| decade | | |
| deciliter | one tenth of a liter | |
| decimeter | | |

| | | |
|---|---|---|
| ❖ **hecto-**, **centi-** | **hundred** 百; **one hundredth** 百分之一 | |
| hectometer | one hundred meters | |
| centimeter | one hundredth of a meter | |

## Chapter 3  Prefixes

❖ *kilo-*, *milli-*　　　*thousand* 千; *one thousandth* 千分之一
kilogram　　　　　　one thousand grams
milliliter　　　　　　one thousandth of a liter

> **Tips**: The custom in the metric system is to identify fractions of units by systems from the Latin, as in *centimeter*, *decimeter*, *millimeter*; and multiples of units by the similar stems from the Greek, as in *hectometer*, *decameter*, and *kilometer*.

❖ *pan-*　　　　　　　*all* 全
panacea　　　　　　　a cure-all
pangastrectomy

❖ *poly-*, *multi-*　　　*many*, *plenty* 多
polycyte　　　　　　　cell that has many nuclei
polyarthritis
multicellular　　　　　having many cells
multiform

### Exercise 7

***Suffix "-cuspid" means point. Explain the meanings of the following terms.***

1. tricuspid
2. bicuspid
3. multicuspid
4. quadricuspid
5. unicuspid

# English Medical Terminology

**Exercise 8**

*Complete the definitions of the following medical terms with the prefix knowledge you have just learned.*

1. *Polyneuritis* refers to inflammation affecting _____ nerves.
2. *Biceps* refers to the muscle that has _____ head(s).
3. *Bilateral* means affecting _____ side(s) and *unilateral* means affecting _____ side(s).
4. A *triplet* is one of _____ offsprings produced in one birth, and a *quadruplet* is one of _____ offsprings.

## Group 6　General Prefixes

❖ **ana-**　　　　　　　　　　*up*, *back*, *again* 回, 再
　anatomy　　　　　　　　　cutting up (of the body for research)
　anabolism　　　　　　　　building up of the complex substances from simpler ones (literal meaning is 'throw up')

❖ **auto-**　　　　　　　　　*self* 自己, 自动
　autocrine　　　　　　　　self secretion
　autogenesis　　　　　　　_____

❖ **ben(e)-**　　　　　　　　*good* 好
　benign (ign/o = fire)　　referring to the tumor that is noncancerous (the literal meaning is 'good fire')
　beneceptor　　　　　　　good nervous receptor

❖ **cata-**　　　　　　　　　*down* 向下
　catalyst　　　　　　　　　substance that helps breaking down
　catabolism　　　　　　　_____

Chapter 3  Prefixes

❖ **com-**(before b, m, p)    ***together*, *with*** 同,聚集
   **con-**
commissure         joining together
contraction        drawing together

❖ **dys-**          ***bad*, *difficult*** 困难
dysplasia          bad formation
dystrophy          _____

❖ **mal-**          ***bad*** 坏
malignant          pertaining to the tumor that is cancerous
                   (the literal meaning is 'bad fire')
malformation       _____

❖ **meta-**         ***change*** 变; ***beyond*** 远,遥
metabolism         the set of chemical changes in the body
metachromia        _____
metastasis         stopping at a far area
(-stasis = stopping)

❖ **para-**         ***beside*, *near*** 旁,近; ***abnormal*** 异常
parathyroid        (the gland located) near the thyroid gland
parafunction       abnormal function
parakinesia        _____
(kinesia = movement)

❖ **sym-**(before b, m, p)    ***together*, *with*, *same*** 同,聚集
   **syn-**
symbiosis          condition of living together
syndrome(-drome = run)  combination of symptoms (the literal
                   meaning is 'run together')
synergy(erg/o = work)   _____
synchronous        happening at the same time

· 39 ·

(chron/o = time)

synthermal _____

(therm/o = temperature)

## Exercise 9

*Answer the following questions.*

1. "Anaphoria" refers to a tendency of eyes to turn upward. What is the meaning of "cataphoria"?
2. A non-cancerous tumor is described as "benign". What is the term to describe a cancerous tumor?
3. A cancerous tumor usually spreads to secondary areas. What is the term to describe this phenomenon?
4. "-physis" is used to mean "growth". What is the meaning of the term "symphysis"?
5. "Epidemic" is used to describe a disease that spreads quickly to affect many people on land; what is the meaning of "pandemic"?

# Part Three  Integrated Practice

## Exercise 10

*Select the correct answer to each of the following questions.*

1. What is the correct spelling for the prefix meaning bad?
   a. dis-          b. dif-          c. dys-          d. de-
2. Which of the following does not mean big?
   a. macro-        b. mega-         c. megalo-       d. meta-
3. What is the prefix meaning new?
   a. new-          b. neo-          c. pre-          d. meta-
4. What is the meaning of the prefix *sym-*?
   a. together      b. away from     c. same          d. both a and c

5. Which prefix does not mean against or opposite?
    a. anti-      b. counter-      c. contra-      d. dis-
6. Which prefix is not a negative prefix?
    a. uni-       b. a-            c. un-          d. non-
7. Which prefix means different?
    a. homo-      b. hetero-       c. macro-       d. micro-
8. Which prefix does not indicate numbers?
    a. mono-      b. hemi-         c. deca-        d. neo-
9. Which prefix means self?
    a. ana-       b. cata-         c. auto-        d. pan-
10. Which prefix means half?
    a. semi-      b. hemi-         c. di-          d. both a and b

## Exercise 11

*Suffix "-cellular" means pertaining to cells. Explain the meanings of the following terms.*

1. acellular _____
2. bicellular _____
3. endocellular _____
4. exocellular _____
5. heterocellular _____
6. homocellular _____
7. hypercellular _____
8. hypocellular _____
9. intercellular _____
10. intracellular _____
11. monocellular _____
12. multicellular _____
13. pancellular _____
14. pericellular _____
15. polycellular _____

16. precellular _____
17. subcellular _____
18. transcellular _____
19. tricellular _____
20. unicellular _____

# Part Four  Supplementary Readings

**Complication** is a secondary disease or disorder that develops in the course of the primary condition. The original disease could get worse and develops new pathological changes. Sometimes a medical treatment, such as drugs or surgery may have adverse effects on the patient and a new disease may appear as a complication to a previous existing disease. Such a complication may be *iatrogenic*, i.e., brought forth by the physician's treatment.

**Contagious Disease**, also known as communicable disease, is the infectious disease communicable through contact with a person who has it, with a bodily discharge of such a patient, or with an object touched by such a patient.

**Diagnosis** means the identification of the nature of a disease or condition from its outward signs and symptoms as well as from various diagnostic procedures. A *differential diagnosis* is the distinguishing of a disease or condition from others presenting similar symptoms.

**Infectious disease** refers to a clinically evident disease resulting from the presence of pathogenic micro-organisms, including pathogenic viruses, pathogenic bacteria, fungi, protozoa, parasites, and so on. When such pathogens enter the body of organisms, they would grow and multiply there, bringing forth diseases in humans and animals.

**Mortality** refers to the death rate, which is the number of deaths per 100,000 (or 10,000 or 1,000) of the population per year. Mortality is often calculated for specific groups. For example, infant mortality measures the deaths of live-born infants during the first year of life.

## Chapter 3  Prefixes

**Prognosis** is the doctor's prediction of the course of the disease and of how a patient would respond to the treatment. From the usual cause of a disease and by the special features of the case, the doctor can foretell the prospect of survival and recovery for the patient.

**Prodrome** is an early non-specific symptom (or symptoms) indicating the start of a disease before specific symptoms occur. It is the precursor to the onset of disease that would develop later. It is also called *prodroma*.

**Relapse** is the recurrence of a disease after an apparent recovery, or the return of symptoms after a remission.

**Remission** is a temporary disappearance or reduction in the severity of the symptoms of a disease, or the period during which this occurs.

**Sign** is the objective indication of a disease or abnormality that is observed or detected by a physician during physical examination of a patient. It is significant in assisting physician in the making of a diagnosis. *Vital Signs* are the indications of the physiological processes necessary to sustain the life of the organism. They are blood pressure, body temperature, respiration and heart rate.

**Symptom** refers to any abnormal function or feeling that is perceived by patients. It is the subjective evidence indicating the presence of a disease or physical disturbance, such as headache, nausea and fatigue.

**Syndrome** refers to a group of recognizable features, such as signs, symptoms, phenomena or characteristics that occur together to indicate a particular abnormality.

## Part Five  Review Sheet

Here is a collection of the word parts you have learned in this chapter. Write the meaning of each word part without referring to your previous work.

## Combining Forms

| Combining Form | Meaning | Combining Form | Meaning |
|---|---|---|---|
| cis/o | _____ | morph/o | _____ |
| cost/o | _____ | nat/o | _____ |
| crin/o | _____ | odont/o | _____ |
| cusp/o | _____ | ophthalm/o | _____ |
| duct/o | _____ | ox/o | _____ |
| flex/o | _____ | plasi/o | _____ |
| gn/o | _____ | seps/o | _____ |
| hydr/o | _____ | son/o | _____ |
| later/o | _____ | top/o | _____ |
| lingu/o | _____ | troph/o | _____ |

## Prefixes

| Prefix | Meaning | Prefix | Meaning |
|---|---|---|---|
| a-, an- | _____ | auto- | _____ |
| ab- | _____ | bi- | _____ |
| ad- | _____ | ben(e)- | _____ |
| ana- | _____ | cata- | _____ |
| ante- | _____ | cent- | _____ |
| anti-, ant- | _____ | circum- | _____ |
| com-, con- | _____ | mal- | _____ |
| contra- | _____ | mega-, megal(o)- | _____ |
| counter- | _____ | meta- | _____ |
| de- | _____ | micro- | _____ |
| deca- | _____ | milli- | _____ |
| deci- | _____ | mono- | _____ |
| di- | _____ | multi- | _____ |
| dia- | _____ | neo- | _____ |
| dis- | _____ | non- | _____ |

# Chapter 3  Prefixes

| | | | |
|---|---|---|---|
| dys- | _____ | pan- | _____ |
| en-, endo- | _____ | para- | _____ |
| epi- | _____ | peri- | _____ |
| ex-, exo- | _____ | poly- | _____ |
| extra- | _____ | post- | _____ |
| hecto- | _____ | pre- | _____ |
| hemi- | _____ | pro- | _____ |
| hetero- | _____ | quadr- | _____ |
| homo-, homeo- | _____ | semi- | _____ |
| hyper- | _____ | sub- | _____ |
| hypo- | _____ | supra- | _____ |
| im-, in- | _____ | sym-, syn- | _____ |
| infra- | _____ | tetra- | _____ |
| inter- | _____ | trans- | _____ |
| intra- | _____ | tri- | _____ |
| kilo- | _____ | uni- | _____ |
| im-, in- | _____ | | |

# Chapter 4  Body Structures & Directional Terms

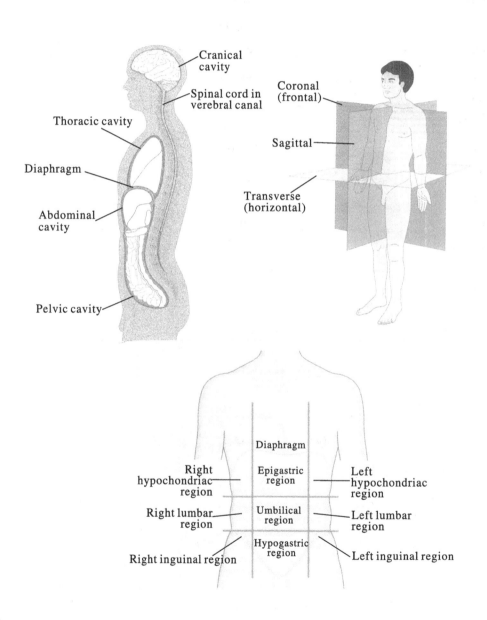

*Chapter 4 Body Structures &Directional Terms*

# Part One  Basic Body Structures & Directional Terms

### *The Body Structure*

The organization of the body from the simplest to the most complex is cell, tissue, organ and system.

The cell is the structural and functional unit of the body. All the physiological activities occur inside the cells. The principal components of cells are **cell membrane**, **cytoplasm**, and **nucleus**.

Cells that are structurally and functionally similar are organized into tissues to perform specific functions. There are four basic tissue types. The **epithelial tissue** covers and protects body surface, and forms the linings of internal organs. The **connective tissue** supports and connects body structures. It contains adipose or fat tissue, cartilage, bone and blood. The **muscle tissue** includes both the voluntary muscle to perform conscious movement and involuntary muscle found in heart and other internal organs. The **nerve tissue** makes up the brain, spinal cord and nerves. It is designed for the transmission of impulses.

An organ is a collection of various tissues integrated into a distinct structural unit to perform specific functions. The medical term for internal organs is **viscera** ( sing. *viscus*).

Systems are groups of organs working together to perform complex functions. The body systems include the digestive, respiratory, urinary, cardiac, immune, nervous, musculoskeletal, endocrine, and reproductive systems as well as special senses.

### *Body Planes*

The body planes are imaginary surfaces that divide the body into two sections. The **frontal** or **coronal** plane vertically divides the body into front and back portions. The **median** or **sagittal** plane divides the body into the left and right sides. If the plane cuts the body into equal right and left halves, it is called **midsagittal** plane. The **transverse** or **horizontal** plane divides the body into upper and lower portions.

### *Body Cavities*

The body cavities are spaces in the body that contains organs. Based on their location in the body, the body cavities can be divided into two posterior cavities, namely the **cranial cavity** and the **spinal cavity**, and three anterior cavities, namely the **thoracic cavity**, the **abdominal cavity** and the **pelvic cavity**.

## *Abdominopelvic Regions and Quadrants*

The abdominopelvic area is divided into nine regions which are called **right hypochondriac region, epigastric region, left hypochondriac region, right lumbar region, umbilical region, left lumbar region, right inguinal region, hypogastric region** and **left inguinal region**.

The abdominopelvic cavity can also be divided into four quadrants, which are **right upper quadrant (RUQ), left upper quadrant (LUQ), right lower quadrant (RLQ)** and **left lower quadrant (LLQ)**.

## *Directional Terms*

Directional terms are used to show the position of one structure in relation to another structure.

anterior (or ventral)——pertaining to the front of the body or a structure

posterior (or dorsal)——pertaining to the back of the body or a structure

superior (or cephalic)——a position that is toward the upper portion

inferior (or caudal)——a position that is toward the lower portion

proximal——toward the trunk of the body

distal——away from the trunk of the body

superficial (or external)——close to the surface of the body

deep (or internal)——close to the center of the body

medial——toward the midline of the body

lateral——away from the midline of the body

### Exercise 1

**Fill in the blanks with the terms you have learned in the above passage.**

1. The body surface and the linings of internal organs are composed of _____ tissue.
2. The four quadrants of the abdominopelvic regions are _____, _____, _____, _____.
3. The medical term for internal organs is _____.

## Chapter 4  Body Structures & Directional Terms

4. The _____ plane divides the body into equal left and right halves.
5. The _____ plane divides the body into upper and lower halves.
6. The spinal cord is made up of _____ tissue.
7. The two posterior cavities of the body are _____ cavity and _____ cavity.
8. The three anterior cavities of the body are _____ cavity, _____ cavity and _____ cavity.

### Exercise 2

*Circle the correct term to complete each of the following statements.*

1. The nose is located (superior, inferior) to the mouth.
2. The elbow is at the (proximal, distal) end of the upper arm.
3. The intestines are situated (superior, inferior) to the stomach.
4. The kidneys are located at the (anterior, posterior) wall of the abdomen.
5. The armpit is at the (proximal, distal) end of the upper arm.

## Part Two  Combining Forms, Prefixes and Suffixes

### Group 1  Combining Forms for Body Parts

| | |
|---|---|
| ❖ *caud/o* | *cauda, tail* 尾 |
| caudal | relating to the tail or lower end of the spine |
| caudad | _____ |
| (-ad = toward) | |
| ❖ *cephal/o* | *head* 头 |
| cephalic | pertaining to the head or upper side |
| cephalalgia | _____ |

| ❖ *cervic/o* | ***neck , cervix*** 颈 |
|---|---|
| cervicodynia | pain of the neck |
| cervical | |

| ❖ *crani/o* | ***cranium , skull*** 头颅 |
|---|---|
| intracranial | pertaining to the inside of the skull |
| craniotomy | |

| ❖ *dors/o* | ***back*** 背 |
|---|---|
| dorsalgia | pain of the back |
| dorsolateral | |

| ❖ *inguin/o* | ***inguina , groin*** 腹股沟 |
|---|---|
| inguinodynia | pain of the groin |
| inguinoabdominal | |

| ❖ *lumb/o* | ***lower back*** 腰 |
|---|---|
| lumbocostal | pertaining to the lower back and ribs |
| lumbodorsal | |

| ❖ *pelv/o , pelv/i* | ***pelvis*** 骨盆 |
|---|---|
| pelvimeter | an instrument to measure pelvis |
| pelvotomy | |

| ❖ *spin/o* | ***spine , the column of back bone*** 脊椎 |
|---|---|
| spinogram | X-ray image of the spinal column |
| spinitis | |

| ❖ *thorac/o* | ***thorax , chest*** 胸 |
|---|---|
| thoracotomy | incision into the chest |
| thoracoabdominal | |

| ❖ *umbilic/o* | ***umbilicus , navel*** 脐,脐带 |
|---|---|
| umbilical | |
| subumbilical | |

| ❖ *ventr/o , abdomin/o* | ***abdomen*** 腹部 |
|---|---|
| ventrad | toward the abdomen |

## Chapter 4  Body Structures & Directional Terms

ventroscopy  _____

abdominocentesis  puncture in the abdomen_____

abdominoscopy  _____

### Exercise 3

*Explain the meanings of the following combining forms.*

1. abdomin/o  _____     7. lumb/o  _____
2. thorac/o  _____     8. inguin/o  _____
3. umbilic/o  _____    9. cephal/o  _____
4. spin/o  _____      10. caud/o  _____
5. pelv/o  _____      11. crani/o  _____
6. dors/o  _____      12. cervic/o  _____

### Exercise 4

*Build a medical term for each of the following definitions.*

1. pertaining to the head  _____
2. pertaining to the skull  _____
3. pertaining to the spine  _____
4. pertaining to the abdomen _____ or _____
5. pertaining to the chest  _____
6. pertaining to the back  _____
7. pertaining to the lower back  _____
8. pertaining to the groin  _____
9. pertaining to the pelvis  _____
10. pertaining to the navel  _____

## Group 2　General Combining Forms

| ❖ *acr/o* | *tip* 尖；*top* 顶；*extremities* 肢端 |
|---|---|
| acromegaly | enlargement of extremities |
| acrodynia | |
| acrophobia | fear of height |
| (-phobia = fear) | |

| ❖ *adip/o* | *adipose*, *fat* 脂肪 |
|---|---|
| adipogenesis | formation of fat |
| adipocyte | |

| ❖ *chrom/o* | *color* 颜色 |
|---|---|
| achromia | colorless, without color |
| chromosome | |

| ❖ *cyt/o* | *cell* 细胞 |
|---|---|
| cytometer | instrument to measure (count) cells |
| cytology | |

| ❖ *epitheli/o* | *epithelium* 上皮 |
|---|---|
| epithelioma | tumor of the epithelium |
| epithelial | |

| ❖ *hist/o* | *tissue* 组织 |
|---|---|
| histolysis | breaking down of the tissue |
| histology | |

| ❖ *morph/o* | *shape* 形状,形态 |
|---|---|
| metamorphosis | change of the shape |
| morphology | |

## Chapter 4  Body Structures & Directional Terms

❖ **nucle/o, kary/o**    **nucleus, kernel** 细胞核
nucleocytoplasmic    pertaining to the nucleus and cytoplasm
nuclear              _____
karyolysis           breaking down of the nucleus
karyomegaly          _____

❖ **somat/o**        **body** 体
somatocyte           body cell
somatology           _____

❖ **viscer/o**       **viscera, internal organs** 内脏
visceroptosis        downward displacement of the internal organs
visceral             _____

### Exercise 5

*Explain the meanings of the following combining forms.*

1. somat/o _____    6. adip/o _____
2. kary/o _____     7. acr/o _____
3. nucle/o _____    8. chrom/o _____
4. epitheli/o _____ 9. hist/o _____
5. cyt/o _____      10. viscer/o _____

### Exercise 6

*Explain the meanings of the following terms.*

1. viscerosomatic _____
2. trichromic _____
3. amorphous _____
4. histologist _____
5. cytolysis _____
6. acrodynia _____
7. adiposis _____
8. karyomegaly _____

## Group 3　Combining Forms for Directions

❖ *anter/o* — *front* 前
anterograd — moving forward
(-grad = moving)
anterior

❖ *dist/o* — *far* 远
distolingual — away from the tongue
distal

❖ *infer/o* — *under* 下
inferonasal — pertaining to under the nose
inferocostal

❖ *later/o* — *side* 旁,侧
laterotorsion — twisting to the side
unilateral — pertaining to one side

❖ *medi/o* — *middle, midline* 中
mediofrontal — pertaining to the middle of the forehead
medial

❖ *poster/o* — *behind, back* 后
posteromedial — pertaining to the middle of the back part
posterior

❖ *proxim/o* — *near* 近
proximolingual — near the tongue
proximolabial
(labi/ = lip)

## Chapter 4  Body Structures & Directional Terms

❖ *tors/i*     *twisting* 扭曲

torsiometer     instrument to measure twisting

extorsion     _____

❖ *vers/o*     *turning* 转

reversion     turning back

inversion     _____

### Exercise 7

*Explain the meanings of the following terms.*

1. anteroinferior _____
2. anterointernal _____
3. anterolateral _____
4. anteromedian _____
5. anteroposterior _____
6. inferolateral _____
7. inferoposterior _____
8. inferomedian _____

### Exercise 8

*Write the opposites of the following terms.*

1. superior _____
2. anterior _____
3. distal _____
4. medial _____
5. entorsion _____

· 55 ·

# Part Three   Integrated Practice

## Exercise 9

**Select the correct answer to each of the following questions.**

1. Which of the following means fat?
   a. adip/o　　b. hist/o　　c. cyt/o　　d. nucle/o
2. Which of the following does not belong to the upper trunk?
   a. cephal/o　　b. inguin/o　　c. cervic/o　　d. crani/o
3. Which of the following does not belong to the lower trunk?
   a. pelv/o　　b. lumb/o　　c. caud/o　　d. cephal/o
4. Which of the following does not belong to the anterior body cavities?
   a. thoracic cavity　　b. abdominal cavity
   c. pelvic cavity　　d. cranial cavity
5. Which of the following does not belong to the connective tissue?
   a. blood　　b. fat　　c. bone　　d. heart muscle
6. Which region is directly below the umbilicus?
   a. epigastric　　b. inguinal　　c. hypogastric　　d. hypochondriac
7. Which term refers to the back of the body?
   a. distal　　b. ventral　　c. dorsal　　d. cephalic
8. Which of the following is the correct spelling for the term denoting internal organs?
   a. vicerus　　b. viscera　　c. visceri　　d. viscerii
9. Cells similar in structure and function are combined together to form ____.
   a. a system　　b. an organ　　c. a tissue　　d. none of the above
10. What is the meaning for the combining form ventr/o?
    a. side　　b. belly　　c. head　　d. tail

## Chapter 4  Body Structures & Directional Terms

**Exercise 10**

*Circle the correct term to complete each of the following statements.*

1. (Sagittal, Frontal) plane is the vertical plane that divides the body into left and right parts.
2. (Sagittal, Frontal) plane is the vertical plane that divides the body into anterior and posterior parts.
3. The kneecap is located on the (anterior, posterior) side of the leg.
4. The shoulder blades are located on the (anterior, posterior) side of body.
5. The big toe is located at the (medial, lateral) side of the body.
6. The (proximal, distal) end of femur joints with the pelvic bone.
7. The wrist is located at the (proximal, distal) end of the forearm.
8. The ribs are (superficial, deep) to the lungs.
9. The umbilicus is at the (ventral, dorsal) side of the body.
10. The spine is at the (ventral, dorsal) side of the body.

## Part Four  Supplementary Readings

**Anatomical position** is a position used as a reference when describing parts of the body in relation to each other. A person in the anatomical position is standing erect with the head, eyes and toes pointing forward, feet together with arms by the side, thumbs lateral to the small finger, and the palms of the hands facing forward.

**Chromosomes** are the thread-like structures in the nuclei of cells. Chromosomes carry inherited information in the form of genes, which govern all cell activity and function. Each chromosome contains up to several thousand genes arranged in single file along a long double filament of DNA. The sequence of chemical units, or bases, in the DNA provides the coded instructions for cellular activities.

**DNA** is the abbreviation for deoxyribonucleic acid, the principal molecule carrying genetic information in almost all organisms; the exceptions are certain viruses that use RNA (ribonucleic acid). DNA is found in the chromosomes of cells; its double helix structure allows the chromosomes to be copied exactly during the process of cell division.

**Homeostasis** is the automatic processes by which the body maintains a constant internal environment despite external changes. Homeostasis regulates conditions such as temperature and acidity by negative feedback. For example, when the body overheats, sweating is stimulated until the temperature returns to normal. Homeostasis also involves the regulation of blood pressure and blood glucose levels.

**Metabolism** is a collective term for all the chemical processes that take place in the body. It is divided into catabolism (breaking down of complex substances into simpler ones) and anabolism (building up of complex substances from simpler ones). Usually, catabolism releases energy, while anabolism uses it. The energy needed to keep the body functioning at rest is called the basal metabolic rate (BMR). It is measured in joules (or kilocalories) per square meter of body surface per hour. The BMR increases in response to factors such as stress, fear, exertion, and illness, and is controlled principally by various hormones, such as thyroxine, adrenaline (epinephrine), and insulin.

**Pronation** is the act of turning the body to a prone (lying facedown) position, or the turning of the hand so that the palm faces downward.

**Supination** is the act of turning the body to a supine (lying faceup) position, or the turning of hand so that the palm faces upward.

## Part Five  Review Sheet

Here is a collection of the word parts you have learned in this chapter. Write the meaning of each word part without referring to your previous work.

**Combining Forms**

| Combining Form | Meaning | Combining Form | Meaning |
| --- | --- | --- | --- |
| abdomin/o | _____ | kary/o | _____ |
| acr/o | _____ | later/o | _____ |

## Chapter 4   Body Structures & Directional Terms

| | | | |
|---|---|---|---|
| adip/o | _____ | lumb/o | _____ |
| anter/o | _____ | medi/o | _____ |
| caud/o | _____ | morph/o | _____ |
| cephal/o | _____ | nucle/o | _____ |
| cervic/o | _____ | pelv/o, pelv/i | _____ |
| chrom/o | _____ | poster/o | _____ |
| crani/o | _____ | spin/o | _____ |
| cyt/o | _____ | somat/o | _____ |
| dist/o | _____ | thorac/o | _____ |
| dors/o | _____ | tors/i | _____ |
| epitheli/o | _____ | umbilic/o | _____ |
| hist/o | _____ | ventr/o | _____ |
| infer/o | _____ | viscer/o | _____ |
| inguin/o | _____ | | |

# Chapter 5  Respiratory System

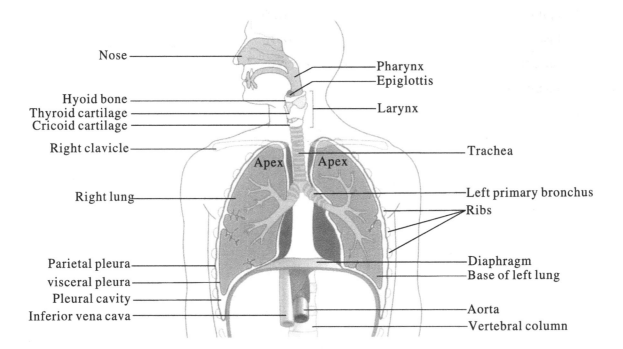

# Chapter 5  Respiratory System

## Part One  Overview of the System

Air enters the body through the **nose**, which is lined with mucous membrane and **cilia** (thin hairs, sing. *cilium*) and acts as a filter to moisten and warm the entering air. The nose is separated into the right and left nasal cavities by the nasal septum. The **paranasal sinuses** are air cavities within the cranial bones that open into the nasal cavities.

Next the air passes through the **pharynx** (also called the throat), which is divided into three regions: the **nasopharynx** behind the nasal cavity, the **oropharynx** behind the mouth and the **laryngopharynx** which is connected to the larynx and esophagus. The pharynx serves as the common passage of food and air and from it, air passes into the **larynx** and food passes into the esophagus. During swallowing, the opening of the larynx is automatically covered with the **epiglottis**, a flap of cartilage, which keeps food from entering the larynx. The larynx is also called the voice box as it is the location of the **vocal cords**.

After passing the larynx, the air enters the **trachea**, which is contained in the **mediastinum**. The mediastinum consists of the space between the lungs together with the organs contained in this space, including the heart, esophagus, aorta, and bronchial tubes.

At its lower end, the trachea branches off into the right and left pulmonary **bronchi** (sing. *bronchus*) that enter the lungs at the **hilum**. These bronchi branch off into smaller bronchi until microscopic bronchi appear, which are called **bronchioles**. The bronchioles carry air into the microscopic air sacs, called **alveoli** (sing. *alveolus*), through which gases are exchanged between the lungs and the blood.

The **lungs** are two sponge-like organs in the thoracic cavity. They are covered by the **visceral pleura** (pl. *pleurae*), which also separates them into lobes. Continuous with the visceral pleura is the **parietal pleura**, which lines the thoracic cavity. The thin space between the two pleural layers is known as the **pleural space**. The pleura is moistened with a serous secretion that facilitates the movements of the lungs within the chest.

The respiratory system is mainly responsible for the exchange of **oxygen** and **carbon dioxide** between the atmosphere and body cells, which is called **respiration**. During

**external respiration**, oxygen passes from the lungs to the blood in the capillaries while carbon dioxide passes from the capillaries back into the lungs to be expelled. This process is aided by the movements of the intercostal muscles and the **diaphragm**, a muscular partition between the chest and abdomen. During **internal respiration**, the body cells take in oxygen from the blood and give back carbon dioxide, which is transported back to the lungs.

### Exercise 1

*Fill in the blanks with the terms you have learned in the above passage.*

1. The _____ are air-filled cavities in the bones that surround the nasal cavity.
2. The _____, also called the windpipe, divides into the right and left _____.
3. The smallest of the bronchial branches are called _____ and at the end of them are clusters of air sacs called _____.
4. _____ refers to the regions in the chest cavity which contains the heart, windpipe, aorta and esophagus and _____ refers to the muscle which separates the chest and the abdomen.
5. The pulmonary arteries, pulmonary veins, lymphatic vessels and the bronchus enter or leave the lungs by way of _____.
6. The lungs are covered with double-folded membrane, consisting of _____ and _____.
7. _____ serves as the common passage of food and air.
8. _____ prevents food from entering larynx in swallowing.
9. There are three regions in the pharynx, respectively the _____, the _____ and the _____.
10. _____ refers to the exchange of gases between the external environment and respiratory organs and _____ refers to the exchanges of gases between blood and tissues.

# Chapter 5  Respiratory System

# Part Two  Combining Forms, Prefixes and Suffixes

## Group 1  Combining Forms for the Respiratory Passageway

❖ *bronch/o, bronchi/o*  *bronchus, bronchial tube* 支气管
bronchogenic   originated from the bronchi
bronchoscopy   _____
bronchiectasis
(-ectasis = dilation)   _____
peribronchial   _____

❖ *bronchiol/o*  *bronchiole, small bronchus* 细支气管
bronchiolar   pertaining to the bronchioles
bronchiolitis   _____

❖ *epiglott/o*  *epiglottis* 会厌软骨
epiglottitis   inflammation of the epiglottis
hypoepiglottic   _____

❖ *laryng/o*  *larynx, voice box* 喉
laryngocentesis   surgical puncture into the larynx
laryngeal   _____

❖ *nas/o, rhin/o*  *nose* 鼻
paranasal   beside the nose
nasopharynx   _____
rhinalgia   pain in the nose
rhinopathy   _____

| ❖ *pharyng/o* | *pharynx* 咽 |
|---|---|
| pharyngotomy | incision into the pharynx |
| pharyngitis | |

| ❖ *sinus/o* | *sinus*, *cavity* 窦, 鼻窦 |
|---|---|
| perisinusitis | inflammation of the tissues around a sinus |
| sinusitis | |

| ❖ *trache/o* | *trachea*, *windpipe* 气管 |
|---|---|
| tracheotome | instrument used to incise the trachea |
| nasotracheal | |

| ❖ *uvul/o*, *staphyl/o* | *uvula* 悬雍垂 |
|---|---|
| uvulitis | inflammation of the uvula |
| uvular | |
| staphylectomy | |
| staphyledema | |

### Exercise 2

*Explain the meanings of the following combining forms.*

1. laryng/o _____    6. sinus/o _____
2. rhin/o _____      7. nas/o _____
3. pharyng/o _____   8. bronch/o _____
4. trache/o _____    9. bronchiol/o _____
5. epiglott/o _____  10. uvul/o _____

### Exercise 3

*Build a medical term for each of the following definitions.*

1. inflammation of the epiglottis _____
2. inflammation of the larynx _____
3. incision into a bronchus _____
4. incision into a sinus _____

5. endoscopic examination of the trachea _____
6. endoscopic examination of the nose _____
7. beside the nose _____
8. pertaining to the small bronchus _____
9. pertaining to the nose and pharynx _____
10. pertaining to the uvula _____

### Group 2  Combining Forms for the Lungs and Chest

❖ *alveol/o*　　　　　　　　*alveolus*, *air sac* 肺泡
bronchoalveolitis　　　　　inflammation of the bronchi and alveoli
interalveolar　　　　　　　_____

❖ *diaphragmat/o*, *phren/o*　　*diaphragm* 膈
diaphragmatic　　　　　　　pertaining to the diaphragm
subdiaphragmatic　　　　　_____
phrenoptosis　　　　　　　_____
phrenalgia

> **Tips**: *Phren/o* is also commonly used to mean mind, as in *phrenology*, *schizophrenia*, etc. The medical adjective *phrenic* can refer either to the mind or the diaphragm. So, you might choose the adjective *diaphrag-matic* over *phrenic* when speaking or writing about the diaphragm.

❖ *lob/o*　　　　　　　　*lobe* 叶, 肺叶
lobule　　　　　　　　　a small lobe
lobectomy　　　　　　　_____

| ❖ *mediastin/o* | *mediastinum* 纵隔 |
|---|---|
| postmediastinal | behind the mediastinum |
| mediastinoscopy | |

| ❖ *pleur/o* | *pleura* 胸膜 |
|---|---|
| interpleural | between the two layers of the pleura |
| pleuritis | |

| ❖ *pneumon/o, pneum/o, pneumat/o* | *air* 气; *lung* 肺 |
|---|---|
| pneumococcus (-coccus = round bacterium) | a berry-shaped bacterium causing pneumonia |
| pneumonia | |
| pneumectomy | |
| pneumatocardia | air in the blood of the heart |
| pneumatometry | |

| ❖ *pulmon/o* | *lung* 肺 |
|---|---|
| intrapulmonary | within the lungs |
| pulmonology | |

| ❖ *thorac/o, pector/o, steth/o* | *chest* 胸 |
|---|---|
| thoracocentesis | surgical puncture into the thoracic cavity |
| thoracoscope | |
| pectoral | pertaining to the chest |
| expectorant | |
| stethalgia | pain of the chest |
| stethoscope | |

## Chapter 5 Respiratory System

### Exercise 4

*Draw a line between the combining forms and their corresponding meanings. Note that different combining forms may have the same meaning.*

1. thorac/o
2. pulmon/o
3. pneum/o
4. mediastin/o
5. pleur/o
6. pector/o
7. alveol/o
8. diaphragmat/o
10. lob/o
11. phren/o

a. air; lung
b. lobe
c. alveolus
d. diaphragm
e. pleura
f. lung
g. chest
h. mediastinum

### Exercise 5

*Divide each of the following terms into its component parts with a slash (/) and then write out its meaning.*

1. pneumology _____
2. phrenogastric _____
3. subdiaphragmatic _____
4. interlobular _____
5. thoracotomy _____
6. pneumography _____
7. mediastinoscopy _____
8. pneumatocele _____
9. bronchopulmonary _____
10. alveolocapillary _____

## Group 3  Combining Forms for Physiology or Pathology

| | | |
|---|---|---|
| ❖ *atel/o* | *imperfect*, *defective* 不完全的,有缺陷的 | |
| atelectasis | incomplete expansion of the lung | |
| atelocardia | | |
| ❖ *capn/o* | *carbon dioxide* 二氧化碳 | |
| eucapnia | normal level of carbon dioxide in the tissue | |
| (eu- = good, normal) | | |
| hypercapnia | | |
| ❖ *coni/o* | *dust* 粉尘 | |
| pneumoconiosis | abnormal condition caused by dust in the lungs | |

> **Tips**: *Pneumoconiosis* refers to a group of lung diseases caused by inhaling dust. Depending on the type of dust, more specific names can be used, including *anthracosis* (coal dust), *asbestosis* (asbestos dust), *silicosis* (silica dust), *siderosis* (iron dust), etc.

| | | |
|---|---|---|
| coniometer | | |
| ❖ *cyan/o* | *blue* 青紫色 | |
| cyanosis | bluish discoloration of the skin | |
| cyanopathy | | |
| ❖ *orth/o* | *straight* 直,端正 | |
| orthopnea | condition in which breathing is comfortable only in the upright position | |
| (-pnea = breathing) | | |
| orthodontics | | |
| (odont/o = teeth) | | |

Chapter 5 Respiratory System

❖ *ox/o , ox/i*  *oxygen* 氧
hypoxia  reduced oxygen level
oximeter  _____

❖ *phon/o*  *sound; voice* 声音
dysphonia  difficulty in speaking
phonology  _____

❖ *py/o*  *pus* 脓
pyothorax  accumulation of pus in the pleural cavity
pyogenic  _____

❖ *spir/o*  *breathing* 呼吸
spirometer  an instrument used to measure the air
respiration  entering and leaving the lungs

**Exercise 6**

*Explain the meanings of the following combining forms.*

1. cyan/o  _____      6. spir/o  _____
2. coni/o  _____      7. orth/o  _____
3. phon/o  _____      8. atel/o  _____
4. ox/o    _____      9. py/o    _____
5. capn/o  _____

**Exercise 7**

*Complete the medical terms according to the definitions given.*

1. an instrument used to measure the oxygen level of the blood: _____ meter
2. an instrument used to measure the breathing capacity of the lungs: _____ meter
3. the state in which there is less than normal level of $CO_2$ in the tissue: hypo _____ ia
4. absence or near absence of $O_2$: an _____
5. voiceless: a _____ ia
6. a weak or whispered voice: hypo _____ ia

· 69 ·

7. presence of pus in the pleural cavity: _____ thorax
8. discharge of pus: _____ rrhea

## Group 4  Prefixes and Suffixes for Pathological Conditions

❖ *-ectasis*, *-ectasia*         *dilation* 扩张
bronchiolectasis                 dilation of the bronchioles
enterectasis                     _____
angiectasia                      _____
lymphectasia                     _____

❖ *-osmia*                       *smelling* 嗅觉
pseudosmia                       false sensation of a smell that does not exist
(pseud/o = false)
anosmia                          _____

❖ *-pnea*, *-pneic*              *breathing* 呼吸
apnea                            lack of breathing
dyspneic                         _____

❖ *-ptysis*                      *spitting* 吐
hemoptysis                       spitting of blood (from the respiratory tract)
pyoptysis                        _____

❖ *-rrhea*                       *flow*, *discharge* 流
rhinorrhea                       discharge from the nose
diarrhea                         _____
(dia- = through)

❖ *-spasm*                       *sudden*, *involuntary contraction* 痉挛
bronchospasm                     involuntary contraction of the bronchi
pharyngospasm                    _____

## Chapter 5  Respiratory System

❖ **-stenosis**                    *constriction, narrowing* 狭窄
  tracheostenosis                 narrowing of the trachea
  laryngostenosis                 _____

❖ **-thorax**                      *chest condition* 胸
  pneumothorax                    presence of air in the pleural cavity
  hemothorax                      _____

❖ **eu-**                          *good, normal* 正常
  eupnea                          normal breathing
  euosmia                         _____

### Exercise 8

*Explain the meanings of the following suffixes and prefixes.*

1. -pnea    _____       5. -ectasis  _____
2. -thorax  _____       6. -ptysis   _____
3. -stenosis _____      7. -osmia    _____
4. -rrhea   _____       8. eu-       _____

### Exercise 9

*Build a medical term for each of the following definitions.*

1. presence of pus in the pleural cavity _____
2. accumulation of water (hydr/o) in the pleural cavity _____
3. absence of breathing _____
4. difficulty in breathing _____
5. narrowing or obstruction in the nasal passage _____
6. narrowing of bronchi _____
7. discharge of pus _____
8. discharge from the pharynx _____
9. abnormal contraction of larynx _____
10. abnormal contraction of bronchioles _____

# Part Three  Integrated Practice

## Exercise 10

*Select the correct answer to complete each of the following statements.*

1. The surgical procedure of _____ creates an artificial opening into the trachea through the neck.
    a. tracheostomy          b. trachelostomy
    c. traceotomy            d. tracheotomy

2. An occupational disease caused by inhalation of coal dust is _____.
    a. siderosis             b. atelectasis
    c. anthracosis           d. silicosis

3. Collection of blood in the pleural cavity is called _____.
    a. hemothorax            b. pleurisy
    c. pneumothorax          d. pyothorax

4. Spitting of blood from the respiratory tract is called _____.
    a. epistaxis             b. hemothorax
    c. hemoptysis            d. hematemesis

5. Pus and air in the pleural cavity are symptomatic of _____.
    a. hydropneumothorax     b. pyopneumothorax
    c. pneumohemothorax      d. pyothorax

6. The reduction of oxygen in body tissues is termed _____.
    a. anoxia                b. anoxemia
    c. cyanosis              d. anosmia

7. _____ refers to the inability to breathe except in an upright position.
    a. Orthopnea             b. Dyspnea
    c. Apnea                 d. Eupnea

8. _____ is an instrument to measure breathing volumes and capacities.
    a. Oximeter              b. Spirometer
    c. Stethoscope           d. Spirograph

# Chapter 5  Respiratory System

9. Surgical repair of a deviated nasal septum is called _____.
   a. rhinoplasty            b. cheiloplasty
   c. septoplasty            d. nasoplasty
10. _____ is a narrowing of the larynx.
    a. Larynostenosis         b. Laryngostenosis
    c. Larynospasm            d. Larygospasm
11. The adjective forms of the lung and bronchus are _____ and _____.
    a. pulmonary; bronchial   b. pulmonary; bronchal
    c. pneumatic; bronchial   d. pneumal; bronchal
12. Excision of the entire lung is termed _____.
    a. lobectomy              b. pneumonectomy
    c. lobotomy               d. pneumonotomy
13. _____ refers to decreased carbon dioxide in the tissues.
    a. Hypercapnia            b. Eucapnia
    c. Acapnia                d. Hypocapnia
14. _____ means incomplete expansion of the lung.
    a. Anectasis              b. Atelostomia
    c. Atelectasis            d. Atelocephaly
15. _____ means near the nose.
    a. Paranasal              b. Intranasal
    c. Endonasal              d. Exonasal

**Exercise 11**

*Fill in the blanks with the correct terms.*

1. The bluish discoloration of the skin and mucous membrane resulting from hypoxia is called _____.
2. Patients with pneumonia often find it difficult or painful to take deep breaths. The term for this is _____.
3. _____ is a term describing coughing up blood from the lungs.
4. The patient with air in the pleural cavity was diagnosed as having _____.
5. The patient reported dizziness brought on by excessive breathing, or _____.

6. The physician informed the patient that the chest pain, or _____, was caused by a heart attack.
7. The patient was able to breathe only in an upright position, so the nurse recorded that he had _____.
8. _____ refers to the condition in which the lungs or part of the lungs are collapsed, usually resulting in breathing difficulty.
9. The patient's difficulty in producing voice, or _____, was caused by acute laryngitis.
10. X-ray examination confirmed the widening of the bronchi, or _____, so the doctor prescribed antibiotics and bronchodilators.

# Part Four  Supplementary Readings

**Asthma** attacks involve spasm and constriction of the airway, accompanied by edema and mucus accumulation on the inner linings of the airway. Symptoms are paroxysmal dyspnea, coughing and wheezing (sound which is usually heard during expiration and is caused by bronchial constriction). Treatment includes removal of allergens, administration of bronchodilators and steroid. Etiology may include allergy and infection. Heredity may also play a role. Asthma is receiving more public attention in the developed world because of its rapidly increasing prevalence, especially among children.

**Auscultation** refers to the process of listening to the internal sounds of the body, usually using a stethoscope. Auscultation is an aid to diagnosis of abnormality in the circulatory system and respiratory system (heart sounds and breath sounds), as well as the gastrointestinal system (bowel sounds).

**Cor pulmonale** is a serious cardiac condition associated with chronic lung disorders, such as emphysema. As a result of the inadequate pulmonary circulation, the right ventricle of the heart changes in structure and function. In chronic cases, right ventricular hypertrophy is the predominant change whereas in acute cases dilation dominates. Both hypertrophy and dilation are the result of increased right ventricular pressure. Elimination of the cause is the most important intervention.

**Croup** refers to a group of respiratory diseases that often affects infants and children under the age of 6. It is characterized by a barking cough, inspiratory stridor (a high-pitched sound heard on inhalation) and hoarseness. It may be mild, moderate or severe, and severe cases, with breathing difficulty, can be fatal if not treated in hospital. Croup is most often caused by parainfluenza virus. Croup can be prevented by immunization for influenza and diphtheria.

**Diphtheria** is a highly contagious infection, caused by the bacterium Corynebacterium diphtheriae, generally affecting the throat but occasionally other mucous membranes and the skin. The disease is spread by direct physical contact or breathing the aerosolized secretions of infected individuals. After an incubation period of 2-6 days, sore throat, weakness and mild fever develop. Later, a soft grey membrane forms across the throat, constricting the airway and causing difficulty in breathing and swallowing; then, a tracheostomy may be necessary. Bacteria multiply at the site of infection and release a toxin into the blood stream, which damages heart and nerves. Treatment includes administration of antitoxin and penicillin as well as prolonged bed rest. The DPT (Diphtheria-Pertussis-Tetanus) vaccine has proved effective in preventing the disease from spreading among children.

**Epistaxis** refers to rapid flow of blood from the nose. It is also called rhinorrhagia, or nosebleed in laymen's words.

**Lobectomy** involves surgical resection of a lobe of an organ or gland, such as the lung, thyroid, or brain. Lobectomy of the lung may be performed for cancer or other diseases of the lung. Depending on the amount of the tissue removed, there are different types of lung resection: pneumectomy, segmental resection, lobectomy, and wedge resection.

**Percussion** means tapping the body to assess the condition of the underlying part by the sounds obtained. Tapping over a solid organ produces a dull sound without resonance. Percussion over an air-filled structure, such as the lung, produces a resonant, hollow note. As the lungs are filled with fluid and become denser, as in pneumonia, resonance is replaced by dullness.

**Pertussis** is a highly contagious bacterial disease causing uncontrollable, violent coughing, which can make it hard to breathe. A deep "whooping" sound is often heard when the patient tries to take a breath. Antibiotics, such as erythromycin and amoxicillin, are used effectively. Pertussis is commonly called whooping cough.

**Pulmonary emphysema** is the condition in which the alveoli of the lungs are enlarged and damaged and the elasticity of the lung tissue is lost, which reduces the surface area for the exchange of oxygen and carbon dioxide. Breathing becomes difficult and is accompanied by a heavy cough. Respiratory acidosis (carbon dioxide building up in the blood) and cor pulmonale may be the result. There is no specific treatment, and the patient may become dependent on oxygen. It is often caused by exposure to toxic chemicals or long-term exposure to tobacco smoke.

**Tuberculosis** is an infectious disease characterized by the formation of tubercles (nodular lesions) in the tissues. In pulmonary tuberculosis, the bacillus is inhaled into the lungs where it sets up a primary tubercle and spreads to the nearest lymph nodes. It may be healed as the result of the body's immune response and the bacilli are encapsulated. Surrounding tissue becomes fibrous and calcified. In other cases, the disease may smoulder for months or years and fluctuate with the patient's resistance. Symptoms of the active disease include fever, night sweats, weight loss and hemoptysis. The inflammation can spread to other parts of the body. Tuberculosis is curable by various combinations of the antibiotics and preventive measures include detection of cases by X-ray screening of vulnerable populations and inoculation with BCG vaccine.

## Part Five  Review Sheet

Here is a collection of the word parts you have learned in this chapter. Write the meaning of each word part without referring to your previous work.

**Combining Forms**

| Combining Form | Meaning | Combining Form | Meaning |
| --- | --- | --- | --- |
| alveol/o | _____ | pharyng/o | _____ |
| atel/o | _____ | phon/o | _____ |

## Chapter 5 Respiratory System

| | | | |
|---|---|---|---|
| bronch/o, bronchi/o | _____ | phren/o | _____ |
| bronchiol/o | _____ | pleur/o | _____ |
| capn/o | _____ | pneumon/o, pneum/o, | _____ |
| coni/o | _____ | pneumat/o | |
| cyan/o | _____ | pulmon/o | _____ |
| diaphragmat/o | _____ | py/o | _____ |
| epiglott/o | _____ | rhin/o | _____ |
| laryng/o | _____ | sinus/o | _____ |
| lob/o | _____ | spir/o | _____ |
| mediastin/o | _____ | steth/o | _____ |
| nas/o | _____ | trache/o | _____ |
| orth/o | _____ | staphyl/o | _____ |
| ox/o, ox/i | _____ | thorac/o | _____ |
| pector/o | _____ | uvul/o | _____ |

## Suffixes

| Suffix | Meaning | Suffix | Meaning |
|---|---|---|---|
| -ectasis, -ectasia | _____ | -spasm | _____ |
| -osmia | _____ | -stenosis | _____ |
| -pnea | _____ | -thorax | _____ |
| -rrhea | _____ | | |

## Prefixes

| Prefix | Meaning |
|---|---|
| eu- | _____ |

# Chapter 6  Digestive System

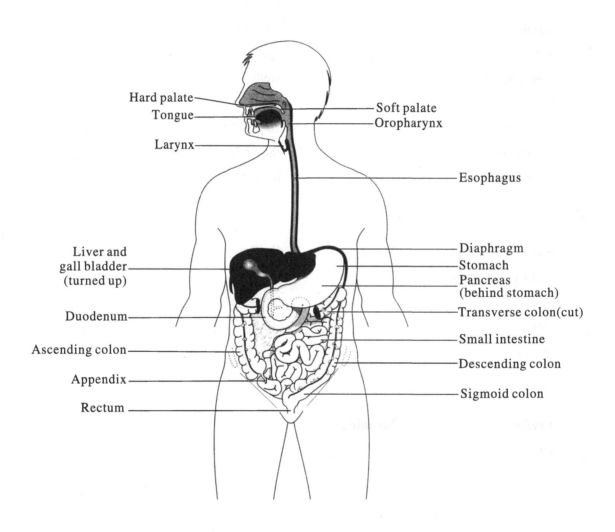

## Chapter 6  Digestive System

## Part One  Overview of the System

The digestive system, also called the **gastrointestinal (GI) tract** or **alimentary canal**, has three major functions, namely, **digestion**, **absorption** and **defecation**.

The **upper GI tract** consists of the mouth, **pharynx**, **esophagus** and **stomach**. In the oral cavity, food is chewed into small pieces (mastication) and is mixed with **saliva** which is secreted from the three pairs of salivary glands, namely the **parotid glands**, **submandibular glands** and **sublingual glands**. The moistened food is swallowed into the pharynx (deglutition) and further into the esophagus. **Peristalsis**, the rhythmic contraction of muscles in the wall of the esophagus, propels food toward the stomach. The stomach has three parts, the **fundus**, **body** and **antrum**. The openings into and out of the stomach are controlled by the **cardiac sphincter** and the **pyloric sphincter** respectively. The inner surface of the stomach is lined with **rugae**, a kind of mucous membrane that appears in folds. The rugae also contain digestive glands that produce the enzyme **pepsin** and **hydrochloric acid**.

The **lower GI tract** comprises the **intestines** and **anus**. The intestine consists of two segments: the small intestine and the large intestine (bowel). The small intestine is subdivided into three parts: the **duodenum**, **jejunum** and **ileum** and here, the vast majority of digestion takes place. Nutrients diffuse through the **villi** (sing. *villus*), projections sticking out of the walls of the small intestine, into the blood. The large intestine is the last part of the GI tract and its function is to absorb the remaining water from indigestible food matter, to store the useless nutrients and wastes and to flush them from the body. It also has three parts: the **cecum**, to which the vermiform **appendix** is attached, the **colon** (further subdivided into the ascending colon, transverse colon, descending colon and sigmoid flexure) and the **rectum**.

Accessory organs of digestion include the liver, gallbladder, and pancreas. The **liver** secretes **bile** into the small intestine via the **biliary system** and aid in digestion of lipids. The **gallbladder** functions as a reservoir of the bile. The **pancreas** secretes pancreatic juice containing digestive enzymes that pass into the small intestine and help in the further breakdown of the carbohydrates, protein, and fat in the **chyme** (the semifluid mass of partly digested food expelled by the stomach into the duodenum).

The **abdominopelvic cavity** and the **visceral organs** are lined with **peritoneum**, which consists of the **parietal layer** and the **visceral layer**. The potential space between the two layers of peritoneum is called the **peritoneal cavity**. When the two folds of peritoneum adhere to one another, they form the **mesentery**, **omenta** (sing. *omentum*), and ligaments.

### Exercise 1

***Fill in the blanks with the terms you have learned in the above passage.***

1. The digestive system serves three major functions: _____, _____ and _____.
2. The upper GI tract consists of mouth, _____, _____, and stomach.
3. The small intestine has three parts: _____, _____, and _____.
4. The large intestine is divided into six parts: _____, ascending colon, _____ colon, descending colon, _____ and _____.
5. The folds in the mucous membrane covering the stomach are called _____; the microscopic projections in the walls of the small intestine are called _____.
6. There are three pairs of salivary glands, respectively _____, _____, and _____.
7. The involuntary, progressive and rhythm-like contractions of tubes of the GI tract are called _____.
8. The double layers of serous membrane covering the abdominopelvic cavity and the visceral organs are called _____.
9. The stomach has three major portions: _____, body and _____.
10. Digestive glands in the inner wall of the stomach can produce _____ and _____.

# Chapter 6  Digestive System

## Part Two  Combining Forms, Prefixes and Suffixes

### Group 1  Combining Forms for the Mouth

❖ *alveol/o*  　　　　　　　*alveolus, tooth socket* 牙槽
alveolotomy　　　　　　　incision into the alveoli
alveolitis　　　　　　　　＿＿＿＿＿＿＿＿＿＿＿＿＿＿＿＿

> **Tips:** The combining form *alveol/o* also means the air sac, as in *bronchoalveolitis* (inflammation of the bronchi and lung tissue).

❖ *bucc/o*　　　　　　　　*cheek* 颊
extrabuccal　　　　　　　outside the cheek
intrabuccal　　　　　　　＿＿＿＿＿＿＿＿＿＿＿＿＿＿＿＿

❖ *cheil/o, labi/o*　　　　　*lip* 唇
cheilosis　　　　　　　　diseased condition of the lips
cheiloplasty　　　　　　　＿＿＿＿＿＿＿＿＿＿＿＿＿＿＿＿
labiodental　　　　　　　＿＿＿＿＿＿＿＿＿＿＿＿＿＿＿＿
interlabial　　　　　　　　＿＿＿＿＿＿＿＿＿＿＿＿＿＿＿＿

❖ *dent/i, dent/o, odont/o*　*tooth* 牙齿
dentistry　　　　　　　　medical science concerned with the teeth and their supporting structures
orthodontist　　　　　　　＿＿＿＿＿＿＿＿＿＿＿＿＿＿＿＿
periodontium　　　　　　＿＿＿＿＿＿＿＿＿＿＿＿＿＿＿＿
endodontics　　　　　　　＿＿＿＿＿＿＿＿＿＿＿＿＿＿＿＿

❖ *gingiv/o*       *gingiva*, *gum* 牙龈

supragingival — above the gingiva

gingivitis

❖ *gloss/o*, *lingu/o*      *tongue* 舌

hemiglossectomy — excision of half of the tongue

stomatoglossitis

sublingual

mesiolingual

> **Tips**: Two different combining forms may have the same meaning. Usually, such pairs of combining forms have developed from different origins, either in Greek or in Latin. For example, both *cheil/o* (Greek) and *labi/o* (Latin) mean lip; both *gloss/o* (Greek) and *lingu/o* (Latin) mean the tongue. As a general rule, Greek word roots are used to build words that describe a disease, condition, treatment, or diagnosis; Latin word roots are used to build words that describe anatomic structures.

❖ *gnath/o*      *jaw* 颌

micrognathia — abnormally small jaws

gnathitis

❖ *or/o*, *stomat/o*      *mouth* 口

perioral — surrounding the mouth

orolingual

stomatopathy — any disease of the mouth

stomatitis

❖ *palat/o*      *palate* 腭

palatine — pertaining to the palate

palatorrhaphy

(-rrhaphy = surgical sewing)

## Chapter 6  Digestive System

❖ **sial/o**       *saliva* 唾液；*salivary glands and ducts* 唾液腺，唾液管

sialorrhea      excessive production of saliva

sialography      _____

❖ **sialoaden/o**      *salivary gland* 唾液腺

sialoadenectomy      removal of the salivary gland

sialoadenotomy      _____

❖ **sialoangi/o**      *salivary ducts* 唾液管

sialoangiitis      _____

sialoangiography      _____

**Exercise 2**

*Explain the meanings of the following combining forms.*

1. stomat/o  _____
2. labi/o  _____
3. odont/o  _____
4. gloss/o  _____
5. lingu/o  _____
6. cheil/o  _____
7. bucc/o  _____
8. gnath/o  _____
9. sial/o  _____
10. or/o  _____

**Exercise 3**

*Build a medical term for each of the following definitions.*

1. pertaining to the teeth and teeth sockets  _____
2. pertaining to the mouth and tongue  _____
3. between the lips  _____
4. pertaining to the cheek and teeth  _____
5. paralysis (-plegia) of the tongue  _____
6. surgical removal of the excess gum tissue  _____
7. X-ray examination of the jaw  _____
8. inflammation of the salivary gland  _____
9. splitting (-schisis) of the palate  _____

10. tumor of the salivary glands _____

## Group 2  Combining Forms for the GI Tract (I)

❖ **abdomin/o, celi/o**  
   **lapar/o**  
         *abdomen* 腹

celiotomy       incision into the abdomen

celiac

laparoscopy       visual examination of the abdominal cavity  
          (also called *celioscopy or abdominoscopy*)

laparotome

abdominocentesis

❖ **an/o**         *anus* 肛门

perianal        surrounding the anus

transanal

❖ **append/o, appendic/o**    *appendix* 阑尾

appendectomy      removal of the appendix

appendicocele

appendicitis

❖ **cec/o**        *cecum* 盲肠

cecocolostomy      surgical connection of the cecum and colon

(-stomy = surgical connection)

cecoptosis

❖ **cholangi/o**      *bile vessel* 胆管

cholangiocarcinoma    malignant tumor of the bile ducts

cholangiography

❖ **cholecyst/o**      *gallbladder* 胆囊

cholecystitis       inflammation of the gallbladder

| | |
|---|---|
| cholecystectomy | |
| ❖ *choledoch/o* | ***common bile duct* 总胆管** |
| choledocholithiasis | presence of stones in the common bile duct |
| (-lithiasis = stone formation) | |
| choledochotomy | |
| ❖ *col/o, colon/o* | ***colon* 结肠** |
| colectomy | excision of all or part of the colon |
| colitis | |
| colonic | |
| colonalgia | |
| ❖ *duoden/o* | ***duodenum* 十二指肠** |
| duodenostomy | surgical creation of an opening into the duodenum |
| duodenoscopy | |
| ❖ *enter/o* | ***small intestine* 小肠** |
| parenteral | outside the intestines |
| enterospasm | |
| ❖ *esophag/o* | ***esophagus* 食管** |
| retroesophageal | behind the esophagus |
| esophagology | |
| ❖ *gastr/o* | ***stomach* 胃** |
| epigastric | above the stomach |
| gastrocele | |

## Exercise 4

*Spell out the combining forms for the following meanings.*

1. esophagus _____
2. stomach _____
3. anus _____
4. common bile duct _____
5. duodenum _____
6. gallbladder _____
7. small intestine _____
8. cecum _____
9. colon _____ or _____
10. abdomen _____ or _____

## Exercise 5

*Build a medical term for each of the following definitions.*

1. inflammation of the appendix _____
2. inflammation of the duodenum _____
3. radiography of the gallbladder _____
4. radiography of the bile duct _____
5. surgical fixation (-pexy) of the colon _____
6. surgical fixation of the small intestine _____
7. visual examination of the anus _____
8. visual examination of the abdominal cavity _____
9. excision of the stomach _____
10. excision of the cecum _____

## Group 3  Combining Forms for the GI Tract (Ⅱ)

❖ *hepat/o* — ***liver* 肝**
hepatogenic — originating in the liver
hepatitis — 

❖ *ile/o* — ***ileum* 回肠**
ileopexy — surgical fixation of the ileum
(-pexy = surgical fixation)
ileectomy — 

❖ *jejun/o* — ***jejunum* 空肠**
gastrojejunostomy — surgical communication between the stomach and jejunum
jejunitis — 

❖ *pancreat/o* — ***pancreas* 胰腺**
pancreatolysis — destruction of the pancreas
pancreatalgia — 

❖ *peritone/o, periton/o* — ***peritoneum* 腹膜**
peritoneocentesis — surgical puncture into the peritoneum
peritonitis — 

❖ *proct/o* — ***anus and rectum* 直肠**
proctology — medical science dealing with the structure and diseases of the anus and rectum
proctoscope — 

❖ *pylor/o* — ***pylorus* 幽门**
pylorostenosis — constriction of the pylorus
pyloroplasty —

❖ **rect/o**   ***rectum* 直肠**
rectocele   prolapse of the rectum (also called *proctocele*)
colorectum   _____

❖ ***sigmoid/o***   ***sigmoid colon* 乙状结肠**
sigmoidopexy   surgical fixation of the sigmoid
ileosigmoidostomy   _____

## Exercise 6

**Draw a line between the combining forms and their corresponding meanings.**

1. ile/o          a. peritoneum
2. hepat/o       b. pylorus
3. jejun/o       c. sigmoid
4. sigmoid/o    d. liver
5. peritone/o   e. rectum
6. rect/o        f. pancreas
7. pancreat/o   g. rectum and anus
8. proct/o       h. ileum
9. pylor/o       i. jejunum

## Exercise 7

**Divide each of the following terms into its component parts with a slash (/) and then explain its meaning.**

1. proctalgia _____
2. pancreatogenic _____
3. pylorospasm _____
4. hepatomegaly _____
5. cholangiopancreatography _____
6. ileojejunitis _____
7. peritoneotomy _____
8. hepatoma _____
9. proctoptosis _____

## Chapter 6  Digestive System

10. sigmoidopexy _____

### Group 4  Combining Forms and Suffixes for Substances

❖ *amyl/o*  *starch* 淀粉
amylogenesis  formation of starch
amyloid  _____

❖ *bil/i, chol/e*  *bile* 胆汁
biliary  pertaining to bile
biligenesis  _____
cholemesis  vomiting of bile
(-emesis = vomiting)
choleperitonitis  _____

❖ *bilirubin/o*  *bilirubin, bile pigment* 胆红素
hyperbilirubinemia  increased level of bilirubin in blood
(-emia = blood)
hypobilirubinemia  _____

❖ *fec/o, copr/o*  *feces* 粪便
defecation  discharge of wastes from the large intestine
fecal  _____
coprolith  mass of hard feces
coprophagia  _____
(-phagia = eating)

❖ *gluc/o, glyc/o*  *glucose* 葡萄糖
gluconeogenesis  production of glucose from substances other than carbohydrates
glucometer  instrument to measure level of glucose
hyperglycemia  _____

| | | |
|---|---|---|
| hypoglycemic | | |
| ❖ *lip/o , steat/o* | *fat* 脂肪 | |
| lipoprotein | a biochemical assembly that contains both proteins and lipids | |
| lipoma | | |
| steatolysis | breaking down of fats | |
| steatorrhea | | |
| ❖ *lith/o , -lith* | *calculus , stone* 结石 | |
| sialolith | calculi formed in the salivary glands and ducts | |
| cholelith | | |
| litholysis | dissolution of calculi | |
| lithectomy | | |
| ❖ *prote/o* | *protein* 蛋白 | |
| proteopepsis (-pepsis = digestion) | digestion of protein | |
| proteolytic | | |
| ❖ *-ase* | *enzyme* 酶 | |
| protease | enzyme that breaks down protein | |
| amylase | | |

### Exercise 8

**Explain the meanings of the following combining forms or suffixes.**

1. chol/e  _____
2. amyl/o  _____
3. lip/o  _____
4. prote/o  _____
5. lith/o  _____

6. glyc/o  _____
7. steat/o  _____
8. -ase  _____
9. bilirubin/o  _____
10. fec/o  _____

Chapter 6  Digestive System

**Exercise 9**

*Build a medical term for each of the following definitions.*

1. an enzyme to break down protein _____
2. an enzyme to break down starch _____
3. an enzyme to break down lipid _____
4. production of glucose _____
5. production of starch _____
6. production of lipid _____
7. a drug that causes increased flow (-agogue) of bile _____
8. gallstone _____
9. reduced level of sugar in the blood _____
10. raised level of bilirubin in the blood _____

### Group 5  Suffixes and Prefixes

| | |
|---|---|
| ❖ **-chezia** | ***defecation, elimination of wastes*** 排便 |
| hematochezia | presence of bright red blood in the feces |
| ❖ **-emesis** | ***vomiting*** 呕吐 |
| hyperemesis | excessive vomiting |
| hematemesis | _____ |

> **Tips**: *Hemoptysis* refers to coughing up blood from the respiratory tract and lungs; *hematemesis* refers to vomiting blood from the digestive tract.

| | |
|---|---|
| ❖ **-orexia** | ***appetite*** 食欲 |
| anorexia | having no appetite |
| hyperorexia | _____ |

❖ *-pepsia*　　　　　　　　*digestion* 消化
dyspepsia　　　　　　　　painful, difficult digestion
apepsia　　　　　　　　　_____

❖ *-phagia*　　　　　　　　*condition of eating or swallowing* 进食；吞咽
hyperphagia　　　　　　　excessive eating
dysphagia　　　　　　　　_____

❖ *-plasty*　　　　　　　　*surgical repair* 整形术，修复手术
cheiloplasty　　　　　　　surgical repair of the lips
jejunoplasty　　　　　　　_____

❖ *-prandial*　　　　　　　*meal* 餐
anteprandial　　　　　　　before a meal (also called *preprandial*)
postprandial　　　　　　　_____

❖ *-stomy*　　　　　　　　*surgical creation of an opening or a communication* 造口术
duodenostomy　　　　　　_____
sigmoidoproctostomy　　　_____

> **Tips**: When the suffix, *-stomy*, is used with one organ, it means surgical creation of an opening between the organ and the surface of the body, e.g. *gastrostomy*, *bronchostomy*, etc. When it is used with two organs, it means surgical creation of a passage between these two organs or two parts of the same organ (i.e. *anastomosis*), e.g. *gastroenterostomy*, *duodenoileostomy*, etc.

❖ *dia-*　　　　　　　　　*through, across* 通过
diarrhea　　　　　　　　　abnormally frequent discharge
diagnosis　　　　　　　　_____

## Chapter 6 Digestive System

❖ **neo-**      new 新,异

neostomy      creation of an opening

neonate      _____

( nat/o = birth )

### Exercise 10

*Explain the meanings of the following suffixes.*

1. -chezia _____
2. -prandial _____
3. -phagia _____
4. -pepsia _____
5. -orexia _____
6. -emesis _____
7. -stomy _____
8. -plasty _____
9. neo- _____
10. dia- _____

### Exercise 11

*Build a medical term for each of the following definitions.*

1. ingestion of stones _____
2. swallowing of air ( aero- ) _____
3. refusal or inability to eat or swallow _____
4. after meal _____
5. surgical creation of an opening into the stomach _____
6. surgical creation of an opening into the trachea _____
7. surgical connection of the ileum and rectum _____
8. surgical connection of the stomach and intestine _____
9. surgical repair of the palate _____
10. surgical repair of the anus _____

## Part Three  Integrated Practice

### Exercise 12

*Write the adjective forms for the following nouns.*

1. jejunum  _____
2. pancreas  _____
3. esophagus _____
4. palate    _____
5. bile      _____
6. ileum     _____
7. duodenum  _____
8. saliva    _____
9. choledoch _____
10. colon    _____

### Exercise 13

*Match the terms in Column I with their meanings in Column II. Place the letter of the definition to the left of the term.*

**Column I**

____ 1. jejunotomy
____ 2. megacolon
____ 3. emetic
____ 4. palatoplasty
____ 5. lipase
____ 6. proctopexy
____ 7. hyperphagia
____ 8. dysentery
____ 9. mesentery
____ 10. cholecystectomy
____ 11. peristalsis
____ 12. hepatopathy
____ 13. hepatopexy

**Column II**

a. study of the GI tract
b. inflammation of the intestine
c. pertaining to meal
d. a drug to induce vomiting
e. surgical fixation of the liver
f. involuntary, rhythmic muscle contraction
g. inflammation of the ileum
h. incision into the jejunum
i. excision of gallbladder
j. excessive production of saliva
k. peritoneum over the intestines
l. one part of the stomach
m. surgical fixation of the rectum

_____ 14. sialorrhea          n. liquefied food entering the duodenum
_____ 15. enterology          o. surgical repair of the palate
_____ 16. cholecystography    p. any disease of the liver
_____ 17. prandial            q. an extremely enlarged colon
_____ 18. ileitis             r. radiography of gallbladder
_____ 19. chyme               s. enzyme of lipid
_____ 20. fundus              t. increased appetite

## Part Four  Supplementary Readings

**Achalasia** occurs when the smooth muscle layer of the esophagus loses normal peristalsis, and the lower esophageal sphincter (LES) fails to relax properly in response to swallowing. Typical symptoms include dysphagia, regurgitation, and sometimes chest pain. Diagnosis is reached with esophageal manometry and barium swallow X-ray studies.

**Ascites** refers to the condition in which an excessive amount of fluid accumulates in the peritoneal cavity. Ascites is frequently a complication of cirrhosis and other severe liver diseases in which the portal veins and lymphatics become obstructed in the cirrhotic liver. Treatment may be with diuretics, paracentesis, or other treatments directed at the cause.

**Cirrhosis** is a chronic liver disease characterized by hepatomegaly, edema, ascites, and jaundice. As the disease progresses there is splenomegaly, internal bleeding, and brain damage caused by changes in the composition of the blood. A complication of cirrhosis is increased pressure in the portal system that brings blood from the abdominal organs to the liver, a condition called portal hypertension. It is most commonly caused by heavy consumption of alcohol.

**Constipation** occurs when stools (feces) are dry and hard and are difficult to expel. This usually happens because the colon absorbs too much water from the food. Severe constipation that prevents passage of both stools and gas is also called obstipation. In treatment, laxatives are used to encourage movement of feces from colon.

**Dental caries** (also called tooth decay) is caused by dental plaque, which is the accumulation of foods, proteins from saliva, and necrotic debris on the tooth enamel. Bacteria grow in the plaque and cause the production of acid that dissolves the tooth enamel, resulting in a cavity. If the bacterial infection reaches the pulp of the tooth and causes pulpitis, root canal therapy may be necessary.

**Diverticula** (sing. *diverticulum*) are small pouches in the wall of the intestine, most commonly in the colon. If these pouches are present in large number the condition is termed diverticulosis, which has been attributed to a diet low in fiber. Collection of waste and bacteria in these sacs leads to diverticulitis, which is accompanied by pain and sometimes bleeding. Diverticula can be seen by radiographic studies of the lower GI tract using barium as a contrast medium, a so-called barium enema. Although there is no cure, diverticulitis is treated with diet, stool softeners, and antispasmodics (drugs to reduce motility).

**Hemorrhoids** are varicosities or swelling and inflammation of veins in the rectum and anus. The condition is often caused by increased straining on anal veins, such as in chronic constipation or diarrhea. It can be external (within the wall of the rectum) or external (in the anal area).

**Ileus** is a partial or complete blockage of the small and/or large intestine due to failure of peristalsis from non-mechanical mechanism. It is often caused by surgical, traumatic, or bacterial injury to the peritoneum.

**Intussusception** refers to the medical condition in which a section of the small intestine has invaginated into another section, causing intestinal obstruction. It occurs most commonly in children and in the ileocecal region. Treatment involves resection of the intussusception and anastomosis.

**Jaundice** is yellowish discoloration of the skin, sclera and mucous membranes caused by hyperbilirubinemia. It can occur in three major ways: (1) excessive destruction of erythrocytes; (2) malfunction of hepatocytes to excrete bilirubin; (3) obstruction of bile flow.

**Melena** refers to the black, "tarry" feces that are associated with gastrointestinal hemorrhage, especially bleeding originating from the upper GI tract (such as the stomach and jejunum). The black color is caused by oxidation of the iron in hemoglobin during its passage through the ileum and colon. In contrast, bleeding originating from the lower GI tract (such as the sigmoid colon and rectum) is generally associated with the passage of bright red blood, or hematochezia.

**Peptic ulcer** is a lesion of the skin or a mucous membrane marked by inflammation and tissue damage. Peptic ulcers are caused by the destruction of mucosa by peptic acid. Most peptic ulcers appear in the distal portion of the stomach or in the first portion of the duodenum. Severe hemorrhage, especially of a duodenal ulcer, is the most common complication of an ulcer. Ulcers can be diagnosed by endoscopy and by radiographic study of the GI tract using a contrast medium, usually barium sulfate. A barium study can reveal a variety of GI disorders in addition to ulcers, including tumors and obstructions. A barium swallow is used for study of the pharynx and esophagus; an upper GI series examines the esophagus, stomach, and small intestine. Vagotomy or gastrectomy can be performed to correct the oversecretion of hydrochloric acid in the stomach; in severe cases, gastrojejunostomy may be performed to bypass an ulcerated duodenum.

**Volvulum** refers to the condition in which a loop of bowel abnormally twists on itself, resulting in a life-threatening bowel obstruction. Acute manifestations may include abdominal distention and vomiting. Acute volvulus requires immediate surgical intervention to untwist the affected segment of bowel and possibly resect any unsalvageable portion.

## Part Five   Review Sheet

Here is a collection of the word parts you have learned in this chapter. Write the meaning of each word part without referring to your previous work.

**Combining Forms**

| Combining Form | Meaning | Combining Form | Meaning |
| --- | --- | --- | --- |
| abdomin/o | _____ | esophag/o | _____ |
| alveol/o | _____ | fec/o | _____ |
| amyl/o | _____ | gastr/o | _____ |
| an/o | _____ | gingiv/o | _____ |
| append/o, appendic/o | _____ | gloss/o | _____ |

| | | | |
|---|---|---|---|
| bil/i | _____ | gluc/o, glyc/o | _____ |
| bucc/o | _____ | gnath/o | _____ |
| cec/o | _____ | hepat/o | _____ |
| celi/o | _____ | ile/o | _____ |
| cheil/o | _____ | jejun/o | _____ |
| cholangi/o | _____ | labi/o | _____ |
| chol/e | _____ | lapar/o | _____ |
| cholecyst/o | _____ | lingu/o | _____ |
| choledoch/o | _____ | lip/o | _____ |
| col/o, colon/o | _____ | lith/o | _____ |
| copr/o | _____ | odont/o | _____ |
| dent/i, dent/o | _____ | or/o | _____ |
| duoden/o | _____ | palat/o | _____ |
| enter/o | _____ | pancreat/o | _____ |
| peritone/o | _____ | sialoaden/o | _____ |
| proct/o | _____ | sialoangi/o | _____ |
| prote/o | _____ | sigmoid/o | _____ |
| pylor/o | _____ | steat/o | _____ |
| rect/o | _____ | stomat/o | _____ |
| sial/o | _____ | | |

## Suffixes

| Suffix | Meaning | Suffix | Meaning |
|---|---|---|---|
| -ase | _____ | -pepsia | _____ |
| -chezia | _____ | -phagia | _____ |
| -emesis | _____ | -plasty | _____ |
| -lith | _____ | -prandial | _____ |
| -orexia | _____ | -stomy | _____ |

## Prefixes

| Prefix | Meaning | Prefix | Meaning |
|---|---|---|---|
| dia- | _____ | neo- | _____ |

# Chapter 7  Cardiovascular System

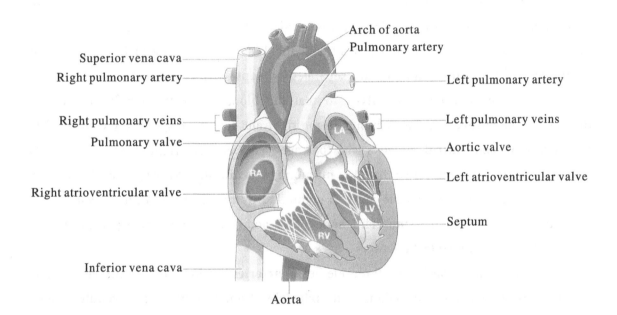

## Part One  Overview of the System

The cardiovascular system brings nutrients and other essential elements to the cells throughout the body and carries away wastes. The function is achieved mainly by the **heart**, **blood**, and **blood vessels**.

The heart is located in the **mediastinum** and serves as the pump of blood circulation. It is contained in the **pericardium** and consists of three portions, the **endocardium**, **myocardium** and **epicardium**. The heart is divided into four chambers: the left and right **atria** (sing. *atrium*) in the upper heart and the left and right **ventricles** in the lower heart. The atria and the ventricles are separated by **septa** (sing. *septum*). The openings in the heart are controlled by **valves** so that the blood flows through it in a certain direction. The atrioventricular openings in the right and left are respectively controlled by the **tricuspid** and **mitral valves**; the passage between the right ventricle and the pulmonary artery is controlled by the **pulmonary semilunar valve**; and the passage between the left ventricle and the aorta is controlled by the **aortic semilunar valve**. The heartbeat is initiated by the **sinoatrial node** (S-A node) and entails two phases: **systole** (contraction) and **diastole** (dilation).

Vascular system consists of three elements: **arteries**, **veins**, and **capillaries**, which join arteries and veins by connecting with **arterioles** (small arteries) and **venules** (small veins). Blood flows in two closed circuits, the **pulmonary circulation** and the **systemic circulation**, also called the **peripheral circulation**. As part of the systemic circulation, oxygen-rich blood flows from the **aorta** (the largest blood vessel in the body) to the **coronary artery** to nourish the heart. Blood pressure is the force that the blood exerts on the arterial walls and can be measured with **sphygmomanometer**.

**Whole blood** consists of two parts: the liquid portion, or **plasma**, and formed elements, or blood cells. Plasma contains water, nutrients, electrolytes, proteins, clotting factors, etc. **Serum** refers to the plasma without the clotting factors. Blood cells fall into three general types: **erythrocytes** (red blood cells), **leukocytes** (white blood cells) and **platelets** (thrombocytes). Erythrocytes contain **hemoglobin**, which combines with

## Chapter 7 Cardiovascular System

oxygen in the lungs and transports it to body cells. Leukocytes help the body fight against bacteria and infection and can be classified into **granulocytes** (characterized by the presence of granules in the cytoplasm) and **agranulocytes** (characterized by the absence of granules). Granulocytes are further divided into **neutrophils**, **basophils**, and **eosinophils**, which are named according to their staining properties. Agranulocytes include **monocytes** and **lymphocytes**. Platelets, though called thrombocytes, are actually fragments of cells and they initiate **blood clotting**, also called **coagulation**, when injury occurs.

### Exercise 1

*Fill in the blanks with the terms you have learned in the above passage.*

1. The heart wall consists of _____, _____ and _____ from the inside to the outside.
2. The chambers in the upper heart are called _____ and those in the lower heart are called _____.
3. The medical term for heart contraction and dilation is _____ and _____, respectively.
4. The largest blood vessel in the body is _____ and the artery supplying the heart is the _____ artery.
5. The atrioventricular valves on the right and the left are termed _____ and _____, respectively.
6. _____ refers to the liquid portion of blood and _____ refers to the liquid portion of blood that remains after the removal of clotting factors.
7. The medical terms for red blood cells and white blood cells are _____ and _____ respectively.
8. According to their affinity for different dyes, granulocytic white blood cells are divided into _____, _____ and _____.
9. Both monocytes and lymphocytes belong to _____.
10. The medical term for blood clotting is _____.

# Part Two  Combining Forms, Prefixes and Suffixes

## Group 1  Combining Forms and Prefixes for the Heart

❖ *atri/o* — *atrium* 心房
interatrial — between the atria
atriomegaly —

❖ *cardi/o* — *heart* 心脏
endocarditis — inflammation of the innermost lining of the heart
electrocardiogram —

❖ *ech/o* — *sound reverberation* 回声
echocardiograph — instrument for recording heart functions with the use of ultrasound waves
echogram —

❖ *electr/o* — *electricity* 电
electrocardiography — process of recording the electrical activity of the heart
electrosurgery —

❖ *pericardi/o* — *pericardium* 心包膜
pericardiocentesis — surgical puncture into the pericardium
pericarditis —

❖ *sept/o* — *septum* 隔膜
atrioseptoplasty — surgical repair of an atrial septum
septostomy —

## Chapter 7  Cardiovascular System

> **Tips**: *Septum* (pl. *septa*) refers to a thin dividing wall within or between parts of the body, e.g. in the nose, heart, etc. So *septoplasty* means surgical procedure to correct the shape of septum of the nose whereas *septostomy* often means the creation of an opening in the heart septum.

❖ ***sphygm/o***       ***pulse* 脉搏**

sphygmomanometer      an instrument to measure blood pressure (*manometer* meaning pressure meter)

sphygmology      _____

❖ ***valv/o, valvul/o***      ***valve* 瓣膜**

valvuloplasty      surgical repair of the valve

valvotomy      _____

❖ ***ventricul/o***      ***ventricle* 心室**

ventriculoscopy      endoscopic examination of a heart ventricle

interventricular      _____

❖ ***brady-***      ***slow* 缓慢；迟钝**

bradycardia      abnormally slow heart beat

(-cardia = heart condition)

bradysphygmia      _____

❖ ***tachy-***      ***fast* 快速**

tachyarrhythmia      abnormally rapid heart rhythm

tachypnea      _____

**Exercise 2**

*Explain the meanings of the following combining forms and prefixes.*

1. cardi/o  _____    2. atri/o  _____

3. ventricul/o _____
4. pericardi/o _____
5. sphygm/o _____
6. valvul/o _____
7. electr/o _____
8. sept/o _____
9. tachy- _____
10. brady- _____

### Exercise 3

**Build a medical term for each of the following definitions.**

1. inflammation of the inner lining of the heart _____
2. inflammation of the heart muscle _____
3. inflammation of the fibrous sac around the heart _____
4. surgical repair of a heart valve _____
5. surgical repair of a heart ventricle _____
6. surgical repair of an atrial septum _____
7. enlargement of the heart _____
8. enlargement of an atrium _____
9. rapid heart beat _____
10. abnormally slow heart rhythm _____

## Group 2  Combining Forms for Blood Vessels

❖ *angi/o, vas/o, vascul/o*          *vessel* 管道

angiography          radiography of a blood vessel _____
angioplasty
endovascular          within the vessels
vasculopathy
vasospasm          sudden contraction of the vessel
vasoconstriction

# Chapter 7  Cardiovascular System

> **Tips**: Although *angi/o* and *vas/o* usually refer to blood vessels, they have other meanings. For example, *angi/o* is commonly used for other types of vessels, as can be found in *cholangiography* and *lymphangiectomy*; *vas/o* is also used to refer to the vas deferens, as in *vasectomy* and *vasovasostomy*.

❖ *aort/o*      *aorta* 主动脉
aortoplasty      surgical repair of the aorta
aortostenosis

❖ *arter/o*, *arteri/o*      *artery* 动脉
endarterectomy      removal of the fatty deposits on the inner lining of the artery
polyarteritis
arteriorrhaphy      surgical suture of an artery
arteriotomy

❖ *arteriol/o*      *arteriole*, *small artery* 小动脉
arteriolosclerosis      hardening of the walls of small arteries
(-sclerosis = hardening)
arteriolar

❖ *ather/o*      *fatty plaque* 脂肪斑, 粥样斑
atheroma      abnormal mass of fatty deposits on the arterial wall
atherectomy

❖ *embol/o*      *embolus* (pl. *emboli*) 栓子
embolectomy      removal of the embolus
embolic

❖ **phleb/o, ven/o**       **vein** 静脉

phlebectasia            dilation of a vein

phlebotomy             _____

intravenous             within the vein

venogram              _____

❖ **thromb/o**           **thrombus, blood clotting** 血栓

thrombosis             condition caused by blood clotting

thrombolytic            _____

❖ **venul/o**            **venule, small vein** 小静脉

venular               pertaining to small veins

venulitis              _____

### Exercise 4

**Spell out the combining forms for the following meanings.**

1. vessel: _____  _____  _____
2. artery: _____  _____
3. vein: _____  _____
4. arteriole: _____
5. venule: _____
6. aorta: _____
7. fatty plaque: _____
8. thrombus: _____
9. embolus: _____

### Exercise 5

**Complete each of the medical terms according to the definitions given.**

1. surgical reshaping of the vessels: _____ plasty
2. pertaining to the heart and blood vessels: cardio _____
3. pertaining to blood vessels in the brain: cerebro _____
4. incision of an artery: _____ tomy

5. excision of a vein: _____ ectomy
6. within a vein: intra _____
7. within the aorta: intra _____
8. inflammation of a vein with blood clotting: _____ phlebitis
9. narrowing of an artery: _____ stenosis
10. narrowing of the aorta: _____ stenosis

## Group 3  Combining Forms for Blood Components

❖ *bas/o*  *base* 碱

basophil  granulocyte with special affinity for basic dyes

(-phil = affinity)

basophilous  _____

❖ *erythr/o*  *red* 红; *red blood cell* 红细胞

erythrocyte  red blood cell

erythropoiesis  _____

(-poiesis = formation)

❖ *granul/o*  *granule* 颗粒

granulocyte  white blood cell with cytoplasmic granules

agranulocytic  _____

❖ *hem/o, hemat/o*  *blood* 血

hemopathy  any disease with blood

hemolysis  _____

hematoma  collection of blood outside the blood vessels

hematopoiesis  _____

| ❖ *kary/o*, *nucle/o* | *nucleus* 核 |
|---|---|
| karyotype | arrangement of chromosomes in the nucleus |
| megakaryocyte | |
| mononuclear | having only one nucleus |
| nucleoid | |
| ❖ *leuk/o* | *white* 白；*white blood cell* 白细胞 |
| leukemia | condition characterized by unrestrained increase of white blood cells |
| leukocyte | |
| ❖ *morph/o* | *form* 形式 |
| morphology | study dealing with form and structure of organisms |
| polymorphonuclear | |
| ❖ *neutr/o* | *neutral* 中性；*neutrophil* 中性细胞 |
| neutralization | |
| neutropenia (-penia = deficiency) | |
| ❖ *poikil/o* | *varied* 异,变；*irregular* 不规则 |
| poikilocyte | an irregularly-shaped red blood cell |
| poikilothrombocyte | |
| ❖ *sider/o* | *iron* 铁 |
| hemosiderosis | increase of iron in tissues |
| siderophil | |

**Exercise 6**

*Explain the meanings of the following combining forms.*

1. bas/o  _____
2. granul/o  _____
3. erythr/o  _____
4. hem/o  _____
5. leuk/o  _____
6. poikil/o  _____
7. kary/o  _____
8. sider/o  _____
9. neutr/o  _____
10. morph/o  _____

# Chapter 7  Cardiovascular System

## Exercise 7

*Divide each of the following terms into its component parts with a slash (/) and then write out its meaning.*

1. histomorphology _____
2. eosinophilia _____
3. mononucleosis _____
4. antisideric _____
5. hemopathy _____
6. leukocytology _____
7. karyolysis _____
8. poikilocytosis _____
9. granuloma _____
10. amorphous _____

## Group 4  Suffixes

❖ **-apheresis**  *removal* 除去
plasmapheresis  removal of plasma from the other blood parts
plateletpheresis  _____

❖ **-emia**  *abnormal blood condition* 血症
ischemia  insufficient blood supply
(isch- = hold back, suppression)
anemia  _____

❖ **-cytosis**  *slight increase in cell numbers* 细胞增加
erythrocytosis  increase in the number of red blood cells
leukocytosis  _____

❖ **-penia**  *deficiency* 缺乏
pancytopenia  deficiency in all blood cells
(pan- = all)

| | | |
|---|---|---|
| granulopenia | | |
| ❖ -phil | one having affinity for something 亲, 嗜 | |
| chromophil | a cell or cell structure that stains readily | |
| (chrom/o = color) | | |
| neutrophil | | |
| ❖ -rrhage, -rrhagia | excessive discharge of blood 血流过多 | |
| hemorrhage | excessive bleeding | |
| gastrorrhagia | | |
| rhinorrhagia | | |
| ❖ -sclerosis | hardening 硬化 | |
| atherosclerosis | hardening of blood vessels due to fatty deposits | |
| arteriosclerosis | | |
| ❖ -stasis | control 停止; stoppage 淤滞 | |
| hemostasis | control of bleeding | |
| cholestasis | | |

### Exercise 8

*Draw a line between the suffixes and their corresponding meanings.*

1. -rrhage          a. blood condition
2. -stasis          b. deficiency
3. -sclerosis       c. affinity
4. -apheresis       d. a slight increase in cell number
5. -emia            e. control
6. -penia           f. removal
7. -cytosis         g. hardening
8. -phil            h. excessive discharge

## Chapter 7 Cardiovascular System

### Exercise 9

*Build medical terms according to the descriptions given.*

1. *Leukemia* refers to an increase in leukocytes; then, the condition marked by general increase in erythrocytes is _____.
2. *Hypertension* refers to high blood pressure; then, low blood pressure is called _____.
3. *Leukapheresis* refers to the separation of leukocytes from the rest of the blood; then, the separation of plasma from the blood cells is called _____.
4. *Granulocytosis* refers to an increase in granulocytes; then, an increase in monocytes is called _____.
5. *Arteriosclerosis* refers to the hardening of the arterial wall; then, the hardening of the venous wall is called _____.
6. *Oligosideremia* refers to a blood condition marked by insufficient iron (*olig/o* means scanty); then, a blood condition marked by increased sugar level (*glyc/o*) is _____.
7. *Splenorrhagia* is the discharge of blood from a ruptured spleen; then, the hemorrhage from liver is _____.
8. A *basophil* refers to a cell that stains readily with basic dyes; then, a/an _____ refers to a cell or other element that stains easily with red dyes.
9. *Eosinopenia* refers to a deficiency in eosinophils; then, a deficiency in neutrocytes is termed as _____.
10. *Hemostasis* refers to the stop/control of bleeding; then, the control of the growth of bacteria (*bacteri/o*) is _____.

# Part Three  Integrated Practice

## Exercise 10

Match the terms in Column I with their definitions in Column II. Place the correct letter of the definition to the left of the term.

**Column I**

_____ 1. venogram
_____ 2. atheroma
_____ 3. arteriotomy
_____ 4. thrombogenic
_____ 5. poikilocytosis
_____ 6. aortitis
_____ 7. hemostasis
_____ 8. diastole
_____ 9. tachycardia
_____ 10. hypertension
_____ 11. sphygmomanometer
_____ 12. granulocytopoiesis
_____ 13. leukemia
_____ 14. hemorrhage
_____ 15. plasma
_____ 16. embolectomy
_____ 17. hemolysis
_____ 18. vasculitis
_____ 19. neutropenia
_____ 20. neutrocytosis

**Column II**

a. inflammation of the aorta
b. incision of the artery
c. stop of bleeding
d. X-ray record of veins
e. destruction of blood cells
f. fatty deposit on the artery wall
g. deficiency in neutrophils
h. producing blood clot
i. fluid part of unclotted blood
j. uncontrolled bleeding
k. increase in neutrophils
l. period of ventricular filling
m. inflammation of blood vessels
n. production of granulocytes
o. high blood pressure
p. malignant neoplasm of WBCs
q. fast heart beat
r. removal of the embolus
s. presence of irregularly-shaped RBCs
t. instrument to measure blood pressure

## Part Four  Supplementary Readings

**Aneurysm** is the local widening of an artery caused by weakness in the arterial wall or breakdown of the wall owing to atherosclerosis. Common sites of aneurysm include cerebral arteries, abdominal aorta and carotid arteries. As the size of an aneurysm increases, there is an increased risk of rupture, which can result in severe hemorrhage or other complications. It may be possible to repair a dissecting aneurysm with a graft.

**Angina Pectoris**, commonly known as angina, is severe chest pain due to ischemia of the heart muscle, generally due to obstruction or spasm of the coronary arteries. Coronary artery disease, the main cause of angina, is due to atherosclerosis of the cardiac arteries. Beta blockers have a large body of evidence in morbidity and mortality benefits and short-acting nitroglycerin medications are used for symptomatic relief of angina.

**Cardiac Catheterization** is a procedure in which a catheter, by way of a peripheral artery, is introduced into a chamber of the heart or one of the major vessels so that the anatomy of the heart can be visualized and specific function tests performed. In addition, an angiocardiography, the injection of a special dye into the heart for further testing of function and possible occlusion, can also be performed during cardiac catheterization.

**Cholesterol** is a waxy fat like substance that travels in the blood in packages called lipoproteins. Some cholesterol in the blood is necessary; however, excessively high levels can lead to heart disease.

**Congenital Heart Diseases** refer to various congenital malformations in the structure of the heart and great vessels of a newborn. Major categories include (a) patent ductus arteriosus in which the blood vessel in the fetus that connects the pulmonary trunk with the aorta remains open, (b) septal defects in which there may be a hole in the interatrial or interventricular septa and (c) tetralogy of Fallot which involves four anatomic abnormalities, i.e. pulmonary stenosis, ventricular septal defect, right-sided aortic arch, and hypertrophy of the right ventricle.

**Electrophoresis** (*-phoresis* meaning carrying) refers to the movement of electrically charged particles suspended in a colloid solution under the influence of an electric current.

The direction, distance, and rate of movement of the particles vary according to their size, shape, and electrical charge. It is used to separate components of blood.

**Fibrillation** and **Flutter** refer to rapid and incomplete atrioventricular contractions and very rapid atrial contractions, respectively. Several areas of the heart act as pacemakers and heartbeat is weak and uncoordinated. Usually the use of external shock, called defibrillation, can bring back normal coordination.

**Hemophilia** is a group of hereditary genetic disorders that impair the body's ability to control blood clotting or coagulation. It occurs almost entirely in males. Major complications include hemarthrosis, hemorrhage, gastrointestinal bleeding, and menorrhagia.

**Palpitation** is a pounding or racing heart with or without irregularity in rhythm. It may be brought on by overexertion, adrenaline, alcohol, caffeine, cocaine, amphetamines, and other drugs, disease (such as hyperthyroidism) or as a symptom of panic disorder. It can also happen in mitral stenosis.

**Percutaneous Transluminal Coronary Angioplasty** is also called balloon angioplasty. In this procedure, a small balloon on the end of a catheter is used to open a partially blocked coronary artery by flattening the plaque deposit and stretching the lumen. After the plaque has been flattened, the balloon is deflated and the catheter and balloon are removed. *Percutaneous* means through the skin and *transluminal* means within the lumen of an artery.

**Varicose Veins** describe a swollen and twisted condition of veins, especially in the legs, due to damaged valves that fail to prevent the backflow of blood. As a result, blood collect in the veins and the veins are abnormally enlarged. This condition can impede blood flow and lead to edema, thrombosis, hemorrhage, or ulceration. A varicose vein near the anus is called a hemorrhoid.

*Chapter 7   Cardiovascular System*

# Part Five   Review Sheet

Here is a collection of the word parts you have learned in this chapter. Write the meaning of each word part without referring to your previous work.

## Combining Forms

| Combining Form | Meaning | Combining Form | Meaning |
|---|---|---|---|
| angi/o | _____ | neutr/o | _____ |
| aort/o | _____ | nucle/o | _____ |
| arter/o, arteri/o | _____ | pericardi/o | _____ |
| arteriol/o | _____ | phleb/o | _____ |
| ather/o | _____ | poikil/o | _____ |
| atri/o | _____ | sept/o | _____ |
| bas/o | _____ | sider/o | _____ |
| cardi/o | _____ | sphygm/o | _____ |
| ech/o | _____ | thromb/o | _____ |
| electr/o | _____ | valv/o | _____ |
| embol/o | _____ | valvul/o | _____ |
| erythr/o | _____ | vas/o | _____ |
| granul/o | _____ | vascul/o | _____ |
| hem/o, hemat/o | _____ | ven/o | _____ |
| kary/o | _____ | ventricul/o | _____ |
| leuk/o | _____ | venul/o | _____ |
| morph/o | _____ | | |

## Suffixes

| Suffix | Meaning | Suffix | Meaning |
|---|---|---|---|
| -apheresis | _____ | -phil | _____ |

| -emia | _____ | -rrhage, -rrhagia | _____ |
| -cytosis | _____ | -sclerosis | _____ |
| -penia | _____ | -stasis | _____ |

## Prefixes

| Prefix | Meaning | Prefix | Meaning |
| --- | --- | --- | --- |
| brady- | _____ | tachy- | _____ |

# Chapter 8  Lymphatic System and Immunity

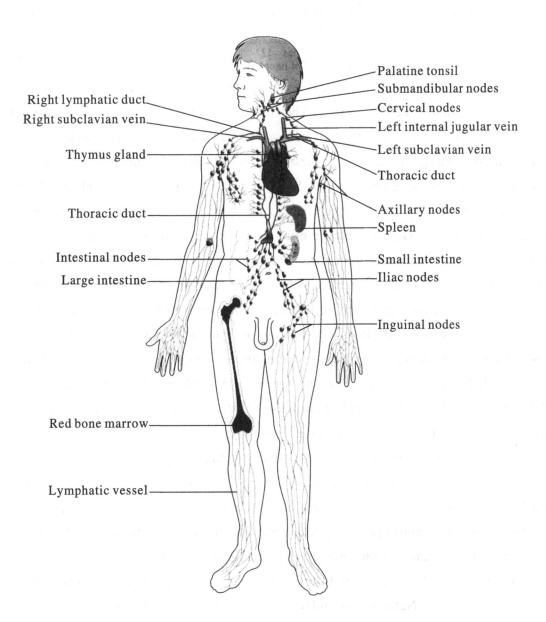

## Part One    Overview of the System

The lymphatic system has three primary functions. First of all, it returns **interstitial fluid** (ISF) to the blood. Next, it absorbs fats and fat-soluble vitamins from the digestive system and transports them to the blood. The last function is defense against invading micro-organisms and diseases.

The system consists of lymph, lymphatic vessels and lymphatic organs. **Lymph** is a clear, watery fluid collected from **interstitial spaces**, the spaces between cells, and has a composition similar to that of plasma. The fluid is picked up by the **lymphatic capillaries** found in almost all body regions and then moved away in the lymph vessels. Lymphatic vessels in the lining of the small intestines, called **lacteals**, are also responsible for absorption and transportation of fats. Such enriched lymph is called **chyle**. With the merging of smaller vessels into larger ones, the lymph is finally drained into two large **lymphatic ducts**: the **right lymphatic duct** receiving lymph from the upper right quadrant of the body and the **thoracic duct** receiving lymph from the rest of the body. From the lymphatic ducts, the fluid is returned to venous circulation. Along the path of lymphatic vessels are small masses of lymphoid tissue, or the **lymph nodes**. They filter and remove unwanted or infectious products out of the lymph as it passes through. They are concentrated in the **cervical**, **axillary**, **mediastinal** and **inguinal** regions. Other lymphatic organs include the spleen, thymus and tonsils. The **spleen**, located in the upper left abdomen, is similar to the lymph node except that it is larger and filled with blood. It filters the blood, removes old worn-out erythrocytes, produces lymphocytes and stores blood. The **thymus gland**, located in the mediastinum, partly controls the immune system by transforming lymphocytes into T cells, the cells responsible for cellular immunity. The **tonsils**, at the back of the throat, and the **adenoids**, at the back of nasal passage, act together to defend against upper respiratory tract infections. At puberty, the thymus begins to shrink gradually and the adenoids usually disappear altogether.

**Immunity** is the body's ability to resist infection, disease, or other unwanted biological invasions. **Natural immunity** is present from birth and includes skin, mucous

# Chapter 8  Lymphatic System and Immunity

membrane, tears, phagocytes, etc. ; **acquired immunity** develops later through natural exposure to invading microorganisms or through **immunization** (inducing immunity to prevent infections). In the case of acquired immunity, the body first must recognize the invading organisms as an **antigen** and then complex immune responses are mounted to produce **antibodies**, macrophages and other cells or substances against the antigenic material.

### Exercise 1

*Fill in the blanks with the terms you have learned in the above passage.*
1. The interstitial fluid that is drained into the lymph capillaries is called _____.
2. The lymph enriched by fats is called _____.
3. Lymph is finally emptied into venous circulation from two large lymph vessels: _____ and _____.
4. Lymph nodes are concentrated in cervical, _____, mediastinal and _____ regions.
5. Lymph organs include lymph nodes, _____, _____ and tonsils.

## Part Two  Combining Forms, Prefixes and Suffixes

### Group 1  Combining Forms and Suffixes for Lymphatics and Immunity

❖ *adenoid/o*      *adenoids* 腺样体
adenoidectomy     removal of the adenoids
adenoiditis     _____

❖ *immun/o*     *defense* 抵御
autoimmunity     defense against oneself
immunologist     _____

❖ ***lymph/o***      *lymph* 淋巴

lymphedema      swelling (of tissues) caused by lymphatic obstruction

lymphocyte      _____

❖ ***lymphaden/o***      *lymph node* 淋巴结

lymphadenectomy      removal of the lymph node

lymphadenopathy      _____

❖ ***lymphangi/o***      *lymphatic vessel* 淋巴管

lymphangiitis      infection of the lymphatic vessels (also spelled as *lymphangitis*)

lymphangiography      _____

❖ ***phag/o, -phage***      *eating, swallowing* 吞噬

phagocyte      cell that swallows microorganisms

phagocytosis      _____

macrophage      _____

❖ ***splen/o, lien/o***      *spleen* 脾脏

hypersplenism      overactivity of the spleen

splenomalacia      _____

lienomalacia      _____

hepatolienal      _____

---

**Tips**: As mentioned earlier, combining forms of different origins may have the same meaning. For examples, *lien/o* (Latin) and *splen/o* (Greek) refer to the spleen. Such combining forms always compete for usage. In some cases, only one can be used, e.g. *nephrology* but never \**renology*. In other cases, both can be used, but with different popularity. For example, you can see both *lienomalacia* and *splenomalacia* in the dictionary, but the latter may be more often used by your professors. So you have to refer to the dictionary to decide which one is correct.

## Chapter 8  Lymphatic System and Immunity

❖ *thym/o*  *thymus gland* 胸腺
thymoma  tumor of the thymus gland
thymotoxic  _____

❖ *tonsill/o*  *tonsils* 扁桃体
tonsillitis  inflammation of the tonsils
tonsillectomy  _____

❖ *-blast*  *embryonic cell* 胚细胞
lymphoblast  embryonic lymphocyte
osteoblast  _____

❖ *-rrhexis*  *rupture* 破裂
angiorrhexis  rupture of the vessels
lymphocytorrhexis  _____

### Exercise 2

*Spell out the combining forms or suffixes for the following meanings.*

1. defense _____          6. spleen _____
2. lymph node _____      7. eating _____
3. lymph vessel _____    8. rupture _____
4. thymus _____          9. adenoids _____
5. tonsils _____         10. embryonic cell _____

### Exercise 3

*Divide each of the following terms into its component parts with a slash (/) and then write out its meaning.*

1. immunogenic _____
2. immunodeficiency _____
3. lymphadenosis _____
4. lymphangioadenography _____
5. lymphangiectasis _____

· 121 ·

6. karyorrhexis _____
7. thymopathy _____
8. splenalgia _____
9. perisplenitis _____
10. hepatosplenomegaly _____

## Group 2  Combining Forms and Suffixes for Pathogenic Organisms

❖ *bacill/i*      *bacillus*（pl. *bacilli*），*rod-shaped bacterium* 杆菌
bacilliform      having the appearance of a bacillus
bacillary      _____

❖ *bacteri/o*      *bacterium*（pl. *bacteria*）细菌
bacteriemia      presence of bacteria in the blood
bacteriology      _____

❖ *fung/i*, *myc/o*      *fungus*（pl. *fungi*）真菌
antifungal      destroying or inhibiting the growth of fungi（also called antimycotic）
fungitoxic      _____
mycosis      any disease caused by fungi
mycology      _____

❖ *phyt/o*      *plant* 植物
phytotoxin      the poisonous substance produced by a plant
phytogenesis      _____

❖ *vir/o*      *virus* 病毒
viremia      presence of virus in the blood
antiviral      _____

## Chapter 8  Lymphatic System and Immunity

| | |
|---|---|
| ❖ -cide | ***killing; an agent that kills or destroys*** 杀 |
| bactericide | an agent that kills bacteria |
| fungicide | |
| | |
| ❖ -coccus | ***round bacteria***（pl. *cocci*）球菌 |
| streptococcus | a round bacterium occurring in twisted chains |
| (strepto- = twisted) | |
| staphylococcus | a round bacterium occurring in grapelike clusters |
| (staphylo- = a bunch of grapes) | |
| | |
| ❖ -gen | ***origin, producer*** 源 |
| antigen | producer of defense |
| pathogen | |
| | |
| ❖ -static | ***inhibiting*** 抑制; ***an agent that inhibits the growth of an organism*** 抑制剂 |
| bacteriostatic | an agent inhibiting the growth of bacteria |
| fungistatic | |

### Exercise 4

*Draw a line between the combining forms or suffixes and their corresponding meanings.*

1. myc/o          a. round bacteria
2. bacteri/o      b. rod-shaped bacteria
3. bacill/i       c. fungi
4. -coccus        d. virus
5. vir/o          e. bacteria
6. -cide          f. producer
7. -static        g. an agent that kills
8. -gen           h. an agent that inhibit

# Exercise 5

**Build a medical term for each of the following definitions.**

1. the study of bacteria _____
2. the study of viruses _____
3. an agent that inhibits the growth of rickettsiae (rickettsi/o) _____
4. inhibiting the growth of fungi (fung/i) _____
5. an agent that kills bacteria _____
6. an agent that kills bacilli _____
7. a substance that causes allergic reaction _____
8. a substance that causes fever (pyr/o) _____

## Group 3  Combining Forms and Suffixes for Oncology

| | |
|---|---|
| ❖ *carcin/o* | *cancer* 癌 |
| carcinoma | cancerous tumor |
| carcinogen | _____ |
| | |
| ❖ *chem/o* | *chemistry* 化学; *drug* 药物 |
| chemotherapy | treatment by using drugs |
| chemolysis | _____ |
| | |
| ❖ *mut/a* | *change* 变化 |
| mutagenic | producing genetic change |
| mutation | _____ |
| | |
| ❖ *onc/o* | *tumor* 肿瘤 |
| oncogenesis | development of tumor |
| oncology | _____ |
| | |
| ❖ *radi/o* | *rays*, *X-rays* 放射 |
| radiologist | _____ |
| radiotherapy | |

# Chapter 8  Lymphatic System and Immunity

❖ *sarc/o*　　　　　*flesh, connective tissue* 肉
sarcoma　　　　　tumors arising from connective tissues
osteosarcoma　　_____

❖ *-oma*　　　　　*mass, tumor* 肿块,肿瘤
myoma　　　　　tumor of muscles
myeloma　　　　_____

❖ *-plasia*　　　　*formation* 发展,形成
hyperplasia　　　excessive formation
dysplasia　　　　_____

❖ *-plasm*　　　　*anything formed or molded* 组成物
neoplasm　　　　new formation; tumor
cytoplasm　　　　_____

❖ *-therapy*　　　　*treatment* 治疗
hydrotherapy　　　treatment by using water
hormonotherapy　_____

**Exercise 6**

*Draw a line between the combining forms or suffixes and their corresponding meanings. Note that different combining forms may have the same meaning.*

1. onc/o　　　　　a. chemistry
2. -oma　　　　　b. cancer
3. carcin/o　　　　c. treatment
4. sarc/o　　　　　d. flesh
5. mut/a　　　　　e. formation
6. -plasia　　　　　f. anything that is formed
7. -plasm　　　　　g. tumor
8. radi/o　　　　　h. change
9. chem/o　　　　　i. rays
10. -therapy

## Exercise 7

*Choose the appropriate term from the following list for each of the given definitions.*

| radiosensitive | aplasia | physiotherapy | carcinoma | mutant |
| osteosarcoma | hypoplasia | sarcoma | osteoma | carcinogen |

1. An individual in which a mutation has occurred is _____.
2. Defective development resulting in the absence of all or part of an organ or tissue is called _____.
3. The cancer-causing gene is called _____.
4. Malignant tumor of bone is _____.
5. Benign tumor of bone is _____.
6. Cancer cells that are particularly susceptible to radiation is described as being _____.
7. Cancer that arises in epithelial cells is _____.
8. Any cancer of connective tissue is _____.
9. Treatment involving physical methods, such as the use of light, heat, electric current, etc., is termed _____.
10. Incomplete development of an organ or a part is called _____.

## Group 4  Singular and Plural Endings

Many medical terms originate from Greek and Latin words and their plurals are thus derived by the rules of these languages. Other words are changed from singulars to plurals by following English rules. Thus, each medical term needs to be considered individually when they are changed from the singular to the plural form. The table below shows some general rules in producing plural forms.

## Chapter 8  Lymphatic System and Immunity

| Singular Endings | Plural Endings | Examples Singular →Plural |
|---|---|---|
| -a | -ae | *vertebra →vertebrae* |
| -ax | -aces | *thorax →thoraces* |
| -en | -ina | *lumen →lumina* |
| -ix, -ex | -ices | *appendix →appendices* |
| -sis | -ses | *diagnosis →diagnoses* |
| -on | -a | *ganglion →ganglia* |
| -um | -a | *ovum →ova* |
| -us | -i | *nucleus →nuclei* |
| -y | -ies | *deformity →deformities* |
| -ma | -mata | *carcinoma →carcinomata* |
| -nx | -ges | *phalanx →phalanges* |

### Exercise 8

*Write out the plural forms of the following terms.*

1. sarcoma  _____
2. biopsy  _____
3. cortex  _____
4. patella  _____
5. metastasis  _____
6. digitus  _____
7. ileum  _____
8. spermatozoon  _____
9. foramen  _____
10. larynx  _____

# Part Three  Integrated Practice

## Exercise 9

**Select the correct answer to complete each of the following statements.**

1. The ability of the body to resist foreign organisms and toxins is known as _____.
   a. antitoxicity            b. immunity
   c. phagocytosis            d. resistance

2. Clusters of small oval-shaped tissue along the path of lymph vessels are _____.
   a. antibodies              b. lymph nodes
   c. macrophages             d. tonsils

3. Lymphadenitis is defined as _____.
   a. any disease of the lymph nodes      b. enlargement of the lymph nodes
   c. inflammation of the lymph nodes     d. stoppage of lymph flow

4. _____ is rupture of the heart.
   a. cardiorrhaphy           b. cardiorrhexis
   c. cardiodynia             d. cardioplegia

5. _____ refers to unusually large immature red blood cell.
   a. erythropoietin          b. macrophage
   c. megaloblast             d. erythremia

6. In emergency cases of ruptured spleen, _____ is sometimes performed to remove the spleen.
   a. splenorrhaphy           b. splenectomy
   c. splenorrhexis           d. splenotomy

7. _____ is benign tumor composed of a mass of dilated lymph vessels.
   a. Lymphangioma            b. Lymphoma
   c. Thymoma                 d. Hodgin disease

8. The term for the process of white blood cells clearing away pathogens and debris is _____.
   a. leukopoiesis            b. phagocytosis
   c. immunization            d. macrophage

9. _____ is the substance that induces sensitivity or an immune response in the form of antibodies.
   a. Autoimmunity            b. Immunology
   c. Antigen                 d. Mutant

10. Inflammation of a lymph node is _____.
    a. lymphadenitis          b. lymphangitis
    c. lymphatitis            d. tonsillitis

11. The process of cancer formation is medically called _____.
    a. metastasis             b. carcinogenesis
    c. metaplasia             d. oncogenesis

12. _____ refers to the procedure to destroy tumor cells or tissues.
    a. Thymolysis             b. Thymectomy
    c. Oncolysis              d. Oncotomy

13. An agent inhibiting the growth of bacteria is called _____.
    a. bacteriostat           b. bacteriotoxin
    c. bacteriemia            d. bactericide

14. _____ refers to the condition in which the number of red cells, white cells, and platelets in the blood decreases due to destruction of these cells by an overactive spleen.
    a. Hypersplenism          b. Hyposplenism
    c. Splenomegaly           d. Splenopathy

15. The plural forms of *calyx* and *alveolus* are _____.
    a. calyxes, alveoluses    b. calyces, alveoli
    c. calyses, alveoli       d. calyces, alveoluses

# Part Four  Supplementary Readings

**AIDS**, acquired immunodeficiency syndrome, is a set of symptoms and infections resulting from the damage to the human immune system caused by the human immunodeficiency virus (HIV). This condition progressively reduces the effectiveness of the immune system and leaves individuals susceptible to opportunistic infections and tumors. HIV is transmitted through direct contact of a mucous membrane or the bloodstream with a bodily fluid containing HIV, such as blood, semen, vaginal fluid, preseminal fluid, and breast milk. AIDS is now a pandemic disease. Although antiretroviral treatment reduces both the mortality and the morbidity of HIV infection, these drugs are expensive and routine access to antiretroviral medication is not available in all countries.

**Allergy** is an overreaction of the immune system to a substance that is harmless to most people, such as pollens, dust mites, molds, danders, and certain foods. Allergic reactions occur only on second or subsequent exposure to the allergen, once first contact has sensitized the body. Common allergic reactions include eczema, hives (urticaria), hay fever, asthma, food allergies, and anaphylactic shock. Treatments for allergies include allergen avoidance, use of anti-histamines, steroids or other oral medications, immunotherapy to desensitize the response to allergen, and targeted therapy.

**Anaphylaxis** is a severe and generalized allergic response that can lead rapidly to death as a result of shock and respiratory distress. It must be treated by immediate administration of epinephrine (adrenaline), maintenance of open airways, and antihistamines. Common causes of anaphylaxis are drugs, especially penicillin and other antibiotics, vaccines, diagnostic chemicals, foods and insect venom.

**Bacteria** (sing. *bacterium*) are a group of single-celled microscopic organisms abundant in the soil, air and water. Most bacteria are harmless to humans and some bacteria, such as those in the intestine, are beneficial and help to break down food for digestion. Bacteria that cause diseases are known as *pathogens* and are classified by shape into three main groups: cocci (spherical), bacilli (rod-shaped), and spirochetes (spiral-shaped).

*Chapter 8   Lymphatic System and Immunity*

**ELISA**, abbreviation for Enzyme-Linked ImmunoSorbent Assay, is a sensitive immunoassay that uses an enzyme linked to an antibody or antigen as a marker for the detection of a specific protein, especially an antigen or antibody. It is often used as a diagnostic test to determine exposure to a particular infectious agent, such as the AIDS virus, by identifying antibodies present in a blood sample.

**Hodgkin Disease**, also known as Hodgkin lymphoma, is a malignancy affecting the lymphatic system. Symptoms include night sweats, fatigue, anorexia, swollen lymph nodes, splenomegaly, hepatomegaly, pain following alcohol consumption and itching. The survival rate is generally around 90% when the disease is detected relatively early.

**Viruses** are very small infectious agents that live only by invading cells. Within the cell, the virus reproduces and then breaks the cell wall. The newly formed viruses are released so they can spread to other cells. Viral infection can be prevented with the use of a vaccine. Antibiotics are not effective against a virus. Common diseases caused by viruses include herpes, varicella, measles, AIDS, mumps, influenza, etc.

**Western blot assay** is an immunological technique for the detection of specific proteins. After separation by electrophoresis, the proteins are bound to radioactively labelled antibodies and identified by X-ray. Currently, it is used as a confirmatory test for HIV exposure.

## Part Five   Review Sheet

Here is a collection of the word parts you have learned in this chapter. Write the meaning of each word part without referring to your previous work.

**Combining Forms**

| Combining Form | Meaning | Combining Form | Meaning |
|---|---|---|---|
| adenoid/o | _____ | mut/a | _____ |
| bacill/i | _____ | myc/o | _____ |
| bacteri/o | _____ | onc/o | _____ |

| | | | |
|---|---|---|---|
| carcin/o | _____ | phag/o | _____ |
| chem/o | _____ | phyt/o | _____ |
| fung/i | _____ | radi/o | _____ |
| immune/o | _____ | sarc/o | _____ |
| lien/o | _____ | splen/o | _____ |
| lymph/o | _____ | thym/o | _____ |
| lymphaden/o | _____ | tonsill/o | _____ |
| lymphangi/o | _____ | vir/o | _____ |

**Suffixes**

| Suffix | Meaning | Suffix | Meaning |
|---|---|---|---|
| -blast | _____ | -phage | _____ |
| -cide | _____ | -phasia | _____ |
| -coccus | _____ | -plasm | _____ |
| -gen | _____ | -rrhexis | _____ |
| -static | _____ | -therapy | _____ |
| -oma | _____ | | |

# Chapter 9  Nervous System

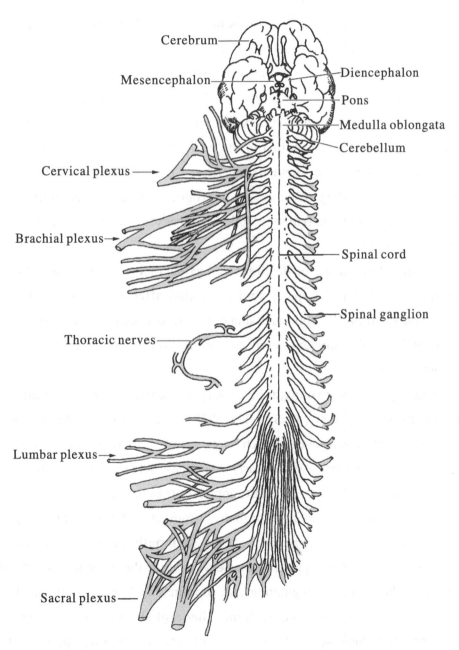

## Part One  Overview of the System

The nervous system is responsible for regulating body functions and body movements, keeping us aware of the changes in the external and internal environments and enabling us to carry on higher mental processes.

The basic unit of the nervous system is the **neurons** (nerve cells). Each neuron has a cell body and, extending from it, two types of fibers: **axons** and **dendrites**. The **impulse** travels along a neuron only in one direction: from the dendrite, to the cell body and then to the axon. The impulse is transmitted to the next neuron across the **synapse** through the release of a chemical substance, **neurotransmitter**. Except neurons, the nervous system has several types of supporting cells, called **neuroglia**, which are supportive, connective and phagocytic in function. **Astrocytes**, **oligodendrocytes**, and **microglia** are the three major types of neuroglia.

A **nerve** refers to a bundle of dendrites and axons that travel together. **Nerves** which carry impulses to the brain and spinal cord are called **afferent** (sensory) **nerves**; those which carry impulses from the brain and spinal cord to organs are called **efferent** (motor) **nerves**. A **ganglion** (pl. *ganglia*) refers to a collection of nerve cell bodies outside the brain and spinal cord.

The nervous system has two major divisions: the **central nervous system** (CNS) and the **peripheral nervous system** (PNS). The CNS consists of the **brain** and **spinal cord**; the PNS consists of **cranial nerves**, which carry impulses between the brain and the head and neck, and **spinal nerves**, which carry messages between the spinal cord and the chest, abdomen and extremities. The **autonomic nerves** in the PNS control involuntary body functions and automatically carry impulses from the CNS to muscles, glands, and internal organs. In the autonomic nervous system, **sympathetic nerves** stimulate the body in times of stress whereas **parasympathetic nerves** return the body to a steady state.

The brain is the center for regulating and coordinating body activities and consists of four major parts: the **cerebrum**, **cerebellum**, **diencephalons** (containing **thalamus** and **hypothalamus**) and **brainstem** (composed of the **midbrain**, **pons** and **medulla**

# Chapter 9  Nervous System

**oblongata**). Each of the different parts controls different body functions. The **cortex**, the grey matter on the surface of cerebrum, is the main region for conscious thought, sensation and movement. The spinal cord carries all the nerves that affect the limbs and lower part of the body. The brain and spinal cord are surrounded by three membranes, called the **meninges**, which are the **dura mater**, **arachnoid membrane** and **pia mater** from the outside to the inside. A watery fluid called the **cerebrospinal fluid** (CSF) circulates the brain and spinal cord and protects them from shock.

### Exercise 1

***Fill in the blanks with the terms you have learned in the above passage.***

1. The nervous system consists of the nerve cells and the supporting cells, also called _____ and _____.
2. _____ is a fiber of a neuron that conducts impulses toward the cell body whereas _____ is the fiber of a neuron that conducts impulses away from the cell body.
3. The junction between two nerve cells is called _____. The impulse is transmitted between nerve cells with the aid of _____.
4. Nerves that transmit impulse from the brain and spinal cord to organs are motor nerves, also called _____ and nerves that transmit impulse to the brain and spinal cord are sensory nerves, also called _____.
5. The four major parts of the brain include _____, _____, _____, and _____.
6. The entire cerebrum is covered with a thin layer of grey matter, called _____.
7. Vital centers for control of respiration, heart rate, and blood pressure are found in _____.
8. Diencephalon is composed of many smaller parts and two of them are _____ and _____.
9. The brain and spinal cord are covered by three layers of _____, respectively called _____, _____ and _____ from the outside to the inside.
10. The autonomic nervous system innervates glands, smooth muscles and cardiac muscles and is further divided into _____ and _____.

# Part Two  Combining Forms, Prefixes and Suffixes

## Group 1  Combining Forms for the Nervous System and the Spinal Cord

❖ *astr/o*      *star shaped* 星形
astrocyte      star-shaped cells
astrocytoma

❖ *gangli/o*, *ganglion/o*      *ganglion* 神经节
ganglionectomy      removal of a ganglion
gangliopathy

❖ *gli/o*      *glue* 胶质；*neuroglia* 神经胶质
glioma      tumor of neuroglial cells
gliotoxin

❖ *medull/o*      *medulla* 髓
intramedullary      within the medulla
extramedullary

> **Tips**: *Medulla* (*medull/o*) refers to the middle of something, and derives from the Latin word for "marrow" (the Latin equivalent of the Greek root *myel/o*). In medicine, it refers to medulla oblongata, bone marrow, the spinal cord, or more generally, the middle part of a structure (as opposed to the cortex).

## Chapter 9 Nervous System

❖ **meningi/o, mening/o** — **meninges** 脑脊膜
- meningocele — herniation of the meninges
- meningioma — _____
- meningeal — _____

❖ **myel/o, spin/o** — **spinal cord** 脊髓
- poliomyelitis — inflammation of the gray matter of the spinal cord
  ( polio- = gray )
- myelography — _____
- cerebrospinal — _____
- supraspinal — _____

❖ **neur/o** — **nerve** 神经
- neurolysis — destruction of a nerve
- polyneuritis — _____

❖ **radicul/o** — **root of the spinal nerve** 脊神经根
- polyradiculitis — inflammation of many nerve roots ( also called *polyradiculopathy* )
- radiculalgia — _____

❖ **thec/o** — **sheath** 鞘; **meninges** 脑脊膜
- intrathecal — within the meninges
- extrathecal — _____

### Exercise 2

*Explain the meanings of the following combining forms.*

1. mening/o _____
2. thec/o _____
3. radicul/o _____
4. gangli/o _____
5. gli/o _____
6. neur/o _____
7. myel/o _____
8. astr/o _____

## Exercise 3

*Build a medical term for each of the following defintions.*

1. inflammation of the meninges _____
2. inflammation of the spinal cord _____
3. condition (-ia) in which there is hemorrhage (hemat/o) into the spinal cord _____
4. pain in a nerve _____
5. pain in the spinal cord _____
6. excision of the nerve root _____
7. excision of a ganglion _____
8. surgery to repair a nerve _____
9. study of the nerve system and the related diseases _____
10. a surgeon who specializes in operations on the nervous system _____

### Group 2  Combining Forms for the Brain

❖ *cerebell/o* — *cerebellum* 小脑
decerebellation — removal of cerebellum
supracerebellar — _____

❖ *cerebr/o* — *cerebrum* 大脑
cerebrovascular — pertaining to the blood vessels in the brain
cerebrotomy — _____

❖ *cortic/o* — *cortex* 皮质
subcortical — below the cortex
corticospinal — _____

❖ *dur/o* — *hard* 硬；*dura mater* 硬脑膜
subdural — below the dura mater
epidural — _____

# Chapter 9  Nervous System

| | | |
|---|---|---|
| ❖ *encephal/o* | ***brain*** 脑 | |
| encephalomalacia | softening of the brain tissue | |
| electroencephalogram | | |
| ❖ *lept/o* | ***thin , slender*** 薄；软；细 | |
| leptomeningitis | inflammation of the leptomeninges | |
| leptomeningopathy | | |
| ❖ *pont/o* | ***pons*** 脑桥 | |
| cerebellopontine | pertaining to the cerebellum and pons | |
| pontomedullary | | |
| ❖ *thalam/o* | ***thalamus*** 丘脑 | |
| hypothalamic | below the thalamus | |
| thalamotomy | | |
| ❖ *ventricul/o* | ***ventricle*** 脑室 | |
| ventriculometry | measurement of the intraventricular cerebral pressure | |
| supraventricular | | |

**Tips**: As you may remember, *ventricul/o* also means *ventricles* in the heart. Thus, *ventriculography* can refer to radiography of the brain ventricles or of that of the heart ventricles. You need to determine the specific meaning by the context.

# Exercise 4

**Draw a line between the combining forms and their corresponding meanings.**

1. dur/o            a. cortex
2. encephal/o       b. thin
3. pont/o           c. ventricle
4. cerebr/o         d. brain
5. cortic/o         e. cerebellum
6. thalam/o         f. cerebrum
7. ventricul/o      g. thalamus
8. lept/o           h. pons
9. cerebell/o       i. dura matter

# Exercise 5

**Divide each of the following terms into its component parts with a slash (/) and then explain its meaning.**

1. cerebrothalamic _____
2. pontoencephalic _____
3. extracorticospinal _____
4. peridurography _____
5. encephalocele _____
6. meningoencephalopathy _____
7. epicerebral _____
8. electrocorticogram _____
9. ventriculostomy _____
10. hydrocephalus _____

# Chapter 9　Nervous System

## Group 3　Combining Forms for Functions

❖ *ambul/o*     *walking* 走动

| | |
|---|---|
| somnambulism | sleepwalking |
| ( somn- = sleep ) | |
| ambulatory | |

❖ *hypn/o , somn/o*     *sleep* 睡眠

| | |
|---|---|
| hypnosis | a sleeplike state |
| hypnotize | |
| polysomnograph | instrument for recording various body parameters in sleep |
| somnolence | |

❖ *kinesi/o , -kinesis*     *movement* 运动

| | |
|---|---|
| hyperkinesis | state of overactivity |
| kinesiology | |

❖ *narc/o*     *stupor* ; *sleep* ; *numbness* 昏迷;昏睡

| | |
|---|---|
| narcosis | state of stupor induced by drugs |
| antinarcotic | |

❖ *psych/o*     *mind* 心理

| | |
|---|---|
| psychiatrist | a specialist intreatment of mental disorders |
| ( iatr/o = treatment ) | |
| psychologist | |

❖ *schiz/o*     *a split or division* 分裂

| | |
|---|---|
| schizophrenia | "split mind", used to describe a severe mental disorder |
| ( -phrenia = mind condition ) | |
| schizophasia | |
| ( -phasia = speech condition ) | |

❖ *somat/o*        *body* 身体

psychosomatic      pertaining to the mind and body

somatotype         _____

❖ *ton/o*           *tension* 紧张; *tone* 张力

dystonia           any abnormality in muscle tone

tonometer         _____

### Exercise 6

**Draw a line between the combining forms and their corresponding meanings.**

1. ambul/o        a. body
2. ton/o           b. splitting
3. hypn/o         c. stupor
4. somn/o         d. sleep
5. narc/o          e. sleep
6. psych/o       f. walking
7. schiz/o         g. tension
8. somat/o       h. mind

### Exercise 7

**Build a medical term for each of the following definitions.**

1. pertaining to the mind and body _____
2. pertaining to the study of mental disorders and their treatment _____
3. pertaining to the study of movements _____
4. pertaining to the movement of white blood cells _____
5. not able to fall asleep or to remain asleep for an adequate length of time _____
6. extremely sleepy _____
7. pertaining to the treatment (-therapy) conducted in hypnosis _____
8. pertaining to the absence of muscle tension _____

## Chapter 9 Nervous System

> **Group 4  Suffixes for Conditions**

❖ **-asthenia**          ***weakness*, *debility* 无力,虚弱**

neurasthenia           "weakness of the nervous system", used to describe a psychological disorder characterized by chronic fatigue and weakness, anxiety, pains, etc.

myasthenia            _____

> **Tips**: Human knowledge in medicine is constantly improving and increasing. Thus, you may find that the literal interpretation of some age-old medical terms reflects people's understanding at a certain time, which in our eyes today, may be partial, limited, or even misleading. For example, *neurasthenia* literally means nervous exhaustion; but now, it has acquired more exact medical definitions. You can compare the literal meanings of *orthopedics* and its medical meanings. For this reason, a responsible medical student should always be ready to refer to medical textbooks or encyclopedia to find the exact meanings of some confusing terms.

❖ **-esthesia**          ***feeling*, *sensation* 感觉**

anesthesia             loss of feeling

hyperesthesia          _____

❖ **-lexia**             ***word*, *phrase* 词语**

dyslexia              difficulty with words

alexia                _____

❖ **-mania**            ***obsession* 躁狂,迷恋**

kleptomania           obsessive impulse to steal
(klept/o = stealing)

nosomania            _____
(nos/o = disease)

| | | |
|---|---|---|
| ❖ *-paresis* | ***slight paralysis*** 轻瘫 | |
| hemiparesis | slight paralysis of one side of the body | |
| myoparesis | | |
| ❖ *-phasia* | ***speech*** 言语 | |
| aphasia | loss of the ability to speak properly | |
| monophasia | | |
| ❖ *-phobia* | ***fear*** 恐惧 | |
| photophobia | abnormal fear of light | |
| hydrophobia | | |
| ❖ *-plegia* | ***paralysis*** 瘫痪 | |
| paraplegia | paralysis of the lower half of the body | |
| diplegia | | |
| ❖ *-praxia* | ***action*** 行动 | |
| apraxia | loss of the ability to perform purposeful movements | |
| eupraxia | | |
| ❖ *-taxia* | ***order, coordination*** 调节,协调 | |
| ataxia | lack of muscle coordination | |
| hemiataxia | | |

### Exercise 8

***Explain the meanings of the following suffixes.***

1. -esthesia  _____
2. -asthenia  _____
3. -mania  _____
4. -taxia  _____
5. -lexia  _____
6. -paresis  _____
7. -phasia  _____
8. -phobia  _____
9. -praxia  _____
10. -plegia  _____

Chapter 9   Nervous System

### Exercise 9

*Complete the terms for the following definitions.*

1. lack of coordination: a _____
2. weakness of muscles: my _____
3. paralysis of one side of the body: hemi _____
4. partial paralysis of one side of the body: hemi _____
5. abnormal fear of diseases: noso _____
6. disorder or difficulty in speech communication: dys _____
7. pertaining to loss of sensation: an _____
8. false sensation: pseudo _____
9. abnormal slowness in reading: brady _____
10. excessive movements: hyper _____

## Part Three   Integrated Practice

### Exercise 10

*Write the plural or adjective form of each of the following terms as required.*

1. thalamus _____ ( adj. )
2. pons _____ ( adj. )
3. coma _____ ( adj. )
4. meninges _____ ( adj. )
5. cortex _____ ( adj. )
6. psychosis _____ ( adj. )
7. syncope _____ ( adj. )
8. ganglion _____ ( pl. )
9. plexus _____ ( pl. )
10. stimulus _____ ( pl. )
11. sulcus _____ ( pl. )
12. gyrus _____ ( pl. )

# Exercise 11

**Select the correct answer to complete each of the following statements.**

1. Paralysis of a single limb is termed _____.
   - a. monoplegia
   - b. quadriplegia
   - c. hemiplegia
   - d. monopathy

2. _____ is the thin surface layer of gray matter of the cerebrum.
   - a. Medulla
   - b. Meninges
   - c. Cortex
   - d. Ganglion

3. Abnormal fear of high places is termed _____.
   - a. hydrophobia
   - b. acrophobia
   - c. nosomania
   - d. kleptomania

4. Abnormal slowness in reading is termed _____.
   - a. dyslexia
   - b. bradylexia
   - c. dysphasia
   - d. alexia

5. The surgical excision of a part of the nerve is termed _____.
   - a. neurolysis
   - b. neurectomy
   - c. neuroplasty
   - d. neurotomy

6. _____ cells are nerve cells that do not carry impulses.
   - a. Neuroglial
   - b. Parenchymal
   - c. Efferent
   - d. Afferent

7. A collection of nerve cell bodies outside the CNS is _____.
   - a. ganglion
   - b. microglia
   - c. synapse
   - d. plexus

8. Excessively large size of head is termed _____.
   - a. macrocephaly
   - b. anencephaly
   - c. hydrocephalus
   - d. hemicephalia

9. _____ refers to any disorder of the brain.
   - a. Gangliopathy
   - b. Encephalopathy
   - c. Radiculopathy
   - d. Cerebropathy

## Chapter 9 Nervous System

10. Protrusion of the meninges is termed _____ .
    a. myelocele            b. meningioma
    c. meningocele          d. meningitis

11. _____ is a general term covering severe mental and emotional disorders.
    a. Neurosis             b. Psychosis
    c. Narcosis             d. Thrombosis

12. A _____ is a physician who studies nerve system disorders.
    a. psychologist         b. psychiatrist
    c. neurologist          d. neurosurgeon

13. _____ is the malignant tumor originating from the supporting cells of the CNS.
    a. Glioma               b. Meningioma
    c. Hematoma             d. Neuroma

14. Inability to perform a particular movement or task as a result of brain dysfunction is _____ .
    a. agnosia              b. aphasia
    c. apraxia              d. apoplexy

15. _____ is characterized by brief, uncontrollable sleep during the day.
    a. Narcolepsy           b. Insomnia
    c. Somnambulism         d. Hypnosis

16. Nutritional deficiencies, especially of Vitamin B, may cause _____, inflammation of many nerves at once.
    a. radiculitis          b. meningitis
    c. myelitis             d. polyneuritis

17. The procedure to record brain electric activity is termed _____ .
    a. electrocardiography  b. electromyography
    c. electroencephalography d. electrospinography

18. _____ means above cerebellum.
    a. Supracerebellar      b. Extracerebellar
    c. Supracerebral        d. Extracerebellar

19. _____ refers to the procedure in which contrast medium is injected into the subarachnoid space and X-rays are taken of the spinal cord.
   a. Ventriculography            b. Myelography
   c. Encephalography             d. Cerebral angiography
20. _____ means muscle weakness.
   a. Gangliasthenia              b. Hypasthenia
   c. Neurasthenia                d. Myasthenia

# Part Four  Supplementary Readings

**Alzheimer's disease (AD)** is the most common form of dementia beginning in middle age. It results from unexplained degeneration of neurons and atrophy of the cerebral cortex. These changes cause progressive loss of recent memory, followed by impairment of cognition and personality changes. AD is diagnosed by CT or MRI scans and confirmed at autopsy. Histological studies show deposits of amyloid in the tissues.

**Cerebral concussion** is a limited period of unconsciousness caused by injury to the head. It may last for a few seconds or a few hours. Severe concussion may lead to coma.

**Coma** is a profound state of unconsciousness. A comatose person cannot be awakened, fails to respond normally to pain or light, does not have sleep-wake cycles, and does not take voluntary actions. Comas may result from intoxication, metabolic abnormalities, stroke, hypoxia, head trauma, etc.

**Epilepsy** is recurrent, unprovoked seizures due to abnormal electric activity of the brain. The more severe seizure, called a *grand mal* is accompanied by convulsions and unconsciousness; the less severe seizure, called a *petit mal*, is accompanied by a minor lapse in consciousness. Epileptic seizures are controlled with antiepileptics and anticonvulsants.

**Migraine** is a neurological syndrome characterized by altered bodily experiences, painful headaches, and nausea. The typical migraine headache is one-sided and throbbing, lasting 4 to 72 hours. Accompanying complaints are nausea and vomiting, and photophobia and hyperacusis. Approximately one third of migraineurs get a preceding aura, in which a patient may sense a strange light or unpleasant smell. The treatment of migraine includes painkillers for headache, anti-emetics for nausea, and avoidance of triggers if present.

**Palsy** is paralysis. Cerebral palsy is partial paralysis and lack of muscular coordination caused by damage to the cerebrum during gestation or in the perinatal period. Bell's palsy involves unilateral facial paralysis, which is due to the temporary paralysis of the seventh cranial nerve and causes drooping only on the affected side of the face.

**Parkinson's disease** (**PD**) is a degenerative disorder of the central nervous system that often impairs the sufferer's motor skills, speech, and other functions. Motor disturbances include shuffling gait, muscle rigidity, tremor of hands, bradykinesia and, in extreme cases, akinesia. The chronic, progressive condition is caused by the insufficient formation and action of dopamine, which is produced in the dopaminergic neurons of the brain. PD can be idiopathic and secondary, as due to drug toxicity, head trauma, etc.

**Sciatica** is inflammation of the sciatic nerve that results in pain, burning, and tingling along the course of this nerve through the thigh and leg.

**Spina Bifida** is a congenital defect affecting the embryonic development of the spinal column. The spinal cord does not form completely and the vertebrae overlying the open portion of the spinal cord remain unfused and open. Through the opening, the abnormal portion of the spinal cord may stick out. Spina bifida falls into several categories, including spina bifida occulta, spina bifida cystica (also called myelomeningocele) and meningocele. Spina bifida usually occurs in the lumbar and sacral areas of the spinal cord.

**Stroke** (**apoplexy**) is the rapidly developing loss of brain functions due to a disturbance in the blood vessels supplying blood to the brain. This can be due to ischemia caused by thrombosis or embolism or due to a hemorrhage. As a result, the function of the affected area of the brain is impaired or lost. Aphasia and hemiplegia are among the common aftereffect.

**Syncope** (also called **fainting**) is a sudden, usually temporary, loss of consciousness induced by insufficient oxygen in the brain through cerebral hypoxia, hypotension, hypoglycemia and other factors.

**Tetanus**, is a medical condition that is characterized by a prolonged contraction of skeletal muscle fibers. The primary symptoms are caused by tetanospasmin, a neurotoxin produced by the Gram-positive, obligate anaerobic bacterium *Clostridium tetani*. Infection

generally occurs through wound contamination, and often involves a cut or deep puncture wound. As the infection progresses, muscle spasms in the jaw develop, followed by difficulty in swallowing and general muscle stiffness and spasms in other parts of the body. Infection can be prevented by proper immunization and by post-exposure prophylaxis.

## Part Five  Review Sheet

Here is a collection of the word parts you have learned in this chapter. Write the meaning of each word part without referring to your previous work.

**Combining Forms**

| Combining Form | Meaning | Combining Form | Meaning |
| --- | --- | --- | --- |
| ambul/o | _____ | myel/o | _____ |
| astr/o | _____ | narc/o | _____ |
| cerebell/o | _____ | pont/o | _____ |
| cerebr/o | _____ | psych/o | _____ |
| cortic/o | _____ | schiz/o | _____ |
| dur/o | _____ | somat/o | _____ |
| encephal/o | _____ | somn/o | _____ |
| gangli/o, ganglion/o | _____ | spin/o | _____ |
| gli/o | _____ | neur/o | _____ |
| hypn/o | _____ | radicul/o | _____ |
| kinesi/o | _____ | thalam/o | _____ |
| lept/o | _____ | thec/o | _____ |
| medull/o | _____ | ton/o | _____ |
| meningi/o, mening/o | _____ | ventricul/o | _____ |

## Chapter 9 Nervous System

**Suffixes**

| Suffix | Meaning | Suffix | Meaning |
|---|---|---|---|
| -asthenia | _____ | -phobia | _____ |
| -esthesia | _____ | -plegia | _____ |
| -lexia | _____ | -praxia | _____ |
| -mania | _____ | -taxia | _____ |
| -paresis | _____ | | |

# Chapter 10   Endocrine System

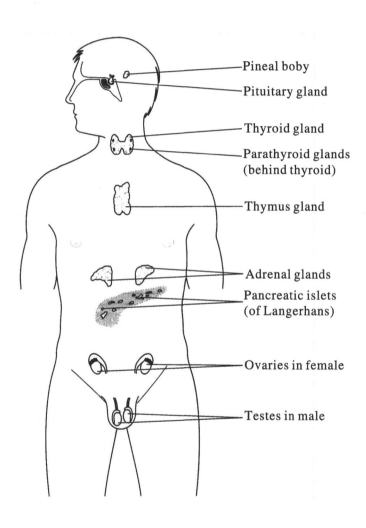

*Chapter 10  Endocrine System*

# Part One  Overview of the System

The endocrine system includes a group of glands located in different parts of the body. These glands produce and secrete **hormones** to regulate the body's growth, metabolism and sexual development and function. The endocrine glands are ductless, which means that the hormones are released directly into the bloodstream to be taken up by target organs and cells.

The major glands of the endocrine system include:

## *Pituitary Gland*

The pituitary gland is located at the base of the brain beneath the hypothalamus and is no larger than a pea. Because it grows at the underside of the brain, the pituitary gland is also called **hypophysis**. It is divided into two parts: the anterior lobe called **adenohypophysis** and the posterior lobe known as **neurohypophysis**.

The anterior lobe produces the following hormones under the regulation of the hypothalamus:

- Growth hormone (GH): stimulates growth of bone and tissue

- Thyroid-stimulating hormone (TSH): stimulates the thyroid gland to produce thyroid hormones.

- Adrenocorticotropin hormone (ACTH): stimulates the adrenal gland to produce several related steroid hormones

- Luteinizing hormone (LH) and follicle-stimulating hormone (FSH): control sexual function and production of the sex hormones

- Prolactin: stimulates milk production in females

The posterior lobe produces the following hormones, which are not regulated by the hypothalamus:

- Antidiuretic hormone (vasopressin): controls water loss by the kidneys

❖ Oxytocin: contracts the uterus during childbirth and stimulates milk production

## *Pineal Body*

The pineal body is a small gland in the brain. It secretes hormone melatonin, which is believed to have aregulatory effect on behavior and sexual development in response to environmental light.

## *Thyroid Glands*

The thyroid glands are located on both side of larynx and upper trachea. It produces thyroid hormones that not only regulate the body's metabolism, but also help maintain normal blood pressure, heart rate, digestion, muscle tone, and reproductive functions. The pituitary gland controls the release of thyroid hormones.

## *Parathyroid Glands*

The parathyroid glands are two pairs of small glands embedded in the surface of the thyroid gland, one pair on each side. They release parathyroid hormone, which plays a role in regulating calcium levels in the blood and bone metabolism.

## *Adrenal Glands*

The adrenal glands are triangular-shaped glands located on top of each kidney. The adrenal glands are made up of the outer adrenal **cortex**, and the inner adrenal **medulla**. Adrenal cortex produces corticosteroids, which regulate the body's metabolism, the balance of salt and water in the body, the immune system, and sexual function. Adrenal medulla produces adrenaline and noradrenaline. These hormones help the body cope with physical and emotional stress by increasing the heart rate and blood pressure.

## *Reproductive Glands*

The reproductive glands are the main source of sex hormones. In males, the testes secrete hormones called androgens, the most important of which is testosterone. These hormones affect male characteristics as well as sperm production. In females, the ovaries produce estrogen and progesterone as well as eggs. These hormones control the development of female characteristics, and reproductive functions (for example, menstruation, and pregnancy).

## *Pancreas*

The pancreas is an elongated organ located toward the back of the abdomen behind the stomach. It has both digestive and hormonal functions. The **islet of Langerhans** in the pancreas secretes hormones called insulin and glucagon. These hormones regulate the level of glucose (sugar) in the blood.

> **Exercise 1**

***Fill in the blanks with the terms you have learned in the above passage.***
1. The chemicals secreted by the endocrine glands are called _____.
2. The pituitary gland is divided into two lobes: the anterior lobe is called _____ and the posterior lobe called _____.
3. The two pairs of glands embedded in the thyroid gland are called _____.
4. The release of thyroid hormonesis controlled by _____.
5. The adrenal glands are divided into two parts, the outer part is called _____, and the inner part is called _____.
6. The male hormones are produced by _____, and female hormones are produced by _____.
7. The hormones that help with the regulation of blood sugar are produced by _____.

# Part Two  Combining Forms, Prefixes and Suffixes

### Group 1  Combining Forms for Organs

| | |
|---|---|
| ❖ *adren/o, adrenal/o* | *adrenal glands* 肾上腺 |
| adrenosclerosis | hardening of the adrenal glands |
| adrenalectomy | _____ |
| ❖ *cortic/o* | *cortex* 皮质 |
| corticorenal | pertaining to the cortex of the kidney |
| corticectomy | _____ |
| ❖ *gonad/o* | *sex glands (ovaries and testes)* 性腺 |
| gonadoblastoma | tumor of the immature cells of the sex glands |

| | | |
|---|---|---|
| gonadogenesis | | |
| ❋ **gon/o** | ***sex glands, genetalia*** 性腺,生殖器 | |
| gonocyte | sex cell, reproductive cell | |
| gonoblast | | |
| ❋ ***hypophys/o, pituitar/i*** | ***pituitary gland, hypophysis*** 脑垂体 | |
| hypophysopathy | disease of the pituitary gland | |
| hypophysectomy | | |
| hypopituitarism | deficiency in the hormone secretion of pituitary gland | |
| hyperpituitarism | | |
| ❋ ***parathyroid/o*** | ***parathyroid gland*** 甲状旁腺 | |
| parathyroidectomy | removal of parathyroid gland | |
| parathyroidoma | | |
| ❋ ***thyr/o, thyroid/o*** | ***thyroid gland*** 甲状腺 | |
| thyrocardiac | pertaining to the thyroid gland and heart | |
| thyromegaly | | |
| hyperthyroidism | excessive secretion of the thyroid gland | |
| thyroidopathy | | |

**Exercise 2**

*Explain the meanings of the following combining forms.*

1. hypophys/o _____     5. parathyroid/o _____
2. thyroid/o _____      6. pancreat/o _____
3. gonad/o _____        7. cortic/o _____
4. adren/o _____        8. gon/o _____

# Chapter 10  Endocrine System

## Exercise 3

*The suffix "-ism" is used to denote the endocrine dysfunction and the prefix "hyper-" or "hypo-" is used to describe the overactivity or underactivity of the gland. Build medical terms for the following definitions.*

1. underactivity of the pituitary gland _____
2. overactivity of the parathyroid gland _____
3. underactivity of the thyroid gland _____
4. overactivity of the spleen _____
5. underactivity of the gonad _____
6. overactivity of thyroid gland _____

## Exercise 4

*Build a medical term for each of the following definitions.*

1. incision into the thyroid gland _____
2. tumor of the pancreas _____
3. removal of the pituitary gland ( hypophys/o ) _____
4. enlargement of the adrenal gland ( adren/o ) _____
5. disease of the sex gland _____

### Group 2  Combining Forms for Hormone Secretions

| | |
|---|---|
| ❖ *andr/o* | *androgen, male* 雄性,男性 |
| androgen | male sex hormone |
| andromorphous | (of women) having male forms |
| ❖ *crin/o* | *secretion* 分泌 |
| endocrine | secretion inside the body |
| exocrine | _____ |

| ❖ *estr/o*, *gynec/o* | *female*, *woman* 雌性,女性 |
|---|---|
| estrogen | female sex hormone |
| gynecophobia | |
| gynecology | |
| ❖ *hormon/o* | *hormone* 激素 |
| hormonogenic | pertaining to the formation of the hormone |
| hormonotherapy | |
| ❖ *idi/o* | *self*, *unknown* 自发的 |
| idiopathy | disease of unknown cause |
| idiolysis | |
| ❖ *insulin/o* | *insulin* 胰岛素; *pancreatic islets* 胰岛 |
| insulinoma | tumor of the pancreatic islets |
| insulinopenia | |
| ❖ *lact/o* | *milk* 乳汁 |
| prolactin | chemical to promote the production of milk |
| lactorrhea | |
| ❖ *somat/o* | *body* 体 |
| somatocyte | body cell |
| somatopathy | |
| ❖ *toc/o* | *labor* 生产,分娩 |
| eutocia | normal labor |
| dystocia | |
| ❖ *tox/o*, *toxic/o* | *poison*, *toxin* 毒药,毒素 |
| toxemia | presence of toxins in the blood |
| antitoxin | |
| toxicodermatitis | inflammation of skin due to toxin |
| toxicology | |

# Chapter 10  Endocrine System

**Exercise 5**

*Explain the meanings of the following combining forms.*

1. toxic/o _____
2. lact/o _____
3. insulin/o _____
4. somat/o _____
5. andr/o _____
6. estr/o _____
7. crin/o _____
8. hormon/o _____
9. idi/o _____
10. toc/o _____

**Exercise 6**

*Complete the following statements.*

1. Lactation refers to the production and secretion of _____.
2. Female sex hormones are called _____.
3. Male sex hormones are called _____.
4. Toxicologist refers to specialist in _____.
5. Insulogenic refers to the production of _____.
6. A person with somatomegaly has exceptionally large _____.
7. Hormonotherapy refers to treatment using _____.
8. Bradytocia means slow _____.
9. Endocrine refers to _____ inside the body.

## Group 3  Suffixes and Prefixes

❖ *-agogue*          *inducing, leading* 引导,导出

lactagogue           inducing of the secretion of milk

hormonagogue         inducing of the secretion of hormone

❖ *-fugal*           *away from, flee* 逃逸,离开

corticofugal         away from the cortex

centrifugal          _____

## 医学英语词汇学
### English Medical Terminology

- **-in**
  adrenalin
  pepsin

  *substance* 物质
  a substance produced by the adrenal gland

- **-petal**
  centripetal
  corticopetal

  *toward*, *seek* 移向
  pertaining to toward the center

- **-privia**
  hormonoprivia
  thyroprivia

  *deprivation*, *without* 缺乏
  lack of the secretion of the hormone

- **-tropin**
  somatotropin
  lactotropin

  *hormone to stimulate* 促…激素
  a hormone to stimulate the growth of the body

- **acr(o)-**
  acromegaly
  acrocyanosis

  *extremity*, *tip* 肢端, 尖
  enlargement of the extremities

- **oxy-**
  oxytocin
  (toc/o = labor)
  oxytocia
  oxyopia (-opia = vision)
  oxyphonia (-phonia = sound)
  oxyhemoglobin
  oxyhemograph

  *quick* 快; *sharp* 敏锐, 尖; *acid* 酸; *oxygen* 氧
  a chemical to help contract the uterus to induce quick labor

  sharp vision

  hemoglobin that carries oxygen

- **para-**
  parathyroid
  paraneural
  parasecretion
  paraphasia

  *beside*, *near* 旁; *abnormal* 异常
  the gland that sits near the thyroid gland

  abnormal secretion

Chapter 10  Endocrine System

### Exercise 7

*Explain the meanings of the following suffixes and prefixes.*

1. para- _____
2. -privia _____
3. acro- _____
4. -tropin _____
5. -therapy _____

6. oxy- _____
7. -petal _____
8. -fugal _____
9. -agogue _____
10. -in, -ine _____

### Exercise 8

*Draw a line between the chemicals and their corresponding functions.*

1. somatotropin
2. thyrotropin
3. corticotrophin
4. oxytocin
5. gonadotropin
6. leuteinizing hormone
7. prolactin
8. antidiuretic hormone

a. stimulating ovulation
b. stimulating the thyroid gland
c. stimulating milk production
d. stimulating sex hormone production
e. promoting reabsorption of water in kidney
f. stimulating growth
g. stimulating the cortex of adrenal glands
h. stimulating contraction of uterus during childbirth

## Group 4  Combining Forms for Minerals and Chemicals

❖ *calc/o, calc/i*    *calcium* 钙
calcipexy            fixation of calcium
calcipenia           _____

❖ *carb/o*           *carbon* 碳
carbocyclic          having a ring composed of carbon
carbonic             _____

· 161 ·

| | | |
|---|---|---|
| ❖ *cupr/o* | *copper* 铜 | |
| cupriuria | presence of copper in urine | |
| cupremia | | |
| ❖ *iod/(o)* | *iodine* 碘 | |
| iodemia | presence of iodine in blood | |
| iodimetry | | |
| ❖ *kal/i* | *potassium* 钾 | |
| cytokalipenia | lack of potassium in the cell | |
| hyperkalemia | | |
| ❖ *natr/o* | *sodium* 钠 | |
| hypernatremia | excessive amount of sodium in blood | |
| hyponatremia | | |
| ❖ *phosph/o, phosphor/o* | *phosphorus* 磷 | |
| phosphopenia | lack of phosphorus | |
| phosphoruria | | |
| phosphorolysis | | |
| ❖ *sacchar/(o)* | *sugar* 糖 | |
| sacchariferous | containing sugar | |
| saccharase | | |
| ❖ *sider/o* | *iron* 铁 | |
| siderogenous | pertaining to producing iron | |
| sideropenia | | |

# Chapter 10  Endocrine System

### Exercise 9

*Explain the meanings of the following combining forms.*

1. natr/i  _____
2. kal/i  _____
3. iod/o  _____
4. cupr/o  _____
5. carb/o  _____
6. sider/o  _____
7. calc/i  _____
8. phosph/o  _____
9. racchar/o  _____

### Exercise 10

*Complete the following definitions.*

1. Calcipexy is the fixation of _____.
2. Natriuresis is the excessive loss of _____ in urine.
3. Kaliuresis is the excessive loss of _____ in urine.
4. Sideroderma refers to the brownish discoloration of the skin due to the deposit of _____.
5. Saccharimeter is the instrument to measure _____.
6. Triiodide contains three _____.
7. Cupriuria is the presence of _____ in urine.
8. Phosphopenia refers to the lack of _____.

# Part Three  Integrated Practice

### Exercise 11

Match the terms in Column I with their definitions in Column II. Place the correct letter of the definition to the left of the term.

**Column I**

_____ 1. gonadotropin (FSH)
_____ 2. adenogenous
_____ 3. antidiuretic hormone
_____ 4. adrenalin
_____ 5. hypophysis
_____ 6. parathyroid gland
_____ 7. thyrotropin (TSH)
_____ 8. thyromegaly
_____ 9. adenohypophysitis
_____ 10. pituitarism
_____ 11. parathyroidectomy
_____ 12. adenomalacia
_____ 13. adrenalopathy
_____ 14. hypopituitarism
_____ 15. adenectomy

**Column II**

a. synonym for epinephrine
b. thyroid-stimulating hormone,
c. an anterior pituitary hormone that stimulates estrogen production
d. synonym for pituitary gland
e. originating in a gland
f. hormone secreted by the posterior pituitary to prevent the kidneys from expelling too much water
g. disease of the adrenal glands
h. condition of diminished hormone secretion from the pituitary gland
i. inflammation of the anterior pituitary gland
j. softening of the gland
k. enlargement of the thyroid gland
l. excision of parathyroid gland
m. any pituitary dysfunction
n. excision of a gland
o. one of the four glands embedded in the thyroid gland

## Chapter 10  Endocrine System

### Exercise 12

*Build a medical term for each of the following definitions.*

1. anterior pituitary gland _____
2. inflammation of the hypophysis _____
3. medical specialty of the endocrine system _____
4. hormone secreted by the posterior pituitary gland to prevent the kidneys from expelling too much water _____
5. synonym for adrenaline _____
6. excessive hormone secretion by the pituitary gland _____
7. surgical removal of one or both adrenal glands _____
8. excision of the thyroid and parathyroid glands _____
9. hormone to stimulate quick labor _____
10. underactivity of the thyroid gland _____

## Part Four  Supplementary Readings

**Diabetes Insipidus** is the result of a lack of (hyposecretion) antidiuretic hormone of the neurohypophysis. Water is not reabsorbed by the kidneys. Polyuria and polydipsia occur as a result of water not being reabsorbed by the kidneys.

**Diabetes Mellitus** is a disorder of glucose metabolism caused by deficiency of insulin production or failure of the tissues to respond to insulin. The word mellitus comes from the Latin root for honey, referring to the sugar content of the urine. Type 1 is juvenile-onset or insulin-dependent diabetes mellitus (IDDM). It involves destruction of the islet cells of the pancreas and complete deficiency of insulin in the body; Type 2 is adult-onset or non-insulin-dependent diabetes mellitus (NIDDM). The islet cells are not destroyed and there is a relative deficiency of insulin secretion with a resistance by target tissues to the action of insulin.

**Acromegaly** refers to the enlargement of the extremities due to the excessive secretion of growth hormone (GH) from the anterior pituitary gland in adults. There is overgrowth of bones and soft tissues, especially in the hands, feet, face and jaw. The cause of the disease could be the benign pituitary adenoma which suppresses the anterior lobe to result in an excess of GH.

**Gigantism** happens when the benign adenoma of pituitary gland occurs before puberty. The excessive growth hormone can lead to abnormal overgrowth of the body. Prognosis of the disease could be favorable with early detection and surgical removal of the pituitary tumor.

**Addison Disease** is a chronic disorder caused by a deficiency of cortical hormones, which occurs when the adrenal cortex is damaged or atrophied. Atrophy of the adrenal glands is probably the result of an autoimmune process in which circulating adrenal antibodies slowly destroy the gland. Hypofunction of the adrenal cortex interferes with the body's ability to handle internal and external stress. In severe cases, the disturbance of sodium and potassium metabolism may be marked by depletion of sodium and water through urination, resulting in severe chronic dehydration. Other clinical manifestations include muscular weakness, anorexia, gastrointestinal symptoms, fatigue, hypoglycemia, hypotension, hyponatremia, and hyperkalemia. The disease is now curable by replacement hormone therapy.

**Cushing Syndrome** is a hormonal disorder caused by high level of corticosteroid hormones in the blood. Cushing's syndrome is characterized by a red moon-shaped face, wasting of the limbs, thickening of the trunk, and a humped upper back. Other symptoms include weakening of the bones by osteoporosis, susceptibility to infection and peptic ulcers, and, in women, increased hairiness. The excess hormones are due to prolonged treatment with corticosteroid drugs or overactivity of the adrenal glands as a result of an adrenal tumor or a pituitary tumor affecting production of ACTH, which stimulates the adrenal glands.

**Hyperthyroidism** refers to the overproduction of thyroid hormones by an overactive thyroid gland. The most common form of hyperthyroidism is Graves' disease, which is an autoimmune disorder. The characteristic signs of hyperthyroidism include weight loss, increased appetite, increased sweating, intolerance to heat, a rapid heart rate, and protruding eyes. In severe cases, the thyroid gland often becomes enlarged (goiter) and

## Chapter 10  Endocrine System

there is physical and mental hyperactivity and muscle wasting.

**Hypothyroidism** refers to the underproduction of thyroid hormones by the thyroid gland. Symptoms include tiredness and lethargy. There may also be muscle weakness, cramps, a slow heart rate, dry skin, hair loss, a deep and husky voice, and weight gain. A syndrome called myxoedema, in which the skin and other tissues thicken, may develop. Enlargement of the thyroid gland may also occur (goiter). If the condition occurs in childhood, it may retard growth and normal development. The disorder is diagnosed by measuring the level of thyroid hormones in the blood. Treatment consists of replacement therapy with the thyroid hormone thyroxine, usually for life.

## Part Five  Review Sheet

Here is a collection of the word parts you have learned in this chapter. Write the meaning of each word part without referring to your previous work.

**Combining Forms**

| Combining Form | Meaning | Combining Form | Meaning |
|---|---|---|---|
| adren/o, adrenal/o | | iod/o | |
| andr/o | | insulin/o | |
| calc/o | | kal/i | |
| carb/o | | lact/o | |
| cortic/o | | natr/o | |
| crin/o | | pituitar/i | |
| cupr/o | | parathyroid/o | |
| estr/o | | phosph/o, phosphor/o | |
| gonad/o | | sacchar/o | |
| gynec/o | | sider/o | |
| gon/o | | somat/o | |
| hormon/o | | thyr/o, thyroid/o | |
| hypophys/o | | toc/o | |
| idi/o | | tox/o, toxic/o | |

## Suffixes

| Suffix | Meaning | Suffix | Meaning |
|---|---|---|---|
| -agogue | _____ | -petal | _____ |
| -fugal | _____ | -privia | _____ |
| -in | _____ | -tropin | _____ |

## Prefixes

| Prefix | Meaning | Prefix | Meaning |
|---|---|---|---|
| acr(o)- | _____ | para- | _____ |
| oxy- | _____ | | |

# Chapter 11  Urinary System

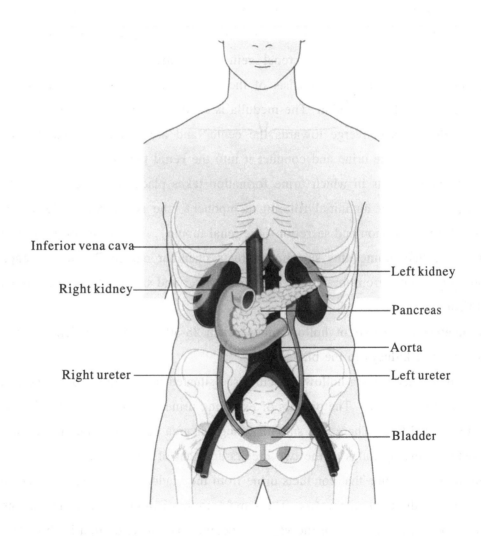

# Part One  Overview of the System

The urinary system is composed of two kidneys, two ureters, a urinary bladder, and a urethra. It is responsible for excreting excess water, urea, uric acid, and other wastes from the blood, and keeping the pH (relation of acids to bases) in balance.

The kidneys are bean shaped organs located between the peritoneum and the posterior abdominal wall. The indented portion of the kidney at the medial direction is the **hilum** through which the renal artery, the renal vein, lymphatic vessels and nerves pass. The internal structure of the kidneys consists of the outer granular area called **cortex** and the inner striated area called **medulla.** The medulla is subdivided into several pyramidal lobes. The tips of the lobes converge towards the center and are cupped by the tubular **renal calices**. They collect the urine and conduct it into the **renal pelvis**.

The functional units in which urine formation takes place are called **nephrons**. Each nephron is composed of an initial filtering component, the **renal corpuscle** and a tubule specialized for reabsorption and secretion (the renal tubule). The renal corpuscle is a clump of capillaries called **glomerulus** surrounded by a chamber named **Bowman's capsule.** It filters out large solutes from the blood, delivering water and small solutes to the renal tubule for modification.

The **ureters** are a pair of hollow tubes, each 25-30 cm long, which conducts urine from the pelvis of kidneys to the bladder.

The urinary bladder is a hollow muscular sac situated behind the pubic bone and serves as a reservoir for the urine. The process of expelling urine through the urethra is also called **micturation** or **voiding**. There is a smooth triangular area called **trigone** at the base of the bladder between the openings of the two ureters and that of the urethra.

The urethra is a tube that conducts urine from the bladder to the exterior. The external opening is called the urethral **meatus**. The female urethra is a thin-walled tube about 3.5cm long and is located just in front of the vaginal opening. The male urethra is about 20cm long and is also a part of the reproductive system.

# Chapter 11 Urinary System

**Exercise 1**

*Fill in the blanks with the terms you have learned in the above passage.*

1. The _____ is the outer, granular area of the kidney; and the _____ forms the inner, striated part of the kidney.
2. The renal corpuscle is a clump of capillaries called _____ surrounded by a chamber named _____.
3. The external opening of the urethra is called _____.
4. The basic structural and functional unit of the kidney is _____.
5. The _____ are a pair of hollow tubes that conducts urine from the kidneys to the bladder.
6. The smooth triangular area at the base of the bladder between the openings of the two ureters and that of the urethra is called _____.
7. The process of urination is also called _____ or _____.

## Part Two  Combining Forms, Prefixes and Suffixes

### Group 1  Combining Forms of Body Parts

❖ *cal/i, calic/o*      calyx, cup 肾盏
caliceal     pertaining to the calyx
calicectomy     _____

❖ *cyst/o, vesic/o*      sac, bladder 囊；膀胱
cystostomy     surgical creation of an opening into the bladder
cystography     _____
vesicorectal     pertaining to the urinary bladder and rectum
vesicostomy     _____

| | |
|---|---|
| ❖ *glomerul/o* | *glomerulus*(pl. glomeruli）肾小球 |
| glomerulopathy | disease of the glomerulus |
| glomerulonephritis | |
| ❖ *meat/o* | *opening*, *meatus* 门；开口 |
| meatoscopy | endoscopic examination of the meatus |
| meatotomy | |
| ❖ *nephr/o*, *ren/o* | *kidney* 肾脏 |
| hydronephrosis | fluid accumulation inside the kidney |
| nephromegaly | |
| suprarenal | pertaining to the glands that located above the kidneys |
| adrenal | |
| ❖ *pyel/o* | *renal pelvis* 肾盂 |
| pyelonephritis | inflammation of the pelvis of the kidney |
| pyelotomy | |
| ❖ *trigon/o* | *trigone* 膀胱三角 |
| trigonitis | inflammation of the urinary trigone |
| ❖ *tubul/o* | *small tube*, *tubule* 小管 |
| tubulopathy | disease of the renal tubules |
| tubular | |
| ❖ *ureter/o* | *ureter* 输尿管 |
| ureterostenosis | narrowing of the ureters |
| ureteroplasty | |
| ❖ *urethr/o* | *urethra* 尿道 |
| urethrodynia | pain of the urethra |
| urethrocystitis | |
| ❖ *ur/o* | *urine* 尿；*urinary system* 泌尿系统 |
| uropenia | lack of urination |

# Chapter 11  Urinary System

( -penia = deficiency )

urology _____

### Exercise 2

*Draw a line between the combining forms and their corresponding meanings.*

1. cyst/o          a. calyx
2. glomerul/o      b. urine
3. nephr/o         c. ureter
4. urethr/o        d. urethra
5. ureter/o        e. renal pelvis
6. meat/o          f. kidney
7. pyel/o          g. glomerulus
8. ur/o            h. bladder
9. calic/o         i. opening

### Exercise 3

*Py/o means pus or suppuration. Explain the meanings of the following terms.*

1. pyuria _____
2. pyonephritis _____
3. pyocalyx _____
4. pyopyelectasis _____
5. pyocystitis _____

### Exercise 4

*Choose the appropriate term from the following list for each of the given definitions.*

| pyelophlebitis | nephroptosis | nephropathy | cystourethrogram | acystia |
| cystotomy | urethralgia | meatoscope | pyelonephritis | glomerulosclerosis |

1. inflammation of the veins of the renal pelvis _____
2. disease of the kidney _____
3. incision into the urinary bladder _____

· 173 ·

4. X-ray record of the urinary bladder and urethra _____
5. an instrument to view the meatus _____
6. congenital absence of bladder _____
7. falling of the kidney _____
8. hardening of the glomerulus _____
9. pain of the urethra _____
10. inflammation of the renal pelvis and kidney _____

### Group 2  Suffixes Related to the System

❖ **-clysis**　　　　　　*washing, irrigation* 灌洗
vesicoclysis　　　　　　washing of the urinary bladder
peritoneoclysis　　　　_____

❖ **-lithiasis**　　　　　*formation of stones* 结石形成
urolithiasis　　　　　　formation of the stones in the urinary tract
rhinolithiasis　　　　　_____

❖ **-lysis**　　　　　　*breaking down, separation* 溶解；分解
dialysis　　　　　　　　complete separation of the harmful substance from the blood
hemolysis　　　　　　　_____

❖ **-pexy**　　　　　　*surgical fixation* 固定术
nephropexy　　　　　　surgical fixation of the kidney
enteropexy　　　　　　_____

❖ **-poiesis**　　　　　*formation, production* 生成，形成
uropoiesis　　　　　　formation of urine
hemopoiesis　　　　　_____

❖ **-poietin**　　　　　*substance to produce* 生成素
erythropoietin　　　　substance to produce red blood cells
leukopoietin　　　　　_____

## Chapter 11  Urinary System

❖ *-rrhaphy*     *surgical suture* 缝合术
ureterorrhaphy     surgical suture of the ureter
urethrorrhaphy     _____

❖ *-rrhexis, -rrhexia*     *rupture* 破裂
urethrorrhexis     rupture of the urethra
cystorrhexis     _____

❖ *-tripsy*     *crushing* 压轧术
lithotripsy     crushing of stones

❖ *-uresis*     *urination, urine* 排尿
enuresis     involuntary urination, bed-wetting (the literal meaning is 'in urine')
polyuresis     _____

❖ *-uria*     *urine, urine condition* 尿
anuria     without urination
polyuria     _____

**Tips**: *Uremia* differs from *hematuria* in that *uremia* refers to the abnormal blood condition in which there is an excessive amount of nitrogenous waste—urea, while *hematuria* refers to the abnormal condition in which blood is detected in urine. Both conditions can indicate the malfunction of the kidney.

## Exercise 5

*Explain the meanings of the following combining forms.*

1. -clysis  _____
2. -lysis  _____
3. -pexy  _____
4. -poiesis  _____
5. -lithiasis  _____
6. -rrhaphy  _____
7. -uresis  _____
8. -uria  _____
9. -tripsy  _____
10. -poietin  _____

## Exercise 6

*The presence of glucose in urine is called "glycosuria". Build terms for the following definitions.*

1. Presence of pus (py/o) in urine _____.
2. Presence of bacteria (bacteri/o) in urine _____.
3. Presence of white blood cells in urine _____.
4. Presence of blood in urine _____.
5. Presence of ketone bodies (ket/o) in urine _____.
6. Presence of protein (protein/o) in urine _____.

## Exercise 7

*Use "nephr/o" to build terms for the following definitions.*

1. surgical suture of kidney _____
2. crushing of stones in the kidney _____
3. formation of stones in the kidney _____
4. surgical fixation of the kidney _____
5. separation of the kidney _____

# Chapter 11　Urinary System

### Group 3　More Combining Forms and Prefixes

❖ *albumin/o*  　　　　　*albumin* 白蛋白
albuminuria　　　　　presence of albumin in urine
hyperalbuminemia

❖ *azot/o*　　　　　　*urea*, *nitrogen* 氮
uroazotometer　　　　an instrument to measure nitrogen in urine
hyperazotemia

❖ *dips/o*　　　　　　*thirst* 渴
polydipsia　　　　　　excessive thirsty feeling
dipsosis　　　　　　　abnormal thirsty feeling

❖ *hydr/o*　　　　　　*water* 水; *fluid* 液体
hydroureter　　　　　fluid accumulation of the ureter
hydronephrosis

❖ *noct/o*　　　　　　*night* 夜
nocturnal　　　　　　pertaining to occurring at night
nocturia

❖ *oligo-*　　　　　　*scanty*, *few* 寡;少
oligodipsia　　　　　scanty thirsty feeling
oliguria

❖ *retro-*　　　　　　*behind*, *backward* 后;向后
retroperitoneal　　　　situated behind the peritoneum
retrovesical

❖ *trans-*　　　　　　*through* 经过,由
transurethral　　　　through the urethra
transnasal

## Exercise 8

*Explain the meanings of the following combining forms and prefixes.*

1. trans- _____
2. noct/o _____
3. olig/o _____
4. albumin/o _____
5. azot/o _____
6. hydr/o _____
7. dips/o _____
8. retro- _____

## Exercise 9

*Choose the appropriate term from the following list for each of the given definitions.*

| noctiphobia | ureterolithiasis | transdermal | azotemia | enuresis |
| retrocardiac | lithotripsy | oligohydruria | polydipsia | polyuria |

1. through the skin _____
2. stone formation in the ureter _____
3. behind the heart _____
4. scanty water in urine _____
5. excessive urination _____
6. presence of nitrogenous waste in blood _____
7. fear of the night _____
8. intense thirsty feelings _____
9. crushing of the stones _____
10. bed-wetting _____

## Group 4  Diminutive Suffixes

In the above part, you have read about "*renal corpuscle*" and "*renal tubule*". In these terms, -*cle* and -*ule* are suffixes to show that something is smaller than things of that type usually are, for example, "tubule" denotes a smaller tube. Below is a list of the commonly used diminutive suffixes.

❖ -cle | *little one* 小,微小
---|---
particle | a little part
denticle | ___

❖ -ette | *little one* 微小
---|---
pipette | a little pipe (to remove fluid)
diskette | ___

❖ -let | *little one* 小
---|---
platelet | a little plate (referring to the shape of the blood cell)
droplet | ___

❖ -ling | *young, small* 幼年,小
---|---
sibling | a brother or sister
footling | ___

❖ -ole | *little, small* 微小
---|---
arteriole | a small artery
centriole | ___

❖ -ule | *little, small* 微小
---|---
venule | a little vein
nodule | ___

### Exercise 10

*Underline the diminutive suffixes in the following words and explain the meanings of the words.*

1. corpuscle ___
2. tubule ___
3. duckling ___
4. droplet ___
5. pedicle ___
6. globule ___

# Part Three  Integrated Practice

## Exercise 11

*Select the correct answer to complete each of the following statements.*

1. The structural and functional unit of the kidney is _____ .
   a. calyx                b. bowman's capsule
   c. nephron              d. glomerulus

2. The outer part of the kidney is called _____ .
   a. capsule              b. glomerulus
   c. cortex               d. medulla

3. The smooth triangular part at the base of bladder is called _____ .
   a. renal pelvis         b. pyramid
   c. apex                 d. trigone

4. The concaved portion of the kidney through which the vessels and nerves enter and leave is called _____ .
   a. medulla              b. hilum
   c. calyx                d. renal pelvis

5. The combining form indicating a collection of capillaries in the kidney is _____ .
   a. calic/o              b. cortic/o
   c. medull/o             d. glomerul/o

6. The temporary reservoir for urine in the body is _____ .
   a. kidney               b. ureter
   c. bladder              d. urethra

7. Frequent urination at night is termed as _____ .
   a. polyuria             b. anuria
   c. enuresis             d. nocturia

8. Urination is a synonym for _____ .
   a. voiding                b. micturation
   c. peristalsis            d. both a and b

9. The patient with _____ has an accumulation of fluid resulting in enlargement of the kidney.
   a. hydroureter            b. hydronephrosis
   c. cystomegaly            d. nehritis

10. The surgical procedure for remove renal adhesions is called _____ .
    a. nephrolysis           b. nephrectomy
    c. ureterolysis          d. nephropexy

11. In renal failure, _____ is used to remove urea from the blood.
    a. nephrotomy            b. nephrectomy
    c. dialysis              d. hemolysis

12. A _____ is a surgical incision into the kidney to remove stones.
    a. nephrostomy           b. nephrotomy
    c. nephrolithotomy       d. nephrolithiasis

13. At the end stage of renal failure, there would be little or no production of urine. This condition is termed _____ .
    a. polyuria              b. hematuria
    c. anuria                d. dysuria

14. The patient receiving _____ has his or her bladder removed.
    a. cystotomy             b. cystostomy
    c. cystectomy            d. cystopexy

15. The condition of excessive nitrogenous substance in the blood is called _____ .
    a. glycosuria            b. hematuria
    c. azotemia              d. hyperglycemia

**Exercise 12**

*Build medical terms according to the descriptions given.*

1. Steven was treated for abnormal narrowing of the urethra, which is known as _____ , and in his case, a surgery, which is called _____ , is required to

repair the malformed urethra.

2. Gill was diagnosed to have a floating kidney. This falling of kidney is also called _____. For this reason, he was scheduled for the surgical fixation of this floating kidney, known as _____.

3. Norma required the surgical removal of a kidney and a ureter, termed as _____.

4. The operation for Kevin includes a surgical incision into the renal pelvis. This procedure is _____.

5. Jennie complained of painful urination. The medical term for this is _____. She was later diagnosed of acute inflammation of urethra, which is called _____.

## Part Four    Supplementary Readings

**Blood urea nitrogen** measures nitrogen in the blood in the form of urea. An increase in BUN indicates an increase in nitrogenous wastes in the blood and renal failure.

**Diuretics** mean the increase of the volume of urine. Diuretics are used in medicine to increase the amount of urine by increasing renal sodium excretion (natriuresis), which is passively followed by water elimination. Diuretics act on specific anatomical sites of the nephron and are accordingly divided into different types, including osmotic diuretics, potassium-sparing diuretics, loop diuretics, carbonic anhydrase (CA) inhibitors and Thiazide diuretics.

**Glomerulonephritis**, also known as glomerular nephritis, abbreviated GN. It is a primary or secondary immune-mediated renal disease characterized by inflammation of the glomeruli, or small blood vessels in the kidneys. It may present with isolated hematuria and/or proteinuria; or as a nephrotic syndrome, a nephritic syndrome, acute renal failure, or chronic renal failure. They are categorized into several different pathological patterns, which are broadly grouped into non-proliferative or proliferative types. Primary causes are one which are intrinsic to the kidney, whilst secondary causes are associated with certain infections (bacterial, viral or parasitic pathogens), drugs, systemic disorders or cancers.

**Hemodialysis** involves pumping the blood through an artificial kidney called hemodialyser. Blood is passed on one side of a semi-permeable membrane, with dialysis fluid being passed in a counter-current direction on the other side. Dialysis occurs across the semi-permeable membrane, removing toxins from the blood.

**Hydronephrosis** is the dilation of the renal pelvis and calyces associated with any obstruction in the urinary tract that prevents the outflow of urine. Hydronephrosis may be unilateral, caused by obstruction at the level of ureter, pelviureteric junction or renal pelvis; or bilateral, caused by obstruction at the level of the bladder or urethra. In both forms, urinary tract obstruction predisposes to infection of the bladder (cystitis) and kidney (pyelonephritis or pyonephrosis) as well as stone formation.

**Peritoneal dialysis** is the procedure that uses the peritoneal membrane as the semi-permeable membrane to remove the soluble substances and water from the body. This requires the insertion of a plastic tube (catheter) through the anterior wall into the peritoneal cavity. Dialysis solution is intermittently introduced into and removed from the peritoneal cavity.

**Polycystic kidney disease (PKD)** is a genetic disease characterized by large cysts in one or both kidneys and a gradual loss of normal kidney tissue which can lead to chronic renal failure. Autosomal dominant PKD occurs in both children and adults, but it is much more common in adults, with symptoms often not showing up until middle age. The disorder may not be discovered unless tests revealing the disease are performed for other reasons. An autosomal recessive form of PKD also exists and appears in infancy or childhood. This type tends to be very serious and progresses rapidly, resulting in end-stage kidney failure and generally causing death in infancy or childhood.

**Renal amyloidosis** is a disease characterized by accumulation of amyloid, an extracellular fibrillar protein, in various organs and tissues of the body. This disorder involves the kidneys in 80-90% of the patients and is called renal amyloidosis or amyloid nephrosis. It is the renal deposits of amyloid, especially in glomerular capillary walls, which may cause albuminuria and nephritic syndrome.

**Uremia** is the accumulation of nitrogenous metabolic waste products in the blood (i.e. urea and creatine). The kidneys are unable to filter and excrete these products. If this disorder develops within a few days, it is known as acute renal failure (ARF). If it occurs over a period of months to years, it is known as chronic renal failure (CRF).

**Urinary stress incontinence** is the leakage of urine as a result of coughing, straining or some sudden voluntary movement, due to weakness of the muscles around the neck of the bladder and surrounding the vagina, resulting in an incompetent internal vesical sphincter.

**Wilm tumor** is also called nephroblastoma, or embryoma of the kidney. It is a malignant renal tumor of young children, composed of small spindle cells and various other types of tissue, including tubules and, in some cases, structures resembling fetal glomeruli, as well as striated muscle and cartilage. It presents with an abdominal mass and occasionally hematuria, abdominal pain and hypertension.

## Part Five  Review Sheet

Here is a collection of the word parts you have learned in this chapter. Write the meaning of each word part without referring to your previous work.

**Combining Forms**

| Combining Form | Meaning | Combining Form | Meaning |
| --- | --- | --- | --- |
| albumin/o | _____ | pyel/o | _____ |
| azot/o | _____ | ren/o | _____ |
| cal/i, calic/o | _____ | retr/o | _____ |
| cyst/o | _____ | trans/o | _____ |
| dips/o | _____ | trigon/o | _____ |
| glomerul/o | _____ | tubul/o | _____ |
| hydr/o | _____ | ureter/o | _____ |
| meat/o | _____ | urethr/o | _____ |
| nephr/o | _____ | ur/o | _____ |
| noct/o | _____ | vesic/o | _____ |
| olig/o | _____ | | |

**Suffixes**

| Suffix | Meaning | Suffix | Meaning |
| --- | --- | --- | --- |
| -cle | _____ | -poiesis | _____ |

## Chapter 11  Urinary System

-clysis  _____          -poietin  _____

-ette  _____            -rrhaphy  _____

-ling  _____            -rrhexis, -rrhexia  _____

-let  _____             -tripsy  _____

-lithiasis  _____       -ule  _____

-lysis  _____           -uresis  _____

-ole  _____             -uria  _____

-pexy  _____

# Chapter 12　Reproductive System

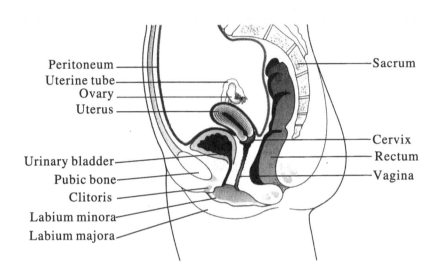

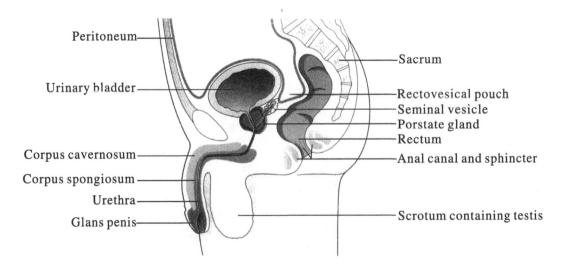

# Chapter 12  Reproductive System

## Part One  Overview of the System

The reproductive system ensures the survival of the species. It comprises the reproductive organs responsible for the forming of reproductive cells and sex hormones.

### *Male reproductive organs*

The **testes** are paired reproductive organs in the **scrotum**, which hangs outside the human body. Each testis contains coiled seminiferous tubules where sperm (male reproductive cells) production occurs. The **epididymis**, a coiled tube next to each testis, receives sperm from the seminiferous tubules. The epididymis stores sperm and propels it toward the penis. The **vas deferens** is the dilated continuation of the epididymis. It passes behind the urinary bladder and expands to form an **ampulla** (expanded end part). Each ampulla joins with a **seminal vesicle** (an accessory gland) to form an **ejaculatory duct**. The ejaculatory ducts pass through the **prostate gland**, where they receive more secretions, and then join with the **urethra.**

The prostate gland lies under the urinary bladder and surrounds the first part of the urethra. Its secretions also help neutralize vaginal acidity and make sperm mobile.

The **penis** deposits semen into the vagina during sexual intercourse and carries urine through the urethra during urination. The penis includes the shaft (tubular portion), glans (penis tip and sexual sensation center), and the prepuce, or foreskin (loose skin fold over glans). In a circumcision procedure, the prepuce is removed.

### *Female reproductive organs*

The female reproductive system produces egg cells, called **ova** (sing. ovum); nourishes, carries, and protects the developing embryo; and nurses the newborn after birth. The system structures are the ovaries, uterine tubes, uterus, vagina, vulva, and mammary glands.

**Ovaries**, a pair of female gonads (sex organs), reside in the pelvic part of the abdomen on either side of the uterus. Ovaries produce ova (sing. *ovum*) and estrogen (female sex hormone).

The **uterine tubes** (oviducts or fallopian tubes) are paired tubes that receive the developing ovum from the ovary. The **infundibulum** end is beside the ovary; its **fimbria** (finger like structures) "sweep" the developing ovum into the tube.

The **uterus** is a hollow muscular organ in front of the rectum and behind the urinary bladder. The uterus has three layers. The outer serous layer, the middle muscular layer and the endometrium inner mucosal lining.

The **vagina** is a muscular tube from the uterus to outside the body. The vagina receives sperm from sexual intercourse, channels menstrual flow out of the body, and is a birth canal for the baby during childbirth. The **vulva**, external genitalia, includes the mons pubis, labia majora, labia minora, and clitoris.

The **mammary glands** provide milk to nourish a baby and are secondary sexual characteristics. The **areola** is the circular area of pigmented skin around the nipple. During pregnancy, estrogen and progesterone, secreted by the ovary and placenta, cause the milk-producing glands to develop. Milk production and its release is stimulated by the hormone prolactin.

### Exercise 1

**Fill in the blanks with the terms you have learned in the above passage.**

1. The testes are located inside the _____, which hangs outside the body.
2. The _____ is a coiled tube near each testis, which receives and stores sperm.
3. The vas deferens and seminalvesicle together forms _____ which pass through the prostate gland.
4. The penis includes _____, _____, and _____.
5. Ovaries are female reproductive organs that produce _____ and _____.
6. _____ is the tube that conducts ova from the ovary to the womb.
7. The uterus is situated in front of _____ and behind the _____.
8. The muscular tube from the uterus to the outside of the body is _____.
9. The female external genitalia are called _____.
10. The pigmented circular area around the nipple is called _____.

*Chapter 12   Reproductive System*

# *Part Two*  Combining Forms, Prefixes and Suffixes

## Group 1  Combining Forms for Male Reproductive System

| | |
|---|---|
| ❖ *balan/o* | *glans (head) penis* 龟头 |
| balanorrhea | flow (of pus) from the glans penis |
| balanitis | |
| ❖ *epididym/o* | *epididymis* 附睾 |
| epididymectomy | removal of the epididymis |
| epididymitis | |
| ❖ *orchid/o, orchi/o* *test/o* | *testis, testicles* 睾丸 |
| orchidectomy | removal of the testis |
| anorchism | congenital anomaly of lack of testes |
| orchidopathy | |
| testicular | |
| ❖ *osche/o, scrot/o* | *scrotum* 阴囊 |
| oscheoma | tumor of the scrotum |
| oscheocele | |
| scrotal | |
| ❖ *pen/o, phall/o* | *penis* 阴茎 |
| penile | pertaining to the penis |
| penitis | |
| phallocampsis (-campsis = bending) | |
| phalloplasty | |

· 189 ·

❖ **perine/o**　　　　　　*perineum* 会阴
perineorrhaphy　　　　　surgical suture of perineum
perineoscrotal

❖ **prostat/o**　　　　　　*prostate gland* 前列腺
prostatomegaly　　　　　enlargement of the prostate gland
prostatodynia

❖ **semin/(o)**　　　　　　*semen, seed* 精子
seminiferous　　　　　　pertaining to carrying semen
inseminate

❖ **sperm/o, spermat/o**　　*sperm, semen* 精子, 精液
spermolysis　　　　　　dissolution of the semen
oligospermia
spermatogenic　　　　　pertaining to semen production
spermatopathy

❖ **vas/o**　　　　　　　　*vessel, vas deferens* 管, 输精管
vasovasostomy　　　　　anastomosis of the vas deferens
vasectomy

❖ **vesicul/o**　　　　　　*seminal vesicle* 精囊
vesiculogram　　　　　　X-ray record of seminal vesicle
vesiculotomy

## Exercise 2

**Explain the meanings of the following terms.**

1. seminal　　　　　　　　5. prostatic
2. oscheal　　　　　　　　6. balanic
3. testicular　　　　　　　7. perineal
4. epididymal　　　　　　8. spermatic

# Chapter 12  Reproductive System

## Exercise 3

*The suffix "-spermia" is used to denote the semen or sperm condition. Build terms for the following definitions.*

1. scanty sperm _____
2. without sperm _____
3. excessive sperm (poly-) _____
4. pus in the sperm (py/o) _____
5. blood in the sperm _____
6. holding back of the sperm (isch/o) _____

## Exercise 4

*Build a medical term for each of the following definitions.*

1. surgical repair of the testis (orchid/o) _____
2. surgical repair of the glans penis _____
3. surgical repair of penis (phall/o) _____
4. removal of the epididymis _____
5. removal of the prostatic gland _____
6. removal of the vas deferens _____

### Group 2  More Combining Forms and Suffixes

| | |
|---|---|
| ❖ *andr/o* | *androgen, male* 雄性,男性 |
| androgen | male sex hormone |
| andromorphous | (of women) having male forms |
| ❖ *blenn/o* | *mucus* 黏液; *pus* 脓 |
| blennurethria | overflow of the pus from the urethra |
| blennorrhea | _____ |

· 191 ·

❖ **crypt/o**     ***hidden* 隐藏的**
cryptorchism     hidden or undescended testicle(s)
cryptomnesia     hidden memory

❖ **gamet/o**     ***gamete, mature reproductive cell* 配子细胞**
gametogenesis     formation of the gamete
gametocide

❖ **genit/o**     ***genitalia, reproductive organs* 生殖器**
genitourinary     pertaining to reproductive and urinary systems
genitoplasty

❖ **-spadias**     ***cutting, tearing* 裂口**
hypospadias     abnormal opening of the male urethra in the under surface of the penis
epispadias

❖ **varic/o**     ***varicose, swollen and twisted veins* 静脉曲张**
varicocele     varicose veins above the testes
varicocelectomy

❖ **zo/o**     ***animal* 动物; *life* 生命**
azoospermia     without spermatozoa in the semen
zoosperm

## Exercise 5

Explain the meanings of the following combining forms.

1. zo/o  _____      5. genit/o  _____
2. crypt/o  _____      6. gamet/o  _____
3. -spadias  _____      7. blenn/o  _____
4. varic/o  _____      8. andr/o  _____

# Chapter 12  Reproductive System

## Exercise 6

*Answer the following questions.*

1. Gynecology (gynec/o = female) is the study of the female's illness. What is the meaning of *andrology*?
2. Cryptorchism refers to the condition in which testis fails to descend into the scortum. What is the meaning of *cryptorchidectomy* and *cryptorchidopexy*?
3. Varicose is the enlarged twisted vein just beneath the skin. What is the meaning of *varicosis* and *varicophlebitis*?
4. The congenital defect of penis may occur in which the opening of the urethra is not in its normal position. Suffix "-*spadias*" is used to describe such condition. Explain the meanings of *hypospadias*, *epispadias* and *paraspadias*.

### Group 3  Combining Forms for Female Reproductive System

| | |
|---|---|
| ❖ *cervic/o* | *neck* 颈部; *uterine cervix* 子宫颈 |
| cervicectomy | removal of the uterine cervix |
| cervicitis | |
| ❖ *clitor/o*, *clitorid/o* | *clitoris* 阴蒂 |
| clitorectomy | removal of the clitoris |
| clitoriditis | |
| ❖ *colp/o*, *vagin/o* | *vagina* 阴道 |
| colpoplasty | surgical repair of the vagina |
| colposcope | |
| vaginectomy | |
| ❖ *episi/o*, *vulv/o* | *vulva* 女阴,外阴 |
| episiotomy | incision into the vulva |
| episiorrhaphy | |

## ❖ hyster/o, metr/(o), uter/o — uterus, womb 子宫

| | |
|---|---|
| hysteromyoma | muscular tumor of the uterus |
| hysteralgia | |
| metrocolpocele | protrusion of the uterus into the vagina |
| metrectasia | |
| uterine | |

## ❖ mamm/o, mast/o — breast 乳房; mammary gland 乳腺

| | |
|---|---|
| mammoplasty | surgical repair of the breast |
| mammectomy | |
| mastoid | resembling breast |
| mastitis | |

## ❖ o/o, ov/i — egg, ovum 蛋, 卵

| | |
|---|---|
| ooblast | immature egg cell |
| oogenesis | |
| ovicide | chemical to kill eggs |
| oviform | |

## ❖ oophor/o, ovari/o — ovary 卵巢

| | |
|---|---|
| oophorrhagia | bursting forth of blood from the ovary |
| oophoroma | |
| ovariectomy | removal of an ovary |
| ovariocentesis | |

## ❖ papill/o — nipple 乳头; nipple-like structure 乳头样

| | |
|---|---|
| papilloma | a nipple-like tumor (this is a non-cancerous growth of epithelium that resembles a wart) |
| papilliform | |

## ❖ salping/o — oviduct, fallopian tubes 输卵管

| | |
|---|---|
| salpingo-ovaritis | inflammation of oviduct and ovary |
| salpingopexy | |

## Chapter 12 Reproductive System

### Exercise 7

*Explain the meanings of the following combining forms.*

1. colp/o and vagin/o both mean _____
2. oophor/o and ovari/o both mean _____
3. o/o and ov/i both mean _____
4. episi/o and vulv/o both mean _____
5. mamm/o and mast/o both mean _____
6. hystr/o, uter/o and metr/o all mean _____
7. clitor/o and clitorid/o both mean _____
8. cervic/o means both _____ and _____

### Exercise 8

*Explain the meanings of the following terms.*

1. papillectomy _____
2. cervicovaginitis _____
3. episioplasty _____
4. clitoroplasty _____
5. salpingorrhaphy _____
6. amastia _____
7. anovulatory _____
8. colporrhaphy _____
9. endocervicitis _____
10. oophoritis _____

## Group 4  Combining Forms for Pregnancy and Birth

| ❖ *amni/o* | *amnion* 羊膜 |
|---|---|
| amniorrhexis | rupture of the amniotic membrane |
| amniocentesis | |

| ❖ *coit/o* | *sexual intercourse, coitus* 性交,交媾 |
|---|---|
| postcoital | after sexual intercourse |
| coitophobia | |

| ❖ *embry/o* | *embryo* 胚胎 |
|---|---|
| embryogenesis | formation of embryo |
| embryology | |

| ❖ *galact/o, lact/o* | *milk* 奶,乳汁 |
|---|---|
| galactophagous | feeding milk |
| galactorrhea | overflow of milk |
| lactodensimeter | instrument to measure the density of milk |
| lactogenesis | |

| ❖ *gynec/o* | *female, woman* 雌性,女性 |
|---|---|
| gynecomastia | (of male) having female breast |
| gynecopathy | |

| ❖ *men/o* | *menstruation, menses* 月经 |
|---|---|
| dysmenorrhea | painful menstruation |
| menorrhagia | excessive menstruation |

| ❖ *nat/o* | *birth* 生产,出生 |
|---|---|
| neonatal | pertaining to the new born baby |
| natality | percentage of birth |

# Chapter 12  Reproductive System

| | | |
|---|---|---|
| ❖ *obstetr/o* | *midwife*, *delivery* 助产 | |
| obstetrics | branch of medicine dealing with the care of woman before and after delivery | |
| obstetrician | | |
| ❖ *omphal/o*, *umbilic/o* | *navel*, *umbilicus* 肚脐;脐带 | |
| umbilical | pertaining to the umbilicus | |
| omphalotomy | cutting of umbilicus | |
| ❖ *placent/o* | *placenta* 胎盘 | |
| placentoma | tumor of placenta | |
| placentopathy | | |
| ❖ *terat/o* | *monster* 怪兽;畸胎 | |
| teratoma | tumor of "monster" | |
| teratoid | | |
| ❖ *toc/o* | *labor* 分娩 | |
| eutocia | normal labor | |
| tocophobia | | |

**Exercise 9**

*Explain the meanings of the following combining forms.*

1. toc/o _____
2. coit/o _____
3. placent/o _____
4. galact/o _____
5. lact/o _____
6. umbilic/o _____
7. men/o _____
8. nat/o _____
9. gynec/o _____
10. terat/o _____
11. obstetr/o _____
12. amni/o _____

## Exercise 10

**Explain the following terms describing menstruation.**

1. amenorrhea _____
2. dysmenorrhea _____
3. cryptomenorrhea _____
4. hypermenorrhea _____
5. menorrhagia _____
6. hypomenorrhea _____
7. oligomenorrhea _____
8. polymenorrhea _____
9. menopause _____
10. menarche ( -arche = first) _____

### Group 5  Suffixes and Prefixes

* **-arche**  *first* 初始，第一
  menarche — first presence of menstruation
  pubarche — first presence of pubic hair

* **-cyesis**  *pregnancy* 妊娠
  monocyesis — pregnancy with one fetus
  polycyesis — _____

* **-didymus**  *joining up of fetuses* 联胎
  craniodidymus — congenital anomaly in which two fetuses join at head
  thoracodidymus — _____

* **-gravida**  *pregnant woman* 孕妇
  multigravida — woman who has been pregnant for many times
  primigravida
  ( primi- = first )

· 198 ·

# Chapter 12  Reproductive System

| ❖ *-para* | ***woman who has given birth*** 产妇 |
|---|---|
| nullipara | woman who has never given birth |
| multipara | |

| ❖ *-pareunia* | ***sexual intercourse*** 性交,交媾 |
|---|---|
| apareunia | unable to have sexual intercourse |
| dyspareunia | |

| ❖ *-partum* | ***birth*** 生产,分娩 |
|---|---|
| peripartum | period of time before and after birth |
| antepartum | |

| ❖ *-salpinx* | ***condition of fallopian tube*** 输卵管 |
|---|---|
| pyosalpinx | accumulation of pus in the fallopian tube |
| hydrosalpinx | |

| ❖ *nulli-* | ***none, zero*** 无,零 |
|---|---|
| nulligravida | woman who has never been pregnant |
| nullipara | |

| ❖ *primi-* | ***first, early*** 初,始 |
|---|---|
| primipara | woman who gives birth for the first time |
| primigravida | |

| ❖ *pseudo-* | ***false*** 假,伪 |
|---|---|
| pseudocyesis | false pregnancy |
| pseudomyopia | |
| (myopia = near sightedness) | |

## Exercise 11

*Explain the meanings of the following prefixes and suffixes.*

1. -cyesis　_____
2. -gravida　_____
3. -arche　_____
4. -pareunia　_____
5. -para　_____
6. pseudo-　_____
7. -salpinx　_____
8. -partum　_____
9. -didymus　_____
10. primi-　_____
11. nulli-　_____

## Exercise 12

*Explain the meanings of the following terms.*

1. pseudocyesis _____
2. eucyesis _____
3. acyesis _____
4. ovariocyesis _____
5. salpingocyesis _____
6. celiocyesis _____
7. monocyesis _____
8. polycyesis _____

Chapter 12 Reproductive System

## Part Three — Integrated Practice

### Exercise 13

*Match the terms in Column I with their definitions in Column II. Place the correct letter of the definition to the left of the term.*

| | Column I | Column II |
|---|---|---|
| _____ | 1. hysteropathy | a. removal of womb |
| _____ | 2. spermatogenesis | b. surgical fixation of the uterus |
| _____ | 3. orchidectomy | c. any disease of the uterus |
| _____ | 4. hysterectomy | d. absence of menses |
| _____ | 5. salpingectomy | e. incision of an ovary |
| _____ | 6. ovarialgia | f. pain of ovaries |
| _____ | 7. hysteropexy | g. pain in the testes |
| _____ | 8. cervicectomy | h. examination of the vagina using an endoscope |
| _____ | 9. oophoritis | i. prolonged or excessive menses |
| _____ | 10. orchalgia | j. puncture into amnionic membrane to remove fluid for diagnosis |
| _____ | 11. amenorrhea | k. production of sperm |
| _____ | 12. colposcopy | l. inflammation of ovary |
| _____ | 13. menorrhagia | m. removal of fallopian tube |
| _____ | 14. ovariotomy | n. excision of the uterine cervix |
| _____ | 15. amnioncentesis | o. removal of one or both testes |

## Part Four — Supplementary Readings

**Endometrosis** refers to the presence of functional endometrial tissue in areas outside the uterus. The endometrial tissue develops into what are called implants, lesions, or growths and can cause pain, infertility, and other problems. The ectopic tissue is usually confined to the pelvic area but may appear anywhere in the abdominopelvic cavity. The symptoms of endometriosis vary greatly, with abnormal or heavy menstrual bleeding being most common. There may also be severe abdominal pain and/or lower back pain during menstruation.

**Chlamydial infection** is a kind of infectious diseases caused by *chlamydie*, a group of microorganisms. The major type, *Chlamydia Trachomatis*, has a number of strains. In men, it is a major cause of nongonococcal urethritis, which may cause a discharge from the penis. In women, the infection is usually asymptomatic, but it can lead to salpingitis. A baby born to a woman with chlamydial infection may acquire an acute eye condition called neonatal ophthalmia. In parts of Africa and Asia, certain strains of *Chlamydia Trachomatis* cause trachoma, serious eye disease. Treatment for chlamydial infections is with antibiotic drugs.

**Gonorrhea** is one of the most common sexually transmitted infections. Caused by the bacterium *Neisseria Gonorrheae*, gonorrhea is most often transmitted during sexual activity. An infected woman may also transmit the disease to her baby during childbirth. In men, symptoms include a discharge from the urethra and pain on passing urine. Many infected women have no symptoms; if symptoms are present, they usually consist of vaginal discharge or a burning sensation on passing urine. Infection acquired by anal sex can cause gonococcal proctitis. Oral sex with an infected person may lead to gonococcal pharyngitis. A baby exposed to infection during its birth may acquire the eye infection gonococcal ophthalmia. Untreated gonorrhea may spread to other parts of the body affecting fertility. Gonorrhea is treated with antibiotic drugs.

**Pelvic inflammatory disease (PID)** is a general term for inflammation of the uterus, fallopian tubes, ovaries, and adjacent pelvic structures and is usually caused by bacterial infection. The infection may be confined to a single organ or it may involve all the internal reproductive organs. As an ascending infection, the pathogens spread from the vagina and cervix to the upper structures of the female reproductive tract. Two of the most common causes of PID are gonorrhea and chlamydia, both of which are sexually transmitted diseases (STDs). Unless treated promptly, PID may result in scarring of the narrow fallopian tubes and of the ovaries, causing sterility. The widespread infection of the reproductive structures can also lead to fatal septicemia.

**Phimosis** refers to the condition in which the foreskin tightens over the glans and cannot be easily pushed back. This can frequently leads to balanitis. Circumcision is performed to remove the foreskin.

**Prostatic hyperplasia** is caused by declining testosterone levels in older male, together with the adrenal production of estrogen. The prostate becomes enlarged, resulting in an obstructed urethra. Nocturia and urinary tract infection are common symptoms. The obstructing prostate tissue can be surgically removed by *curettage*, a scraping or cutting of tissue.

**Syphilis** is caused by infection with the bacterium Treponema pallidum. Syphilis is a chronic, infectious, multisystemic disease acquired through sexual contact or, less commonly, at birth (congenitally). A primary sore (chancre) develops at the point where the bacteria entered the body. The chancre is an ulcerated sore with hard edges that contains contagious organisms for 10 days to 3 months. In pregnancy, the fetus is infected from the mother through the placenta. However, the vast majority of cases are contracted through sexual activity. The danger of transmission is greatest in the early stage of syphilis. If left untreated, the end result is systemic infection that commonly leads to blindness, insanity, and eventual death.

**Teratoma** (pl. *teratomata*) is a primary tumor consisting of cells totally unlike those normally found in that part of the body.

**Vasectomy** is the operation of male sterilization. It is a minor surgical procedure, performed under local anesthesia that consists of cutting out a short length of each vas deferens. After vasectomy, the man continues to achieve orgasm and ejaculate as normal, but the semen no longer contains sperm, which are reabsorbed in the testes. Male sterilization is a safe and effective method of contraception. Some operations to restore fertility after vasectomy are successful, but the process should be regarded as irreversible.

## Part Five  Review Sheet

Here is a collection of the word parts you have learned in this chapter. Write the meaning of each word part without referring to your previous work.

**Combining Forms**

| Combining Form | Meaning | Combining Form | Meaning |
| --- | --- | --- | --- |
| amni/o | _____ | metr/o | _____ |
| andr/o | _____ | nat/o | _____ |
| balan/o | _____ | obstetr/o | _____ |
| blenn/o | _____ | omphal/o | _____ |
| cervic/o | _____ | orchid/o, orchid/o | _____ |
| clitor/o, clitorid/o | _____ | test/o | _____ |
| coit/o | _____ | o/o | _____ |
| colp/o | _____ | oophor/o | _____ |
| crypt/o | _____ | ovari/o | _____ |
| embry/o | _____ | ov/i | _____ |
| epididym/o | _____ | osche/o | _____ |
| episi/o | _____ | papill/o | _____ |
| galact/o | _____ | pen/o | _____ |
| gamet/o | _____ | perine/o | _____ |
| genit/o | _____ | phall/o | _____ |
| gynec/o | _____ | placent/o | _____ |
| hyster/o | _____ | prostat/o | _____ |
| lact/o | _____ | salping/o | _____ |
| mamm/o | _____ | scrot/o | _____ |
| mast/o | _____ | semin/o | _____ |
| men/o | _____ | sperm/o, spermat/o | _____ |

## Chapter 12  Reproductive System

| | | | |
|---|---|---|---|
| terat/o | _____ | varic/o | _____ |
| toc/o | _____ | vas/o | _____ |
| umbilic/o | _____ | vesicul/o | _____ |
| uter/o | _____ | vulv/o | _____ |
| vagin/o | _____ | zo/o | _____ |

## Suffixes

| Suffix | Meaning | Suffix | Meaning |
|---|---|---|---|
| -arche | _____ | -pareunia | _____ |
| -cyesis | _____ | -partum | _____ |
| -didymus | _____ | -salpinx | _____ |
| -gravida | _____ | -spadias | _____ |
| -para | _____ | | |

## Prefixes

| Prefix | Meaning | Prefix | Meaning |
|---|---|---|---|
| nulli- | _____ | primi- | _____ |
| pseudo- | _____ | | |

· 205 ·

# Chapter 13  Musculoskeletal System

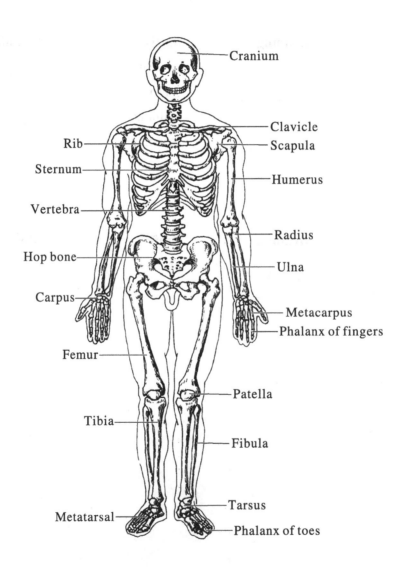

# Chapter 13  Musculoskeletal System

## Part One  Overview of the System

The musculoskeletal system (also known as the locomotive system) consists of the skeletal system and the muscular system. The skeleton provides support and gives shape to the body and protects the brain and internal organs. It also helps in maintaining homeostasis by storing calcium and other minerals in the bone. What's more, bone marrow participates in the blood cell formation (**hematopoiesis**) by producing blood cells.

There are 206 bones in the body. These bones can be divided into five categories: **long bones** (found in arms and legs), **short bones** (found in wrists and ankles), **flat bones** (ribs, shoulder blades, pelvis and skull), **irregular bones** (bones of vertebrae and face) and **sesamoid bones** (round bones found near joints, such as patella). The shaft, or the middle part of a long bone, is called **diaphysis**. Each end of a long bone is called an **epiphysis**. The **periosteum** is a strong, fibrous, vascular membrane that covers the surface of the bones.

The place where two bones meet is a joint. There are three types of joints, **diarthroses** (sing. *diarthrosis*) which allow extensive mobility between two or more articular heads, **synarthroses** (sing. *synarthrosis*) which allow no movement and are predominantly fibrous, and **amphiarthroses** (sing. *amphiarhtrosis*), which are slightly movable joints.

Synovial joints are lubricated by a solution called **synovia** produced by the synovial membranes. This fluid lowers the friction between the articular surfaces and is contained within an articular capsule.

Muscles cover the bones to make movement possible. They also provide a protective covering for internal organs and produce body heat. There are three types of muscles: **smooth**, **skeletal**, and **cardiac**. Smooth muscles function to control the flow of substances within the lumens of hollow organs, and are involuntary. Skeletal and cardiac muscles are striated. Cardiac muscle is the muscle of the heart. It does not belong to the musculoskeletal system, and is under involuntary control (autonomic). **Fascia** is a fibrous white membrane that covers and separates muscles.

A **tendon** is a tough, flexible band of fibrous connective tissue that connects muscles to bones. A **ligament** is a small band of dense, white, fibrous elastic tissue that connects the ends of bones together to form a joint. Most ligaments limit dislocation, or prevent certain movements that may cause breaks.

A **bursa** (pl. *bursae*) is a small fluid-filled sac made of white fibrous tissue and lined with synovial membrane. It provides a cushion between bones and tendons and/or muscles around a joint.

**Exercise 1**

***Fill in the blanks with the terms you have learned in the above passage.***
1. The musculoskeletal system consist of _____ system and _____ system.
2. The formation of the blood cells occurs in the _____.
3. The bones are divided into five types, which are _____, _____, _____, _____ and _____.
4. There are three types of muscles, which are _____, _____ and _____.
5. _____ is the joint which allows full mobility between the joints.
6. The tough, flexible fibrous connective tissues that attach muscles to the bones are called _____.
7. A solution named _____ can lower the friction between articular surfaces.
8. _____ is a sac that provides a cushion around a joint.

*Chapter 13 Musculoskeletal System*

# Part Two  Combining Forms, Prefixes and Suffixes

## Group 1  Combining Forms for Body Parts

❖ ***brachi/o***　　　　　　　　***arm*** 手臂,胳膊
brachiocephalic　　　　　　　pertaining to the arm and head
brachiodynia　　　　　　　　_____

❖ ***cervic/o***　　　　　　　　***neck*** 颈
cervicodorsal　　　　　　　　pertaining to the neck and back
cervicofacial　　　　　　　　_____

❖ ***chir/o***　　　　　　　　　***hand*** 手
chirospasm　　　　　　　　　involuntary contraction of the hand
chiroplasty　　　　　　　　　_____

❖ ***chondr/o***　　　　　　　　***cartilage*** 软骨
achondroplasia　　　　　　　lack of the formation of cartilage
chondrosarcoma　　　　　　_____

❖ ***crani/o***　　　　　　　　　***skull*** 颅骨
cranioslerosis　　　　　　　hardening of the cranium
craniomalacia　　　　　　　_____

❖ ***dactyl/o, phalang/o***　　　***phalanx*** 指(趾); ***finger*** 手指; ***toe*** 脚趾
dactylogram　　　　　　　　fingerprint
syndactyly　　　　　　　　　_____
phalangeal　　　　　　　　　pertaining to the fingers or toes
phalangectomy　　　　　　　_____

❖ *dors/o*　　　　　　　　*back* 背
dorsolateral　　　　　　pertaining to the side of the back
dorsalgia　　　　　　　　_____

❖ *lumb/o*　　　　　　　*lower back* 腰
lumbocostal　　　　　　pertaining to the lower back and ribs
lumbodorsal　　　　　　_____

❖ *oste/o, osse/o*　　　　*bone* 骨
osteoarthropathy　　　　any disease affecting bones and joints
osteoma　　　　　　　　_____
osseous　　　　　　　　pertaining to the bone, bony
osseofibrous　　　　　　_____

❖ *pelv/i, pelv/o*　　　　*pelvis* 骨盆
pelvimetry　　　　　　　measurement of the pelvis
pelvioscopy　　　　　　_____

❖ *pod/o, ped/o*　　　　*foot* 脚,足
chiropodist　　　　　　　specialist in treating hand and foot diseases
pododynia　　　　　　　_____
pedal　　　　　　　　　pertaining to the foot

**Exercise 2**

*Explain the meanings of the following combining forms.*

1. cervic/o _____　　　7. oste/o _____
2. brachi/o _____　　　8. crani/o _____
3. pelv/i _____　　　　9. lumb/o _____
4. chir/o _____　　　　10. pod/o _____
5. dactyl/o _____　　　11. dors/o _____
6. chondr/o _____　　　12. ped/o _____

Chapter 13  Musculoskeletal System

> Exercise 3

*Build a medical term for each of the following definitions.*

1. incision into the back _____
2. malignant tumor of the bones (oste/o) _____
3. surgical repair of the cartilage _____
4. involuntary contraction of the arm _____
5. pain of the hand _____
6. instrument to measure the cranium _____
7. disease of the bone and cartilage _____
8. incision into the pelvis _____
9. treatment of the foot _____

## Group 2  Combining Forms for Specific Bones (I)

| | |
|---|---|
| ❖ *acromi/o* | *acromion*, extension of the shoulder bone 肩峰 |
| acromial | pertaining to the acromion |
| acromiothoracic | _____ |
| ❖ *carp/o* | *carpus*, wrist 手腕; 腕骨 |
| carpoptosis | dropping of the wrist |
| carpectomy | _____ |
| ❖ *clavicul/o* | *clavicle*, collar bone 锁骨 |
| supraclavicular | pertaining to above the collar bone |
| interclavicular | _____ |
| ❖ *cost/o* | *rib* 肋骨 |
| intercostal | pertaining to between the ribs |
| costochondral | _____ |

· 211 ·

| ❖ *humer/o* | *humerus, upper arm bone* 肱骨 |
|---|---|
| humeroscapular | pertaining to the humerus and scapula |
| humeroulnar | |

| ❖ *mandibul/o* | *mandible, lower jaw bone* 下颌骨 |
|---|---|
| bmandibular | pertaining to mandible |
| maxillomandibular | |

| ❖ *maxill/o* | *maxilla, upper jaw bone* 上颌骨 |
|---|---|
| maxillary | pertaining to maxilla |
| maxillodental | |

| ❖ *metacarp/o* | *metacarpus, hand bones* 掌骨 |
|---|---|
| metacarpophalangeal | pertaining to the hand bones and finger bones |
| metacarpectomy | |

| ❖ *palat/o* | *palate, roof of the mouth* 腭 |
|---|---|
| palatoschisis | splitting of the palate |
| palatine | |

| ❖ *radi/o* | *radius, outer bone of the forearm* 桡骨 |
|---|---|
| humeroradial | pertaining to the humerus and radius |
| radial | |

| ❖ *scapul/o* | *scapula, shoulder blade* 肩胛骨 |
|---|---|
| scapulopexy | surgical fixation of the scapula |
| scapulodynia | |

| ❖ *stern/o* | *sternum* 胸骨 |
|---|---|
| sternopericardia | pertaining to the sternum and pericardium |
| sternovertebral | |

| ❖ *uln/o* | *ulna, inner bone of the forearm* 尺骨 |
|---|---|
| ulnocarpal | pertaining to the ulna and carpus |
| ulnoradial | |

## Chapter 13  Musculoskeletal System

### Exercise 4

*Spell out the combining forms and the adjective forms for the following words.*

1. clavicle   _____ , _____
2. scapula    _____ , _____
3. carpus     _____ , _____
4. palate     _____ , _____
5. rib        _____ , _____
6. sternum    _____ , _____
7. maxilla    _____ , _____
8. mandible   _____ , _____

### Group 3   Combining Forms for Specific Bones (II)

❖ *acetabul/o*  —  *acetabulum, part of hipbone* 髋臼
acetabulectomy — removal of the acetabulum
acetabuloplasty — _____

❖ *calcane/o*  —  *calcaneus, heel bone* 跟骨
calcaneodynia — pain of the calcaneus
calcaneitis — _____

❖ *coccyg/o*  —  *coccyx* 尾骨
coccygalgia — pain of the coccyx
coccygectomy — _____

❖ *femor/o*  —  *femur, thigh bone* 股骨
femoro-articular — pertaining to the femur and joint
femoral — _____

❖ *fibul/o*  —  *fibula, smaller lower leg bone* 腓骨
fibular — _____

❖ **ili/o**　　　　　　　　　　***ilium*, *part of the hipbone* 髂骨**
iliocostal　　　　　　　　　pertaining to the ilium and ribs
iliococcygeal　　　　　　　_____

❖ **ischi/o**　　　　　　　　***ischium*, *part of the hipbone* 坐骨**
ischioanal　　　　　　　　pertaining to the ischium and anus
ischioneuralgia　　　　　　_____

❖ **metatars/o**　　　　　　***metatarsals*, *ankle* 跖骨**
metatarsalgia　　　　　　　pain if the ankle
metatarsectomy　　　　　　_____

❖ **patell/o**　　　　　　　　***patella*, *kneecap* 髌骨**
patellopexy　　　　　　　　surgical fixation of the patella
patellectomy　　　　　　　_____

❖ **sacr/o**　　　　　　　　　***sacrum* 骶骨**
sacrolumbar　　　　　　　　pertaining to the sacrum and lower back
sacrolisthesis　　　　　　　_____

❖ **tars/o**　　　　　　　　　***tarsals*, *foot bone* 跗骨**
tarsoptosis　　　　　　　　falling of the footbone
tarsomegaly　　　　　　　　_____

❖ **tibi/o**　　　　　　　　　***tibia*, *shin* 胫骨**
tibiofemoral　　　　　　　　pertaining to tibia and femur
tibialgia　　　　　　　　　　_____

### Exercise 5

*Explain the meanings of the following terms.*

1. calcaneotibial _____
2. ischiococcygeal _____
3. femorofibular _____
4. iliofemoral _____

Chapter 13  Musculoskeletal System

5. ischiosacral _____
6. tibiofibular _____
7. sacrococcygeal _____
8. fibulocalcaneal _____
9. tarsophalangeal _____
10. calcaneofibular _____

**Group 4  Word Parts Related to the Spine**

❖ *-desis*                *binding together* 绑；固定
spondylodesis            binding of the vertebrae
pleurodesis              _____

❖ *kyph/o*                *humped, curved* 弯曲的,拱的
kyphosis                 hump back, posterior curvature of the spine in the thoracic region.

carpokyphosis            _____

❖ *lamin/o*               *lamina, the back of the vertebra* 椎板
laminectomy              surgical removal of lamina
laminoplasty             _____

❖ *-listhesis*            *displacement, slipping* 脱位,滑脱
spondylolisthesis        slipping of a vertebra
prespondylolisthesis     forward displacement of a vertebra

❖ *lord/o*                *bend inward* 内弯的
lordosis                 anterior curvature of the spine in the lumbar region

❖ *myel/o*                *bone marrow, spinal cord* 骨髓,脊髓
osteomyelitis            inflammation of the bones and bone marrow
myeloblast               _____
myeloschisis             fissure of the spinal cord

· 215 ·

| | | |
|---|---|---|
| encephalomyelitis | | |
| ❖ *rachi/o* | *vertebral column*, *spine* 脊柱 | |
| rachiocentesis | surgical puncture into the spine | |
| rachiodynia | | |
| ❖ *-schisis* | *fissure*, *split* 裂开;裂口 | |
| cranioschisis | fissure of the cranium | |
| spondyloschisis | | |
| ❖ *scoli/o* | *curved*, *crooked* 弯曲的 | |
| scoliosis | lateral curvature of the spine | |
| lordoscoliosis | anterior and lateral curvature of the spine. | |
| ❖ *spondyl/o*, *vertebr/o* | *vertebrae* 脊椎 | |
| spondylolysis | loosening of the vertebrae | |
| spondyloarthropathy | | |
| vertebrocostal | pertaining to the vertebrae and ribs | |
| vertebrosternal | | |

**Exercise 6**

Explain the meanings of the following combining forms and suffixes.

1. spondyl/o  _____      6. myel/o  _____
2. scoli/o    _____      7. rachi/o  _____
3. -listhesis _____      8. vertebr/o _____
4. kyph/o     _____      9. -schisis _____
5. lamin/o    _____     10. -desis   _____

# Chapter 13　Musculoskeletal System

## Exercise 7

*Explain the following terms related to the vertebrae.*

1. spondyloschisis _____
2. spondylolisthesis _____
3. spondylomalacia _____
4. spondylotome _____
5. spondylolysis _____
6. spondylosyndesis _____

## Exercise 8

*Complete the definitions of the terms below.*

1. Rhinokyphosis is the _____ of the nose.
2. Lordosis is the _____ curvature of the spinal column in the thoracic region.
3. Rachioscoliosis is the _____ curvature of the spinal column.
4. Kyphoscoliosis refers to the _____ and _____ curvature of the spinal column.

### Group 5  Combining Forms for Joints and Muscles

| | |
|---|---|
| ❖ *arthr/o , articul/o* | *joints* 关节 |
| arthrocentesis | surgical puncture into the joints |
| arthralgia | _____ |
| periarticular | pertaining to surrounding the joints |
| endoarticular | _____ |
| ❖ *burs/o* | *bursa* 关节囊 |
| bursitis | inflammation of bursa |
| bursotomy | _____ |

| ❖ *fasci/o* | *fascia* 筋膜 |
|---|---|
| fasciodesis | binding of the fascia |
| fasciitis | |

| ❖ *fibr/o*, *in/o* | *fiber* 纤维 |
|---|---|
| fibrosclerosis | hardening of fiber |
| fibroid | |
| inoblast | immature fiber cell |
| inomyoma | |

| ❖ *leiomy/o* | *smooth muscle* 平滑肌 |
|---|---|
| leiomyoma | tumor of smooth muscle |
| leiomyosarcoma | |

| ❖ *ligament/o*, *syndesm/o* | *ligament* 韧带 |
|---|---|
| ligamentopexy | surgical fixation of the ligament |
| ligamentotomy | |
| syndesmectomy | removal of ligament |
| syndesmoma | |

| ❖ *my/o*, *muscul/o* | *muscle* 肌肉 |
|---|---|
| myosarcoma | malignant tumor of muscle |
| myomectomy | |
| musculocutaneous | pertaining to muscle and skin |
| muscular | |

| ❖ *sarc/o* | *flesh* 肉 |
|---|---|
| sarcoma | fleshy tumor (malignant) |
| sarcotome | |

| ❖ *synovi/o* | *synovial membrane* 滑膜 |
|---|---|
| synovioblast | embryonic synovial membrane |
| synoviotomy | |

## Chapter 13  Musculoskeletal System

❖ ten/o, tendin/o        tendon 肌腱

tenorrhaphy        surgical suture of tendon

tenodynia        _____

tendinitis        inflammation of tendon

tendinoplasty        _____

### Exercise 9

**Draw a line between the combining forms and their corresponding meanings.**

1. burs/o          a. smooth muscle
2. tendin/o        b. fascia
3. synovi/o        c. tendon
4. my/o            d. joint
5. syndesm/o       e. flesh
6. leiomy/o        f. ligament
7. arthr/o         g. bursa
8. sarc/o          h. fiber
9. in/o            i. muscle
10. fasci/o        j. synovia

### Exercise 10

**Build medical terms for the following definitions.**

1. fiber cell (in/o) _____
2. muscle cell (my/o) _____
3. disease of the smooth muscle _____
4. without synovia _____
5. suture of fascia _____
6. removal of bursa _____
7. pertaining to surround the joint (articul/o) _____
8. resembling flesh _____
9. surgical suture of ligament _____, or _____
10. inflammation of tendon _____

## Group 6  More Combining Forms, Prefixes and Suffixes

| | |
|---|---|
| ❖ *amphi-* | *both* 两边; *around* 周围 |
| amphiarthrosis | joint that permits slight movement in all directions |
| amphibian | animals that can live both on land and in water |
| amphicentric | |
| ❖ *ankyl/o* | *stiff* 僵硬的; *adhesion* 粘连 |
| ankylosis | stiffness (of the joints) |
| ankylodactyly | adhesion of the fingers or toes |
| ❖ *-clasis, -clasia* | *breaking* 破坏, 碎 |
| osteoclasis | breaking of the bone |
| cytoclasis | |
| arthroclasia | breaking of a joint (to allow movement) |
| histoclasia | |
| ❖ *-clast* | *breaker* 破裂 |
| osteoclast | the cell (or instrument) that breaks the bone |
| chondroclast | |
| ❖ *-kinesia* | *movement* 运动 |
| dyskinesia | difficulty in movement |
| hyperkinesia | |
| ❖ *-malacia* | *softening* 软化 |
| craniomalacia | softening of the cranium |
| osteomalacia | |
| ❖ *myx/o* | *mucus* 黏液 |
| fibromyxoma | fibrous tumor of mucous |
| myxadenitis | |
| ❖ *-physis* | *a growing* 生长; 生长物 |
| symphysis | a growing together |

## Chapter 13 Musculoskeletal System

neophysis _____

❖ **-pyesis**    *suppuration, pus* 化脓
empyesis    a pustular eruption (on the skin) (literal meaning is 'in pus')
osteopyesis _____

❖ **-tome**    *instrument to cut* 刀
arthrotome    instrument to cut into joints
osteotome _____

### Exercise 11

*Explain the meanings of the following word parts.*

1. -malacia _____   5. myx/o _____
2. -kinesia _____   6. -clast _____
3. ankyl/o _____   7. -pyesis _____
4. amphi- _____   8. -physis _____

### Exercise 12

*Complete the definitions of the terms below.*

1. Hypokinesia is inadequate _____.
2. Myxorrhea refers to the discharge of _____.
3. Spondylomalacia refers to _____ of vertebrae.
4. Ankylosis refers to the _____ of the joints.
5. Odontoclasis means _____ of teeth.

# Part Three  Integrated Practice

## Exercise 13

*Select the correct answer to complete each of the following statements.*

1. The binding of the end of a tendon to a bone is termed _____.
   a. tenoplasty            b. tenodesis
   c. myodynia              d. myorrhaphy

2. A/An _____ is a benign smooth muscle tumor.
   a. myosarcoma            b. myoma
   c. osteoma               d. leiomyoma

3. The condition of abnormal posterior curvature of the thoracic spine is called _____.
   a. scoliosis             b. spondylosis
   c. lordosis              d. kyphosis

4. All of the following are pelvic bones except the _____.
   a. ilium                 b. ischium
   c. pubis                 d. xphoid

5. A _____ is a tough band of tissue that connects bones at a joint.
   a. fascia                b. ligament
   c. tendon                d. bursa

6. Bone-forming cells are called _____.
   a. osteoblasts           b. osteoclasts
   c. osteomas              d. osteocytes

7. The malignant tumor of muscle is termed _____.
   a. myoma                 b. chondroma
   c. osteoma               d. myosarcoma

8. The _____ are sacs of fluid near the joints to act as cushions and reduce friction.
   a. synovia
   b. bursae
   c. bursa
   d. tendon
9. The _____ is the cell that breaks down the bony tissue.
   a. osteoblast
   b. osteoclast
   c. osteoclasis
   d. osteolysis
10. A person with a lateral curvature of the spine is diagnosed as _____.
    a. scoliosis
    b. kyphosis
    c. lordosis
    d. spondylosis
11. Which of the following muscle is under voluntary control?
    a. cardiac muscle
    b. smooth muscle
    c. skeletal muscle
    d. all of the above
12. The pain at the lower region of the back may be _____.
    a. spondylalgia
    b. osteodynia
    c. arthalgia
    d. lumbodynia
13. All of the following bones are of the arm except the _____.
    a. radius
    b. ulna
    c. tarsals
    d. humerus
14. The defective development of the bone is termed _____.
    a. osteodystrophy
    b. osteoclasia
    c. osteogenesis
    d. osteomalacia
15. The upper jaw bone is called _____.
    a. mandible
    b. maxilla
    c. tarsal
    d. sternum

## Part Four　Supplementary Readings

**Achondroplasia** is a rare genetic disorder of bone growth that leads to short stature. The condition is caused by a dominant gene but often arises as a new mutation. The long bones of the arms and legs are affected mainly. The cartilage that links each bone to its epiphysis is converted to bone too early, preventing further limb growth. Those affected have short limbs, a well-developed trunk, and a head of normal size except for a protruding forehead.

**Bursitis** refers to the inflammation of a bursa, resulting from injury, infection, or rheumatoid synovitis. It causes pain and tenderness and sometimes restricts movement at a nearby joint. Treatment of non-infectious bursitis includes rest and corticosteroid injection.

**Chondrosarcoma** is a cancerous growth of cartilage occurring within or on the surface of large bones, causing pain and swelling. Usually occurring in middle age, the tumor develops slowly from a non-cancerous tumor (chondroma, dyschondroplasia) or from normal bone. Amputation of the bone above the tumor usually results in a permanent cure.

**Gout** is a disease in which a defect in uric acid metabolism causes an excess of the acid and its salts (urates) to accumulate in the bloodstream and the joints. It results in attacks of acute gouty arthritis and chronic destruction of the joints and deposits of urates in the skin and cartilage. The affected joint (most commonly the base of the big toe) is red, swollen and tender. The excess urates also damage the kidneys, in which stones may form. Treatment often includes the drugs that increase the excretion of urates or slows the formation of urates.

**Myasthenia gravis** (**MG**) is a neuromuscular disorder, causes weakness of certain skeletal muscle groups (of the eyes, face and, to a lesser degree, the limbs). It is characterized by destruction of the receptors in the synaptic region that respond to acetylcholine, a neurotransmitter. As the disease progresses, the muscle becomes increasingly weak and may eventually cease to function altogether. Women tend to be affected slightly more than men. Initial symptoms include a weakness of the eye muscles and dysphagia. Later, the individual has difficulty chewing and talking. Eventually, the muscles of the limbs may become involved.

**Osteoarthrosis** is a disease of joint cartilage. It is associated with secondary changes in the underlying bone, which may ultimately cause pain and impair the function of the affected joint (usually the hip, knee, and thumb joints). The condition may result from overuse and is most common in those past middle life; it may also complicate many other diseases involving joints. Osteoarthritis is recognized on X-ray by narrowing of the joint space (due to loss of cartilage) and irregularity at the bone margins. Treatment includes analgesics, corrective and prosthetic surgery.

**Osteomyelitis** refers to the inflammation of the bone marrow due to the infection. This is a hazard following compound fractures and must be rigorously guarded against whenever the marrow is exposed during bone or joint surgery. It may also be caused by blood-borne microorganisms. In acute osteomyelitis, most common in children, there is severe pain, swelling, and redness at the site, often in the shaft of a lone bone, accompanied by general illness and high fever. Chronic osteomyelitis may follow the acute form or develop insidiously. Delay in eradicating the infection may lead to bone shortening and deformity.

**Osteoporosis** is the loss of bony tissue, resulting in bones that are brittle and liable to fracture. In osteoporosis the bone mineral density (BMD) is reduced, bone microarchitecture is disrupted, and the amount and variety of non-collagenous proteins in bone is altered. Osteoporosis is most common in women after menopause, which it is called postmenopausal osteoporosis, but may also develop in men, and may occur in anyone in the presence of particular hormonal disorders and other chronic diseases or as a result of medications, specifically glucocorticoids. Certain medication and lifestyle changes (like exercises) can prevent and treat osteoporosis.

**Osteosarcoma** is a cancerous tumor of the bone that spreads rapidly to the lungs and, less often, to other areas. An osteosarcoma may occur in adolescents for unknown reason (usually in a long bone of the arm or leg or around the knee, hip, or shoulder). In elderly people, osteosarcoma may develop in several bones as a late, rare complication of Paget's disease. The tumor causes pain and swelling of the affected bone if it occurs near the surface. The condition may be treated by radiotherapy, but the affected bone is usually surgically removed. Sometimes it is replaced by a bone graft or artificial bone, but most often, an amputation and an artificial limb (prosthesis) are required.

**Rhematoid arthritis** is a form of arthritis that is the second most common rheumatic disease (after osteoarthritis). It typically involves the joints of the fingers, wrists, feet, and ankles and often the hips and shoulders: the joints are affected symmetrically and there is a considerable range of severity. The condition is diagnosed by a blood test, which shows the presence of the rheumatoid factor, and by X-rays revealing typical changes around the affected joints.

**Talipes** refers to a birth defect (commonly called club-foot) in which the foot is twisted out of shape or position. The cause may be pressure on the feet from the mother's uterus, or a genetic factor. It is treated by repeated manipulation of the foot and ankle, starting soon after birth. A plaster cast, splint, or strapping may be used to hold the foot in position. If this is not successful, surgery will be needed.

## Part Five   Review Sheet

Here is a collection of the word parts you have learned in this chapter. Write the meaning of each word part without referring to your previous work.

**Combining Forms**

| Combining Form | Meaning | Combining Form | Meaning |
| --- | --- | --- | --- |
| acetabul/o | | fibr/o | |
| acromi/o | | fibul/o | |
| ankyl/o | | humer/o | |
| arthr/o | | ili/o | |
| articul/o | | in/o | |
| brachi/o | | ischi/o | |
| burs/o | | kyph/o | |
| calcane/o | | lamin/o | |
| carp/o | | leiomy/o | |
| cervic/o | | ligament/o | |
| chir/o | | lord/o | |
| chondr/o | | lumb/o | |
| clavicul/o | | mandibul/o | |
| coccyg/o | | maxill/o | |
| cost/o | | metacarp/o | |
| crani/o | | metatars/o | |
| dactyl/o | | muscul/o | |

## Chapter 13  Musculoskeletal System

| | | | |
|---|---|---|---|
| dors/o | _____ | myel/o | _____ |
| fasci/o | _____ | my/o | _____ |
| femor/o | _____ | patell/o | _____ |
| phalang/o | _____ | spondyl/o | _____ |
| palat/o | _____ | stern/o | _____ |
| pelv/i, pelvi/o | _____ | syndesm/o | _____ |
| pod/o | _____ | synovi/o | _____ |
| ped/o | _____ | tars/o | _____ |
| rachi/o | _____ | ten/o | _____ |
| radi/o | _____ | tendin/o | _____ |
| sacr/o | _____ | tibi/o | _____ |
| scapul/o | _____ | uln/o | _____ |
| scarc/o | _____ | vertebr/o | _____ |
| scoli/o | _____ | | |

## Suffixes

| Suffix | Meaning | Suffix | Meaning |
|---|---|---|---|
| -clasis, -clasia | _____ | -malacia | _____ |
| -clast | _____ | -physis | _____ |
| -desis | _____ | -pyesis | _____ |
| -kinesia | _____ | -schisis | _____ |
| -listhesis | _____ | -tome | _____ |

## Prefixes

| Prefix | Meaning |
|---|---|
| amphi- | _____ |

# Chapter 14  Integumentary System

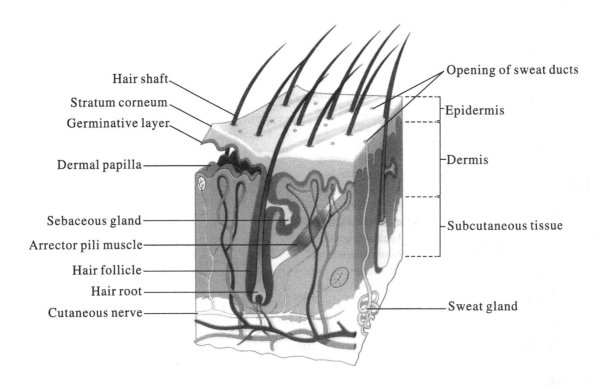

# Chapter 14  Integumentary System

## Part One  Overview of the System

The integumentary system comprises the skin and its accessory organs, including hair, nails, and glands.

The skin covers the external surface of the body and plays an important role in body defense, **thermoregulation**, sensation and vitamin D synthesis. There are three primary layers in the skin: the **epidermis**, **dermis** and **hypodermis** (also called the subcutaneous tissue) from the surface inward. The epidermis is composed of stratified squamous **epithelium** and does not contain blood vessels (described as **avascular**). At the deep layer of the epidermis, new cells are constantly formed and pushed to the surface. As they are moved away from their blood supply, they die and are filled with **keratin**, a protein which toughens the outlayer of the skin. Upon reaching the surface of the epidermis, these cells slough off. Also in the deep part of the epidermis, **melanocytes** can be found, which produce **melanin**, a pigment which gives the skin its color and protects it against the sun's ultraviolet rays. The dermis, the middle layer of the skin, comprises blood vessels, connective tissue, nerves, lymph vessels, sweat glands and hair follicles. So it is directly related to many skin functions and provides nourishment to its own cells and cells in the deep layer of the epidermis. The dermis is composed of interwoven elastic and **collagen** fibers, which give the dermis the properties of strength, extensibility and elasticity. Below the dermis lies **the subcutaneous layer**, which contains around half of the body fat and serves as padding and insulation for the body.

Hair is widespread over the body. Each hair grows in a sac called the **hair follicle** and has two parts: the **root** and **shaft**. The nails protect the dorsal surface of the last bone of toes and fingers and have several parts, including **cuticle**, which is the fold of epidermis at the base and sides of the nail plate, **paronychium**, which is the soft tissue surrounding the border of the nail, **hyponychium**, which is the attachment between the skin of the finger or toe and the distal end of the nail, and **lunula** which is the crescent-shaped whitish area at the base of the nail plate. Both hair and nails are mainly composed of keratin.

Two types of glands are located in the skin. **Sebaceous glands** produce **sebum**, a lipid that lubricates the skin and discourages the growth of bacteria on the skin. **Sweat glands** produce sweat to regulate body temperature and water content and excrete some metabolic wastes.

### Exercise 1

**Fill in the blanks with the terms you have learned in the above passage.**

1. The outmost layer of the skin is called _____ and it is composed of squamous _____.
2. _____ is the middle layer of the skin, which contains blood, lymph vessels, nerve ending, etc.
3. _____ is a pigment that gives the skin color and it is produced by _____.
4. _____ is an oily substance secreted by _____ glands in the skin.
5. The _____ is the whitish area at the base of the nail plate and is where new growth occurs.

## Part Two  Combining Forms, Prefixes and Suffixes

**Group 1   Combining Forms and Suffixes for Skin Structures**

❖ *cutane/o, derm/o*
  *dermat/o*                    *skin* 皮肤

| | |
|---|---|
| subcutaneous | below the skin |
| percutaneous | |
| intradermal | within the skin |
| dermitis | |
| dermatology | |

## Chapter 14  Integumentary System

❖ *diaphor/o* — *profuse sweating* 出汗
diaphoresis — condition of profuse sweating
adiaphoresis

❖ *follicul/o* — *follicle* 小囊
folliculitis

> **Tips**: More often, *follicul/o* is used to mean the ovarian follicle, as in *folliculoma*, *folliculose*, and *folliculosis*.

❖ *hidr/o*, *sudor/o* — *sweat* 汗
anhidrosis — lack of sweating
hidropoiesis
sudorific — sweat producing
sudoriferous
( -ferous = carrying )

❖ *onych/o*, *ungu/o* — *nail* 指(趾)甲
paronychia — infection around a nail
( par(a)- = beside, close to )
onycholysis
ungual — pertaining to the nail
subungual

❖ *pil/o*, *trich/o* — *hair* 毛发
pilosebaceous — pertaining to the hair follicle and the sebaceous gland
piliform
polytrichia — increase in the number of hair
trichosis

❖ *seb/o* — *sebum* 皮脂
seborrhea — excessive secretion of sebum
sebaceous

❖ *-derma*　　　　　　　　*skin condition* 皮肤
　pyoderma　　　　　　　any pyogenic infection of the skin
　scleroderma　　　　　　_____

### Exercise 2

**Draw a line between the combining forms and their corresponding meanings. Note that different combining forms may have the same meaning.**

1. dermat/o　　　　　　a. nail
2. ungu/o　　　　　　　b. skin
3. trich/o　　　　　　　c. profuse sweating
4. hidr/o　　　　　　　d. sweating
5. onych/o　　　　　　 e. follicle
6. seb/o　　　　　　　 f. sebum
7. diaphor/o　　　　　　g. hair
8. pil/o
9. cutane/o
10. follicul/o

### Exercise 3

**Divide each of the following words into its component parts with a slash (/) and then explain its meaning.**

1. onychomalacia _____
2. dermatome _____
3. acrodermatitis _____
4. epidermis _____
5. dermabrasion _____
6. hyperhidrosis _____
7. onychorrhexis _____
8. hidradenitis _____
9. onychotomy _____
10. onychodynia _____

# Chapter 14  Integumentary System

## Group 2  Combining Forms, Suffixes and Prefixes Related to Skin

❖ *adip/o, lip/o, steat/o*    *fat* 脂肪
adipose                       fat tissue
adipocyte                     _____
lipoma                        a tumor composed of the fat cells
liposuction                   _____
steatoma                      any cyst or tumor of a sebaceous gland
steatorrhea                   _____

❖ *coll/a, coll/o*            *glue* 胶
collagen                      a fibrous protein material
colloid                       _____

❖ *cry/o*                     *cold* 冷,冻,低温
cryotherapy                   treatment using low temperature
cryosurgery                   _____

❖ *kerat/o*                   *horny; horny layer of the skin* 角,角质
keratin                       a hard protein material
keratosis                     _____

> **Tips**: *Kerat/o* also means the cornea of the eye in such terms as *keratoplasty*, *keratoscope*, and *keratocentesis*.

❖ *squam/o*                   *scale-like* 鳞状
squamous                      resembling scale
squamatization                _____

❖ *xer/o*  *dry* 干燥
xerostomia  dry mouth
xeroderma  _____

❖ *therm/o*  *heat* 热,温度
thermoregulation  regulation of the temperature
hypothermic  _____

❖ *-mycosis*  *fungal infection* 真菌感染
onychomycosis  fungal infection of the nail
dermatomycosis  _____

❖ *pachy-*  *thick* 厚
pachyderma  thickening of the skin
pachyonychia  _____

**Exercise 4**

**Draw a line between the word parts and their corresponding meanings.**

1. coll/a           a. scale-like
2. cry/o            b. heat
3. kerat/o          c. cold
4. -mycosis         d. horny
5. pachy-           e. thick
6. squam/o          f. dry
7. therm/o          g. glue
8. xer/o            h. fungal infection

**Exercise 5**

**Complete the terms for the following definitions.**

1. instrument for measuring temperature: _____ meter
2. dry eyes: _____ ophthalmia
3. abnormal fear of dryness and dry places: _____ phobia

## Chapter 14  Integumentary System

4. fungal infection of the hair: tricho _____
5. fungal infection of the ear: oto _____
6. use of low temperature to destroy unwanted tissue: _____ surgery
7. an abnormal thickness of the tongue: _____ glossia
8. an abnormal thickness of the lips: _____ cheilia

### Group 3  Combining Forms for Colors

❖ *albin/o , leuk/o*         *white* 白
albinism                    a condition marked by lack of melanin in the skin and its related structures
leukoderma                  _____

❖ *chlor/o*                  *green* 绿
chlorophyll                 a green pigment in leaves
(-phyll = leaf)
chloroma                    _____

❖ *chrom/o*                  *color* 颜色
hypochromic                 having less color than normal (referring to red blood cells)
achromotrichia              _____

❖ *cirrh/o , jaund/o*
  *xanth/o*                 *yellow* 黄
jaundice                    yellow discoloration of the skin, eye whites and mucous membranes
cirrhosis                   _____
xanthoderma                 _____

❖ *cyan/o*                   *blue* 蓝
cyanosis                    bluish discoloration of skin (due to lack of oxygen)
acrocyanosis                _____

| ❖ *eosin/o* | *rose-colored* 玫瑰红 |
|---|---|
| eosinophil | granulocytic white blood cells that are readily stained with eosin, the red acidic dye |
| eosinopenia | |

| ❖ *erythem/o*, *erythr/o*, *rub/o* | *red* 红 |
|---|---|
| rubella | viral infection with red skin rash |
| erythema | |
| erythrocyte | |

| ❖ *glauc/o*, *poli/o* | *gray* 灰 |
|---|---|
| glaucoma | "gray eyes" (a condition in which poor blood flow to the back of the eye causes the optic nerve to appear pale gray) |
| poliomyelitis | |

| ❖ *melan/o* | *black* 黑 |
|---|---|
| melanoderma | abnormally dark skin |
| melanin | |

| ❖ *purpur/o* | *purple* 紫 |
|---|---|
| purpura | purplish skin bruises |
| purpuriferous | |

**Exercise 6**

*Explain the meanings of the following combining forms.*

1. erythem/o _____
2. xanth/o _____
3. cirrh/o _____
4. chlor/o _____
5. cyan/o _____
6. poli/o _____
7. albin/o _____
8. melan/o _____
9. purpur/o _____
10. leuk/o _____

# Chapter 14  Integumentary System

## Exercise 7

*Choose the appropriate term from the following list for each of the given definitions.*

| albino | bilirubin | chloropia | chromohidrosis | erythroderma |
| jaundice | leukoplakia | melanoglossia | poliodystrophy | xanthoma |

1. a deposition of yellowish cholesterol-rich material in tendons and other body parts _____
2. abnormally blackened tongue _____
3. green vision _____
4. abnormal development of the graymatter in the brain _____
5. white patches on mucous membrane of the tongue or cheek _____
6. excretion of colored sweats _____
7. abnormal reddening, flaking and thickening of the skin affecting a wide area of the body _____
8. a person without any skin pigment _____
9. red pigment produced when hemoglobin from dying RBCs is broken down _____
10. yellowing of the skin or white of the eyes _____

## Part Three  Integrated Practice

## Exercise 8

*Match the terms in Column I with their definitions in Column II. Place the correct letter of the definition to the left of the term.*

| Column I | Column II |
|---|---|
| _____ 1. cyanosis | a. resembling a horn |
| _____ 2. onychia | b. excessive sweating |
| _____ 3. dermatomycosis | c. bluish discoloration |
| _____ 4. epidermis | d. removal of a nail |

_____ 5. steatoma               e. dry skin
_____ 6. keratoid               f. abnormally thick lips
_____ 7. trichophagia           g. recording of heat
_____ 8. hyperhidrosis          h. dark pigment
_____ 9. thermography           i. outmost layer of the skin
_____ 10. xeroderma             j. specialization of skin diseases
_____ 11. melanin               k. eating hair
_____ 12. dermatology           l. inflammation of nail
_____ 13. pachycheilia          m. fungal skin infection
_____ 14. onychectomy           n. erection of hair
_____ 15. piloerection          o. tumor of a sebaceous gland

# Part Four    Supplementary Readings

**Acne** is an inflammation of the sebaceous glands and hair follicles. Dried sebum or keratin plugs a sebaceous gland, forming a comedo or blackhead. Bacteria act on the sebum, which spills over into the surrounding tissue, irritating it. Papules, pustules, and cysts can thus form.

**Alopecia**, hair loss, may result from aging, illness, or treatment. Alopecia areata is an idiopathic condition in which hair falls out in patches.

**Cryosurgery** is the application of extreme cold to destroy abnormal or diseased tissue in a number of conditions, especially a variety of benign and malignant skin conditions, such as warts, moles, skin tags, solar keratoses, and small skin cancers.

**Ecchymosis** refers to "black and blue" mark caused by hemorrhage into the skin. Petechiae are smaller versions of ecchymoses. Purpura forms when ecchymoses and petechiae merge over any part of the body.

**Eczema** is a form of dermatitis. The term *eczema* is broadly applied to a range of persistent skin conditions. These include dryness and recurring skin rashes which are characterized by one or more of these symptoms: redness, skin edema, itching and dryness, crusting, flaking, blistering, cracking, oozing, or bleeding. Areas of temporary skin discoloration may appear and are sometimes due to healed lesions, although scarring is rare.

**Lesions** are areas of damaged tissues resulting from disease or injury. Examples of skin lesions include macules (flat, colored spot), papule (raised, solid area of the skin), pustule (pus-containing raised lesion), ulcer (erosion of the skin or mucous membrane), vesicles (fluid-filled raised lesion), wheals (smooth, rounded, slightly raised areas, often accompanied by itching), etc.

**Psoriasis** is chronic, recurrent dermatosis marked by itchy, scaly, red patches covered by slivery gray scales. The scaly patches frequently appear on the skin of elbows and knees. It is believed to have a genetic origin and to be aggravated by stress, smoking and consumption of alcohol. Treatment is palliative and includes topical lubricants, keratolytics, and steroids.

**Systemic lupus erythematosis** (SLE or lupus) is a chronic inflammatory autoimmune disease of connective tissue, which can affect any part of the body, including the skin, joints, and internal organs. The patients may have a characteristic "butterfly pattern" of redness over the cheeks and nose. Corticosteroids and immunosuppressive drugs are used to control symptoms.

**Urticaria** (hives) describes a skin rash notable for red, raised, itchy bumps. Frequently, it is caused by allergic reactions. Antihistamines are used to control the symptoms.

**Vitiligo**, or **leukoderma**, is a chronic skin disease that causes depigmentation in areas of the skin (pale patches). It occurs when the melanocytes die or are unable to function. Some evidence suggests it is caused by a combination of autoimmune, genetic, and environmental factors.

## *Part Five* **Review Sheet**

Here is a collection of the word parts you have learned in this chapter. Write the meaning of each word part without referring to your previous work.

## Combining Forms

| Combining Form | Meaning | Combining Form | Meaning |
|---|---|---|---|
| albin/o | | leuk/o | |
| adip/o | | lip/o | |
| chlor/o | | melan/o | |
| chrom/o | | onych/o | |
| cirrh/o | | pil/o | |
| coll/o | | poli/o | |
| cry/o | | purpur/o | |
| cutane/o | | rub/o | |
| cyan/o | | seb/o | |
| derm/o, dermat/o | | squam/o | |
| diaphor/o | | steat/o | |
| erythem/o, erythr/o | | sudor/o | |
| follicul/o | | therm/o | |
| glauc/o | | trich/o | |
| hidr/o | | ungu/o | |
| jaund/o | | xanth/o | |
| kerat/o | | xer/o | |

## Suffixes

| Suffix | Meaning | Suffix | Meaning |
|---|---|---|---|
| -mycosis | | -derma | |

## Prefixes

| Prefix | Meaning |
|---|---|
| pachy- | |

# Chapter 15  Special Senses: The Eye and The Ear

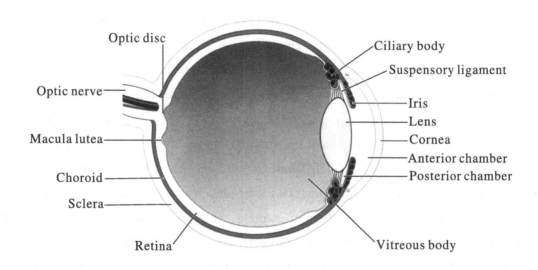

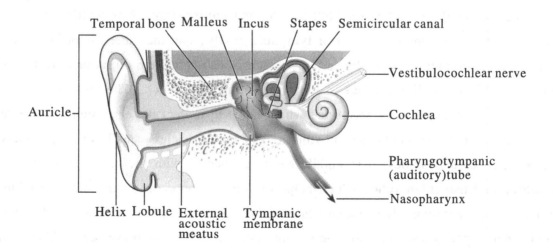

## Part One  Overview of the System

The eye and the ear are sense organs respectively responsible for vision, hearing and balance.

The eyes are paired to provide **stereoscopic** vision (perception of depth and three dimensions). The wall of the eyeball consists of three layers. The outer fibrous layer is the **sclera**, which extends over the front of the eye as the transparent **cornea**. The middle vascular layer, the **uvea**, contains the **choroid**, the **ciliary body**, and the **iris**. At the center of iris is an opening, the **pupil**, through which light rays pass. The inner layer is the **retina**, which contains the photoreceptor cells and specialized areas including the **macula fovea** (the point of the retina with the sharpest vision) and **optic disc**. Nerve cells in the retina receive and transmit visual information via the **optic nerve** to the brain where it is processed. Light rays are refracted and focused on the inner retina by the **anterior aqueous humor**, the **lens** and the **posterior vitreous humor**. In addition, the eye has some accessory structures, which help to protect the eye in one way or another. The eyelid, or **palpebra** (pl. *palpebrae*), protects the anterior portion of the eye. The **conjunctiva** (pl. *conjunctivae*) lines the eyelid and covers the anterior eyeball. The **lacrimal apparatus** cleans and moistens the eye.

The ear has the receptors for both hearing and **equilibrium**. It is divided into three parts: the outer ear, the middle ear or **tympanic cavity**, and the inner ear or **labyrinth**. Sound waves are picked up by the earflap, which is also called the **pinna** or **auricle**, and travel through the **auditory canal** to the **tympanum** (eardrum). The auditory canal is lined with **cerumen**, a waxy secretion, which helps to protect the ear. Sound waves are conducted through the middle ear via vibrations of three **ossicles** (small bones), namely, **malleus**, **incus** and **stapes**. The middle ear is connected with the nasopharynx via the **auditory** or **Eustachian tube**, which helps to equalize pressure on the outer and inner surfaces of the eardrum. The first structure of the inner ear, or the **cochlea**, is filled with fluids, called **perilymph** and **endolymph**, through which the vibrations travel. Also in the cochlea is an auditory receptor area, the **organ of Corti**, where vibrations from the liquids

## Chapter 15   Special Senses: The Eye and The Ear

are received, generating impulses that are transmitted to the brain by way of the auditory nerve. Also within the inner ear are located three **semicircular canals** which function in equilibrium. These canals are placed at right angles to each other and are filled with a fluid called **endolymph**. Any movement of the ear sets this fluid in motion, stimulating nerve endings of the **vestibular nerve**. Nerve impulses are transmitted to the brain for correction of equilibrium as necessary.

**Exercise 1**

*Fill in the blanks with the terms you have learned in the above passage.*

1. The eyeball is composed of three layers: the _____, _____ and _____.
2. The amount of light entering the eye is regulated by the size of the _____, which in turn is controlled by the _____.
3. The light rays entering the eyes are bent by the cornea, _____, _____, and _____.
4. The area in the retina responsible for sharp central vision is _____.
5. The mucous membrane that lines the eyelids and covers the anterior portion of the eyeball is _____.
6. The spiral-shaped organ in the labyrinth that contains the receptors for hearing is the _____.
7. The _____ is a waxy substance secreted in the ear canal.
8. The _____ helps to protect the ear by balancing the pressure between the outer and middle ear.
9. In the middle ear, vibrations of three small bones conduct the sound waves. The three bones are _____, _____ and _____.
10. Ears are responsible for hearing and _____.

# Part Two  Combining Forms, Prefixes and Suffixes

## Group 1  Combining Forms for the Eye (I)

❖ *blephar/o, palpebr/o*  —  *eyelid* 眼睑
- blepharoptosis — drooping of the eyelids
- blepharoplegia
- palpebral
- interpalpebral

❖ *chori/o, choroid/o*  —  *choroids* 脉络膜
- chorioretinal — pertaining to retina and choroid
- choroidopathy

❖ *conjunctiv/o*  —  *conjunctiva* 结膜
- conjunctivoplasty — surgical repair of the conjunctiva
- subconjunctival

❖ *core/o, pupill/o*  —  *pupil* 瞳孔
- corectasis — dilation of the pupil
- coreometer
- pupillography — procedure for recording the reactions of the pupil
- pupillotonia
(ton/o = tension)

❖ *corne/o, kerat/o*  —  *cornea* 角膜
- keratome — an instrument for cutting the cornea
- keratoplasty
- circumcorneal

# Chapter 15  Special Senses: The Eye and The Ear

| | |
|---|---|
| corneosclera | |
| ❖ *cycl/o* | *ciliary body* 睫状体 |
| cycloplegia | paralysis of the ciliary muscle |
| cyclospasm | |
| ❖ *dacry/o , lacrim/o* | *tear* 泪; *lacrimal sac* 泪囊 |
| dacryorrhea | excessive secretion of tears |
| dacryolith | |
| lacrimotomy | incision into the lacrimal sac |
| lacrimation | |
| ❖ *dacryocyst/o* | *lacrimal sac* 泪囊 |
| dacryocystorhinostomy | surgical connection of the lacrimal sac and nose |
| dacryocystitis | |
| ❖ *ir/o , irid/o* | *iris* 虹膜 |
| iridomalacia | softening of the iris |
| iridectomy | |
| iritis | |

**Exercise 2**

*Draw a line between the combining forms and their corresponding meanings.*

1. chori/o            a. iris
2. kerat/o            b. tear
3. core/o             c. cornea
4. conjunctiv/o       d. lacrimal sac
5. blephar/o          e. eyelid
6. irid/o             f. conjunctiva
7. dacryocyst/o       g. choroid
8. lacrim/o           h. pupil

## Exercise 3

*Build a medical term for each of the following definitions.*

1. removal of the lacrimal sac _____
2. inflammation of the eyelid and conjunctiva _____
3. pertaining to the nose and the lacrimal apparatus _____
4. hernia of the iris _____
5. any disease of the choroid _____
6. spasm of the eyelid _____
7. instrument for measuring the curve of the cornea _____
8. surgical repair of the pupil _____

### Group 2  Combining Forms and Suffixes for the Eye (II)

❖ *ocul/o, ophthalm/o*　　*eye* 眼睛
oculodynia　　　　　　　pain in the eyeball
binocular　　　　　　　　_____
ophthalmology　　　　　study of eye diseases and their treatment
ophthalmoscopy　　　　_____

❖ *opt/o, optic/o*　　　*eye* 眼睛；*vision* 视力
optometrist　　　　　　one trained in examining the eyes and prescribing corrective lenses
optician　　　　　　　　one who fills prescription for glasses
optic　　　　　　　　　　_____

❖ *phak/o, phac/o*　　　*lens* 晶状体
aphakia　　　　　　　　absence of the lens in the eyes
phacolysis　　　　　　　_____

## Chapter 15　Special Senses: The Eye and The Ear

| | |
|---|---|
| ❖ *retin/o* | *retina* 视网膜 |
| retinoschisis | splitting of the retina |
| retinopathy | |
| ❖ *scler/o* | *sclera* 巩膜 |
| scleromalacia | softening of the sclera |
| scleroiritis | |
| ❖ *uve/o* | *uvea* 葡萄膜 |
| uveitis | inflammation of the uvea |
| uveoscleritis | |
| ❖ *vitre/o*, *hyal/o* | *glassy* 玻璃样; *vitreous body* 玻璃体 |
| vitreous | pertaining to the vitreous body |
| vitrectomy | |
| hyalosis | disorder of the vitreous body |
| hyaloid | |
| ❖ *-opia*, *-opsia* | *vision* 视力 |
| myopia | nearsightedness |
| (my/o = shut) | |
| hyperopia | far sightedness |
| heteropsia | different vision in each eye |
| ❖ *-tropia* | *turning* 向… |
| esotropia | inward turning of the eyes |
| (eso- = inward) | |
| exotropia | |
| (exo- = outward) | |

## Exercise 4

*Explain the meanings of the following combining forms and suffixes.*

1. ophthalm/o  _____
2. scler/o  _____
3. opt/o  _____
4. hyal/o  _____
5. retin/o  _____
6. phak/o  _____
7. uve/o  _____
8. vitre/o  _____
9. -opsia  _____
10. -tropia  _____

## Exercise 5

*Complete the medical terms for the following definitions.*

1. softening of the lens: p _____
2. inflammation of the sclera and iris: s _____
3. surgical fixation of the retina: r _____
4. pertaining to one eye: m _____
5. a knife used to cut into the sclera: s _____
6. an instrument used to examine the eye: o _____
7. inflammation of the retina: r _____
8. hernia of the lens: p _____
9. protrusion of one or both eyeballs: ex _____ os
10. profession dealing with examining eyes for defects of refraction: o _____

### Group 3  Combining Forms and Suffixes for the Ear

| | | |
|---|---|---|
| ❖ *acous/o* | *sound* 声音; *hearing* 听力 | |
| acoustic | pertaining to hearing | |
| acousimeter | _____ | |
| ❖ *audi/o* | *hearing* 听力 | |
| audiogram | record of hearing ability | |
| audiometry | _____ | |

## Chapter 15  Special Senses: The Eye and The Ear

| | | |
|---|---|---|
| ❖ *aur/o, auricul/o, ot/o* | *ear, ear-like structure* 耳 | |
| postauricular | behind the ear | |
| biaural | | |
| otosclerosis | hardening and the ossicles in the ear | |
| otorrhea | | |
| ❖ *cochle/o* | *cochlea* 耳蜗 | |
| retrocochlear | pertaining to behind the cochlea | |
| cochleitis | | |
| ❖ *labyrinth/o* | *labyrinth* 迷路 | |
| labyrinthotomy | incision into the labyrinth | |
| labyrinthine | | |
| ❖ *myring/o* | *tympanic membrane* 鼓膜 | |
| myringoplasty | repair of the ear drum | |
| myringotomy | | |
| ❖ *ossicul/o* | *ossicle, small bone* 小骨 | |
| ossiculoplasty | surgical repair of the ossicle | |
| ossiculotomy | | |
| ❖ *salping/o* | *tube* 管; *Eustachian tube* 咽鼓管 | |
| salpingoscope | instrument to examine the Eustachian tube | |
| salpingopharyngeal | | |

> **Tips**: *Salping/o* is more often used to refer to the fallopian tube, as in *salpingectomy*, *salpingocyesis*. In other terms, it can refer to either the Eustachian or the fallopian tube, as in *salpingitis*.

| | | |
|---|---|---|
| ❖ *staped/o* | | ***stapes* 镫骨** |
| stapedolysis | | loosening of the stapes |
| stapedectomy | | _____ |
| ❖ *tympan/o* | | ***tympanic membrane or cavity* 鼓膜,鼓室** |
| tympanocentesis | | surgical puncture into the tympanic cavity |
| tympanometry | | _____ |
| ❖ *vestibul/o* | | ***vestibule* 前庭** |
| vestibulopathy | | _____ |
| vestibular | | _____ |
| ❖ *-acusia, -acusis* | | ***hearing condition* 听力** |
| hyperacusis | | abnormal sensitivity to sounds |
| bradyacusia | | _____ |
| ❖ *-otia* | | ***ear condition* 耳** |
| macrotia | | abnormally large ears |
| microtia | | _____ |

### Exercise 6

***Explain the meanings of the following combining forms and suffixes.***

1. aur/o  _____
2. ot/o  _____
3. cochle/o  _____
4. myring/o  _____
5. salping/o  _____
6. staped/o  _____
7. tympan/o  _____
8. vestibul/o  _____
9. -acusia  _____
10. -otia  _____

### Exercise 7

***Divide each of the following terms into its component parts with a slash (/) and then explain its meaning.***

1. otogenic  _____
2. otalgia  _____

# Chapter 15 Special Senses: The Eye and The Ear

3. labyrinthine _____
4. salpingopharyngeal _____
5. audiometer _____
6. vestibulocochlear _____
7. tympanectomy _____
8. anacusis _____
9. otolaryngology _____
10. stapedoplasty _____

## Group 4  Other Related Combining Forms and Prefixes

❖ *ambly/o*　　　　　　*dull*, *dim* 钝,弱
amblyopia　　　　　　dimness of vision
amblyacusis　　　　　　_____

❖ *anis/o*　　　　　　*unequal* 不等
anisocoria　　　　　　unequal size of the pupils
anisocytosis　　　　　　_____

❖ *dipl/o*　　　　　　*double* 双,两倍
diplacusis　　　　　　double hearing
diplopia　　　　　　_____

❖ *nyct/o*　　　　　　*night* 夜
nyctalopia　　　　　　night blindness
nyctophobia　　　　　　_____

❖ *phot/o*　　　　　　*light* 光
photophobia　　　　　　fear of light
photocoagulation　　　　_____

❖ **presby/o, ger/o**
   **geront/o**                    **old age** 老年

presbyopia                    impaired vision due to old age
presbyacusis                  _____
geriatrics                    medicine dealing with treatment of disorders occurring
                              in old age
(iatr/o = treatment)
gerontology                   _____

> **Tips**: *Gerontology* is the study of the aging process itself. *Geriatrics* is the branch of medicine focusing on health care of the elderly. The relation between geriatrics and internal medicine is similar to that between pediatrics and internal medicine.

❖ **dextro-**                 **right side** 右
dextrocular                   having the right eye dominant
dextrocardia                  _____

❖ **sinistro-**               **left side** 左
sinistrocular                 _____
sinistrocerebral              _____

## Exercise 8

Draw a line between the combining forms or prefixes and their corresponding meanings.

1. presby/o          a. right
2. phot/o            b. unequal
3. nyct/o            c. old age
4. dextro-           d. dim
5. dipl/o            e. light
6. anis/o            f. left
7. ambly/o           g. night
8. sinistro-         h. double

# Chapter 15  Special Senses: The Eye and The Ear

### Exercise 9

*Build a medical term for each of the following definitions.*

1. nearsightedness _____
2. farsightedness _____
3. night blindness _____
4. deafness _____
5. complete color blindness _____
6. impairment of visual function due to aging _____
7. impairment of hearing due to aging _____
8. dim vision _____
9. pertaining to the right cerebral hemisphere _____
10. double vision _____

## Part Three  Integrated Practice

### Exercise 10

*Circle the term with the correct spelling in each pair.*

1. keratomy          keratotomy
2. papillary         papilary
3. blepharoptosis    blepharotosis
4. ophthalmical      ophthalmic
5. vetrous           vitreous
6. otopyorrhea       otopyorhea
7. dacryadenitis     dacryoadenitis
8. iral              iridic
9. biocular          binocular
10. corneoscleral    cornoscleral

· 253 ·

11. cerumen          serumen
12. macule           macula

### Exercise 11

*Select the correct answer to complete each of the following statements.*

1. The surgical procedure for correction of a deformed pinna might be noted on the operative record as a/an _____.
   a. otoplasty            b. otocleisis
   c. microsurgery of ear  d. myringoplasty
2. _____ is a condition in which there is a marked intolerance to light.
   a. Diplopia             b. Anisometropia
   c. Nyctalopia           d. Photophobia
3. The ophthalmologist refers to inflammation of the cornea as _____.
   a. keratitis            b. uveitis
   c. scleritis            d. retinitis
4. Measurement of hearing acuity at various sound wave frequencies is termed _____.
   a. tonometry            b. audiometry
   c. otoscopy             d. salpingoscopy
5. The surgical procedure for removing a lesion in the eyelid is termed _____.
   a. dacryocystectomy     b. blepharectomy
   c. dacryoadenectomy     d. retinectomy
6. The surgical repair of the pupil is called _____.
   a. coreoplasty          b. coreopexy
   c. kerotomy             d. keratoplasty
7. The person who is an expert in filling prescription for corrective lenses is called _____.
   a. ophthalmologist      b. oculist
   c. optometrist          d. optician
8. _____ is softening of the lens, as may occur in hypermature cataract.
   a. Iridomalacia         b. Ophthalmomalacia
   c. Phacomalacia         d. Scleromalacia

## Chapter 15   Special Senses: The Eye and The Ear

9. _____ is a general term for eye diseases.
   a. Retinopathy          b. Oculopathy
   c. Otopathy             d. Maculopathy

10. Visual examination of the interior of the eye with a handheld instrument is called _____.
    a. gonioscopy          b. retinoscopy
    c. otoscopy            d. ophthalmoscopy

11. The science of _____ deals with the diagnosis and treatment of ocular diseases.
    a. orthoptics          b. audiology
    c. ophthalmology       d. optometrics

12. An infection of the middle ear is called _____.
    a. otitis media        b. tympanitis
    c. labyrinthitis       d. mastoiditis

13. The clinical term for nearsightedness is _____.
    a. hypermetropia       b. myopia
    c. presbyopia          d. nyctalopia

14. The _____ is a mucous membrane over the anterior surface of the eyeball and eyelid.
    a. choroid             b. sclera
    c. cornea              d. conjunctiva

15. The procedure to drain the middle ear cavity by making a small incision on the tympanic membrane is termed _____.
    a. myringotomy         b. myringotome
    c. tympanostomy        d. tympanectomy

16. A condition of dimness of vision in one eye that is normal on ophthalmoscopic examination is termed _____.
    a. monocular blindness b. amblyopia
    c. ametropia           d. scotoma

17. Secretion of tears is called _____.
    a. dacryosis           b. lacrimation
    c. epiphora            d. stereopsis

18. The clinical term for farsightedness is _____.
    a. emmetropia      b. hyperopia
    c. myopia          d. hypertropia
19. Removal of the innermost small bone in the middle ear is called _____.
    a. stapedectomy    b. adenoidectomy
    c. mastoidectomy   d. incudectomy
20. The procedure commonly referred to as a corneal grafting might appear on an operative record as _____.
    a. basal iridectomy    b. peripheral iridotomy
    c. keratoplasty        d. keratoconus

# Part Four  Supplementary Readings

**Astigmatism** is an irregularity in the curve of the cornea or lens that distorts light entering the eye and blurs vision.

**Cataracts** are opacities that form on the lens and impair vision. These opacities are commonly produced by protein that builds up over time until vision is lost. The most common form of cataract is age related. The usual treatment is removal of the clouded lens by phacoemulsification (fragmenting the lens with ultrasound or a laser probe). An artificial intraocular lens (IOL) is then implanted to compensate for the missing lens.

**Enucleation** is removal of the eyeball from the orbit and is performed to treat cancer of the eye when the tumor is large and fills most of the structure, and **evisceration** is removal of the contents of the eye while leaving the sclera and cornea, which is performed when the blind eye is painful or unsightly. The eye muscles are left intact, and a prosthesis is fitted over the shell.

**Glaucoma** is increased intraocular pressure due to the inability of aqueous humor to drain away from the eye. It can result in damage to the retina and optic nerve. Glaucoma is diagnosed by means of tonometry. And it is usually treated with drugs (miotics) to reduce pressure in the eye and occasionally is treated with laser therapy.

## Chapter 15  Special Senses: The Eye and The Ear

**LASIK** is a method of correcting myopia by using an eximer laser to remove corneal tissue. The top layer of the cornea is lifted and then a laser is used to sculpt the cornea, which is referred to as the refractive ablation. Once it is complete, the corneal flap is repositioned.

**Ménière disease** is a disorder that affects the inner ear. It seems to involve the production and circulation of the fluid that fills the inner ear, but the cause is unknown. The symptoms are vertigo (dizziness), hearing loss, pronounced tinnitus (ringing in the ears), and feeling of pressure in the ear. The course of the disease is uneven, and symptoms may become less severe with time. Ménière disease is treated with drugs to control nausea and dizziness, such as those used to treat motion sickness. In severe cases, the inner ear or part of the eighth cranial nerve may be destroyed surgically.

**Mydriatic drugs** cause the pupil to dilate, such as epinephrine, atropine, and cocaine. **Miotic drugs** cause the pupil to constrict, such as morphine, pilocarpine and physostigmine. Both types of drugs are used to examine the eyes and to treat certain diseases.

**Slit lamp biomicroscope** is an instrument that permits examination of anterior ocular structure under magnification. Devices attached to a slit lamp expand the scope of the examination. For example, a tonometer measure intraocular pressure and a gonioscope visualizes the anterior chamber angle.

**Strabismus**, also called heterotropia or tropia, is a condition in which one eye is misaligned with the other and the eyes do not focus simultaneously when viewing an object. This misalignment may be in any direction—inward (esotropia), outward (exotropia), up, down, or any combination of these. Strabismus commonly causes a loss of stereopsis (binocular perception of depth or three-dimensional space).

## Part Five  Review Sheet

Here is a collection of the word parts you have learned in this chapter. Write the meaning of each word part without referring to your previous work.

## Combining Forms

| Combining Form | Meaning | Combining Form | Meaning |
|---|---|---|---|
| acous/o | | lacrim/o | |
| audi/o | | myring/o | |
| aur/o, auricul/o | | ocul/o | |
| blephar/o | | ophthalm/o | |
| chori/o | | opt/o, optic/o | |
| choroid/o | | ossicul/o | |
| cochle/o | | ot/o | |
| conjunctiv/o | | palpebr/o | |
| core/o | | phak/o, phac/o | |
| corne/o | | pupill/o | |
| cycl/o | | retin/o | |
| dacry/o | | salping/o | |
| dacryocyst/o | | scler/o | |
| hyal/o | | staped/o | |
| ir/o | | tympan/o | |
| iri/o | | ure/o | |
| kerat/o | | vestibul/o | |
| labyrinth/o | | vitre/o | |

## Suffixes

| Suffix | Meaning | Suffix | Meaning |
|---|---|---|---|
| -acusia, -acusis | | -otia | |
| -opia, -opsia | | -tropia | |

## Prefixes

| Prefix | Meaning | Prefix | Meaning |
|---|---|---|---|
| dextro- | | sinistro- | |

# Appendix 1  Glossary

| English Term | Phonetic Symbol | Chinese Term | Chapter |
|---|---|---|---|
| **A** | | | |
| abdominocentesis | /ˌæbdɒmɪnəʊˌsenˈtiːsɪs/ | 腹腔穿刺术 | Ch. 4, 6 |
| abdominoscopy | /ˌæbˌdɒmɪˈnɒskəpɪ/ | 腹腔镜检查 | Ch. 2, 4 |
| abductor | /æbˈdʌktə/ | 外展肌 | Ch. 3 |
| abnormal | /æbˈnɔːml/ | 反常的 | Ch. 3 |
| acetabulectomy | /æsɪtæbjʊˈlektəmɪ/ | 髋臼切除术 | Ch. 13 |
| acetabuloplasty | /æsɪtæbjʊləʊˈplæstɪ/ | 髋臼成形术 | Ch. 13 |
| achondroplasia | /eɪˌkɒndrəʊˈpleɪzɪə/ | 软骨发育不全 | Ch. 13 |
| achromia | /əˈkrəʊmɪə/ | 色素缺乏症 | Ch. 4 |
| achromotrichia | /əˌkrəʊməˈtrɪkɪə/ | 毛发退色 | Ch. 14 |
| acousimeter | /əkuːˈzɪmiːtə/ | 测听计 | Ch. 15 |
| acoustic | /əˈkuːstɪk/ | 听觉的 | Ch. 15 |
| acrocyanosis | /ækrəʊˌsaɪəˈnəʊsɪs/ | 手足发绀 | Ch. 10, 14 |
| acrodynia | /ˌækrəˈdɪnɪə/ | 肢端痛 | Ch. 4 |
| acromegaly | /ˌækrəʊˈmegəlɪ/ | 肢端肥大症 | Ch. 4, 10 |
| acromial | /ˈækrəmɪəl/ | 肩峰的 | Ch. 13 |
| acromiothoracic | /ækrəmɪəʊθɔːˈræsɪk/ | 肩峰胸廓的 | Ch. 13 |
| adductor | /əˈdʌktə/ | 内收肌 | Ch. 3 |
| adenoidectomy | /ˌædɪnɔɪˈdektəmɪ/ | 腺样体切除术 | Ch. 8 |
| adenoiditis | /ædɪnɔɪˈdaɪtɪs/ | 腺样体炎 | Ch. 8 |
| adenopathy | /ædɪˈnɒpəθɪ/ | 腺病 | Ch. 2 |
| adiaphoresis | /ˌeɪdaɪəfəˈriːsɪs/ | 无汗 | Ch. 14 |
| adipocyte | /ˈædɪpəʊsaɪt/ | 脂肪细胞 | Ch. 4, 14 |
| adipogenesis | /ˌædɪpəʊˈdʒenɪsɪs/ | 脂肪生成 | Ch. 4 |
| adipose | /ˈædɪpəʊs/ | 脂肪的 | Ch. 14 |

| | | | |
|---|---|---|---|
| adneural | /ˈædnjurəl/ | 近神经的 | Ch. 3 |
| adrenal | /əˈdriːnl/ | 肾上腺的 | Ch. 11 |
| adrenalectomy | /ˌædrɪnəˈlektəmɪ/ | 肾上腺切除术 | Ch. 10 |
| adrenalin | /əˈdreɪnəlɪn/ | 肾上腺素 | Ch. 10 |
| adrenosclerosis | /ˌædrɪnəskləˈrəʊsɪs/ | 肾上腺硬化 | Ch. 10 |
| agranulocytic | /əˌgrænjʊləˈsaɪtɪk/ | 无粒(白)细胞的 | Ch. 7 |
| albinism | /ˈælbɪnɪzəm/ | 白化病 | Ch. 14 |
| albuminuria | /ˌælbjʊmɪnˈjuːrɪə/ | 蛋白尿 | Ch. 11 |
| alexia | /əˈleksɪə/ | 失读症 | Ch. 9 |
| alveolitis | /ˌælvɪəˈlaɪtɪs/ | 牙槽炎 | Ch. 6 |
| alveolotomy | /ˌælvɪəˈlətəʊmɪ/ | 牙槽切开术 | Ch. 6 |
| amblyacusis | /ˌæmblɪəˈkjuːsɪs/ | 弱听 | Ch. 15 |
| amblyopia | /ˌæmblɪˈəʊpɪə/ | 弱视 | Ch. 15 |
| ambulatory | /ˈæmbjʊlətərɪ/ | 可走动的 | Ch. 9 |
| ameboid | /əmˈbɔɪd/ | 阿米巴样的 | Ch. 2 |
| amniocentesis | /ˌæmnɪəʊsenˈtiːsɪs/ | 羊膜穿刺术 | Ch. 12 |
| amniorrhexia | /ˌæmnɪəˈreksɪə/ | 羊膜破裂 | Ch. 12 |
| amphiarthrosis | /ˌæmfɪɑːˈrəʊsɪs/ | 微动关节 | Ch. 13 |
| amphibian | /æmˈfɪbɪən/ | 两栖类的 | Ch. 13 |
| amphicentric | /ˌæmfɪˈsentrɪk/ | 起止同源的 | Ch. 13 |
| amylase | /ˈæmɪleɪz/ | 淀粉酶 | Ch. 6 |
| amylogenesis | /ˌæmɪləʊˈdʒenəsɪs/ | 淀粉形成 | Ch. 6 |
| amyloid | /ˈæmɪlɔɪd/ | 淀粉样的 | Ch. 6 |
| anabolism | /əˈnæbəlɪzəm/ | 合成代谢 | Ch. 3 |
| anatomy | /əˈnætəmɪ/ | 解剖学 | Ch. 3 |
| androgen | /ˈændrədʒən/ | 雄性激素 | Ch. 10, 12 |
| andromorphous | /ˌændrəˈmɔːfəs/ | (女子)男性形态的 | Ch. 10, 12 |
| anemia | /əˈniːmɪə/ | 贫血 | Ch. 7 |
| anesthesia | /ˌænesˈθiːzɪə/ | 麻醉 | Ch. 9 |
| angiectasis | /ˌændʒɪˈektəsɪs/ | 血管扩张 | Ch. 5 |
| angiogram | /ˈændʒɪəgræm/ | 血管造影片 | Ch. 2 |
| angiography | /ˌændʒɪˈɒgrəfɪ/ | 血管造影术 | Ch. 2, 7 |
| angioid | /ˈændʒɪɒɪd/ | 血管样的 | Ch. 2 |

## Appendix 1  Glossary

| | | | |
|---|---|---|---|
| angioplasty | /ˈændʒɪəʊˌplæstɪ/ | 血管成形术 | Ch. 2, 7 |
| angiorrhexis | /ˌændʒɪəʊˈreksɪs/ | 血管破裂 | Ch. 8 |
| anhidrosis | /ˌænhaɪˈdrəʊsɪs/ | 无汗 | Ch. 14 |
| anisocoria | /ˌænaɪsəʊˈkɔːrɪə/ | 瞳孔不等的 | Ch. 15 |
| anisocytosis | /ˌænaɪsəʊsaɪˈtəʊsɪs/ | 红血球不均 | Ch. 15 |
| ankylodactyly | /ˌæŋkɪləˈdæktɪlɪ/ | 并指/趾 | Ch. 13 |
| ankylosis | /ˌæŋkɪˈləʊsɪs/ | 关节强直 | Ch. 13 |
| anorchism | /æˈnɔːrkɪzəm/ | 无睾 | Ch. 12 |
| anorexia | /ˌænəˈreksɪə/ | 厌食症 | Ch. 6 |
| anosmia | /æˈnɒsmɪə/ | 嗅觉缺失 | Ch. 5 |
| anoxia | /æˈnɒksɪə/ | 缺氧症 | Ch. 3 |
| antacid | /æntˈæsɪd/ | 解酸的;解酸剂 | Ch. 3 |
| anteflexion | /ˌæntəˈflekʃn/ | 前屈 | Ch. 3 |
| antenatal | /ˌæntəˈneɪtl/ | 出生前的 | Ch. 3 |
| antepartum | /ˌæntəˈpɑːtəm/ | 分娩前的 | Ch. 12 |
| anteprandial | /ˌæntəˈprændɪəl/ | 餐前的 | Ch. 6 |
| anterior | /ænˈtɪərɪə/ | 前面的 | Ch. 4 |
| anterograde | /ˈæntərəʊˌgreɪd/ | 顺行的;前进的 | Ch. 4 |
| anticoagulant | /ˌæntɪkəʊˈægjʊlənt/ | 抗凝的;抗凝血剂 | Ch. 3 |
| antifungal | /ˌæntɪˈfʌŋgəl/ | 抗真菌的 | Ch. 8 |
| antigen | /ˈæntɪdʒən/ | 抗原 | Ch. 8 |
| antinarcotic | /ˌæntɪnɑːˈkɒtɪk/ | 抗麻醉的 | Ch. 9 |
| antiseptic | /ˌæntɪˈseptɪk/ | 杀菌的;杀菌剂 | Ch. 3 |
| antitoxin | /ˌæntɪˈtɒksɪn/ | 抗毒素 | Ch. 10 |
| antiviral | /ˌæntɪˈvaɪrəl/ | 抗病毒的 | Ch. 8 |
| anuria | /ənˈjuːrɪə/ | 无尿 | Ch. 11 |
| aortoplasty | /eɪˈɔːtəʊˌplæstɪ/ | 主动脉修复术 | Ch. 7 |
| aortostenosis | /eɪˌɔːtəʊstɪˈnəʊsɪs/ | 主动脉狭窄 | Ch. 7 |
| apareunia | /ˌeɪpərəˈjuːnɪə/ | 性交不能症 | Ch. 12 |
| apepsia | /eɪˈpepsɪə/ | 消化不良 | Ch. 6 |
| aphakia | /əˈfeɪkjə/ | 无晶状体 | Ch. 15 |
| aphasia | /əˈfeɪzɪə/ | 失语症 | Ch. 9 |
| apnea | /ˈæpnɪə/ | 呼吸暂停 | Ch. 5 |

| | | | |
|---|---|---|---|
| appendectomy | /ˌæpenˈdektəmɪ/ | 阑尾切除术 | Ch. 6 |
| appendicitis | /əˌpendəˈsaɪtɪs/ | 阑尾炎 | Ch. 6 |
| appendicocele | /əˈpendɪkəʊˌsiːl/ | 阑尾疝 | Ch. 6 |
| apraxia | /eɪˈpræksɪə/ | 失用症 | Ch. 9 |
| arteriolar | /ɑːˌtɪərɪˈəʊlə/ | 小动脉的 | Ch. 7 |
| arteriole | /ɑːˈtɪərɪəʊl/ | 小动脉 | Ch. 11 |
| arteriolosclerosis | /ɑːˌtɪərɪəʊləskləˈrəʊsɪs/ | 小动脉硬化症 | Ch. 7 |
| arteriorrhaphy | /ˌɑːtɪərɪˈɒrəfɪ/ | 动脉缝合术 | Ch. 7 |
| arteriosclerosis | /ɑːˌtɪərɪəʊskləˈrəʊsɪs/ | 动脉硬化症 | Ch. 7 |
| arteriotomy | /ˌɑːtɪərɪˈɒtəmɪ/ | 动脉切开术 | Ch. 7 |
| arthralgia | /ɑːˈθrældʒɪə/ | 关节痛 | Ch. 13 |
| arthritis | /ɑːˈθraɪtɪs/ | 关节炎 | Ch. 2 |
| arthrocentesis | /ˌɑːθrəʊsenˈtiːsɪs/ | 关节穿刺术 | Ch. 2, 13 |
| arthroclasis | /ɑːˈθrɒkləsɪs/ | 关节破坏 | Ch. 13 |
| arthrography | /ɑːˈθrɒgrəfɪ/ | 关节造影术 | Ch. 2 |
| arthrolysis | /ɑːˈθrɒlɪsɪs/ | 关节松解术 | Ch. 2 |
| arthroscopy | /ɑːˈθrɒskəpɪ/ | 关节内镜检查 | Ch. 2 |
| arthrotome | /ˈɑːθrətəʊm/ | 关节刀 | Ch. 2, 13 |
| aseptic | /eɪˈseptɪk/ | 无菌的 | Ch. 3 |
| astrocyte | /ˈæstrəsaɪt/ | 星形细胞 | Ch. 9 |
| astrocytoma | /ˌæstrəʊsaɪˈtəʊmə/ | 星形细胞瘤 | Ch. 9 |
| ataxia | /əˈtæksɪə/ | 共济失调 | Ch. 9 |
| atelectasis | /ˌætəˈlektəsɪs/ | 肺不张 | Ch. 5 |
| atelocardia | /ˌætɪləʊˈkɑːdɪə/ | 心脏发育不全 | Ch. 5 |
| atherectomy | /ˌæθəˈrektəmɪ/ | 粥样硬化斑切除术 | Ch. 7 |
| atheroma | /ˌæθəˈrəʊmə/ | 动脉粥样化 | Ch. 7 |
| atherosclerosis | /ˌæθərəʊsklɪˈrəʊsɪs/ | 动脉粥样硬化 | Ch. 7 |
| atriomegaly | /ˌeɪtrɪəˈmegəlɪ/ | 心房肥大 | Ch. 7 |
| atrioseptoplasty | /ˌeɪtrɪəˌseptəʊˈplæstɪ/ | 房间隔成形术 | Ch. 7 |
| audiogram | /ˈɔːdɪəʊgræm/ | 听力（阈值）图 | Ch. 15 |
| audiometry | /ˌɔːdɪˈɒmətrɪ/ | 测听术 | Ch. 15 |
| autocrine | /ˈɔːtəʊkren/ | 自分泌的 | Ch. 3 |
| autogenesis | /ˌɔːtəʊˈdʒenəsɪs/ | 自然发生 | Ch. 3 |

## Appendix 1  Glossary

| | | | |
|---|---|---|---|
| autoimmunity | /ɔːtəʊɪˈmjuːnɪtɪ/ | 自身免疫 | Ch. 8 |
| azoospermia | /eɪzəʊəˈspəmɪə/ | 无精子症 | Ch. 12 |

**B**

| | | | |
|---|---|---|---|
| bacillary | /bəˈsɪləri/ | 杆菌的 | Ch. 8 |
| bacilliform | /bəˈsɪlɪfɔːm/ | 杆状的 | Ch. 8 |
| bactericide | /bækˈtɪərɪsaɪd/ | 杀细菌剂 | Ch. 8 |
| bacteriemia | /bæktəˈrɪəmɪə/ | 菌血症 | Ch. 8 |
| bacteriology | /bækˌtɪərɪˈɒlədʒɪ/ | 细菌学 | Ch. 8 |
| bacteriostatic | /bækˌtɪrɪəˈstætɪk/ | 抑菌的 | Ch. 8 |
| balanitis | /bæləˈnaɪtɪs/ | 龟头炎 | Ch. 12 |
| balanorrhea | /bælənəʊˈriːə/ | 龟头脓溢 | Ch. 12 |
| basophil | /ˈbeɪsəʊfɪl/ | 嗜碱性白细胞 | Ch. 7 |
| basophilous | /beɪsəʊˈfɪləs/ | 嗜碱性的 | Ch. 7 |
| beneceptor | /benɪˈseptə/ | 良性感受器 | Ch. 3 |
| benign | /bɪˈnaɪn/ | 良性的 | Ch. 3 |
| biaural | /ˌbaɪˈɔːrəl/ | 双耳的 | Ch. 15 |
| bicuspid | /ˌbaɪˈkʌspɪd/ | 双尖的 | Ch. 3 |
| bilateral | /ˌbaɪˈlætərəl/ | 双侧的 | Ch. 3 |
| biliary | /ˈbɪlɪərɪ/ | 胆的;胆汁的 | Ch. 6 |
| biligenesis | /ˌbɪlɪˈdʒenəsɪs/ | 胆汁生成 | Ch. 6 |
| binocular | /bɪˈnɒkjʊlə/ | 双眼的 | Ch. 15 |
| biology | /baɪˈɒlədʒɪ/ | 生物学 | Ch. 2 |
| biopsy | /ˈbaɪɒpsɪ/ | 活检 | Ch. 2 |
| blennorrhea | /blenəʊˈriːə/ | 黏液溢出 | Ch. 12 |
| blennurethria | /blenjʊˈreθrɪə/ | 淋病 | Ch. 12 |
| blepharoplegia | /blefərəʊˈpliːdʒɪə/ | 睑麻痹 | Ch. 15 |
| blepharoptosis | /blefərəʊˈptəʊsɪs/ | 睑下垂 | Ch. 15 |
| brachiocephalic | /breɪkɪəʊseˈfælɪk/ | 头臂的 | Ch. 13 |
| brachiodynia | /breɪkɪəʊˈdɪnɪə/ | 臂疼 | Ch. 13 |
| bradyacusia | /breɪdɪəˈkjuːzɪə/ | 听力迟钝 | Ch. 15 |
| bradycardia | /breɪdɪˈkɑːdɪə/ | 心搏过缓 | Ch. 7 |
| bradysphygmia | /breɪdɪˈsfɪɡmɪə/ | 脉搏过缓 | Ch. 7 |
| bronchiectasis | /brɒŋkɪˈektəsɪs/ | 支气管扩张 | Ch. 5 |

| | | | |
|---|---|---|---|
| bronchiolar | /ˌbrɒŋkɪˈəʊlə/ | 细支气管 | Ch. 5 |
| bronchiolectasis | /ˌbrɒŋkɪəʊˈlektəsɪs/ | 细支气管扩张 | Ch. 5 |
| bronchiolitis | /ˌbrɒŋkɪəʊˈlaɪtɪs/ | 细支气管炎 | Ch. 5 |
| bronchoalveolitis | /ˌbrɒŋkəʊˌælvɪəˈlaɪtɪs/ | 支气管肺炎 | Ch. 5 |
| bronchogenic | /ˌbrɒŋkəˈdʒenɪk/ | 支气管源的 | Ch. 5 |
| bronchoscopy | /ˌbrɒŋˈkɒskəpɪ/ | 支气管镜检查 | Ch. 5 |
| bronchospasm | /ˈbrɒŋkəˌspæzəm/ | 支气管痉挛 | Ch. 5 |
| bursitis | /ˌbɜːˈsaɪtɪs/ | 黏液囊炎 | Ch. 13 |
| bursotomy | /bɜːˈsɒtəmɪ/ | 黏液囊切开术 | Ch. 13 |

## C

| | | | |
|---|---|---|---|
| calcaneitis | /kælkənɪˈaɪtɪz/ | 跟骨炎 | Ch. 13 |
| calcaneodynia | /ˌkælkæniːəʊˈdɪnɪə/ | 跟痛症 | Ch. 13 |
| calcipenia | /kælsɪˈpiːnɪə/ | 钙质减少 | Ch. 10 |
| calcipexy | /kælsɪˈpeksɪ/ | 钙固定 | Ch. 10 |
| caliceal | /kælɪˈsiːl/ | (肾)盏的 | Ch. 11 |
| calicectomy | /ˌkælɪˈsektəmɪ/ | 肾盏切除术 | Ch. 11 |
| carbocyclic | /ˌkɑːbəʊˈsaɪklɪk/ | 碳环形的 | Ch. 10 |
| carbonic | /kɑːˈbɒnɪk/ | 碳的 | Ch. 10 |
| carcinogen | /kɑːˈsɪnədʒən/ | 致癌物 | Ch. 8 |
| carcinogenesis | /kɑːsɪnəˈdʒenɪsɪs/ | 致癌作用 | Ch. 2 |
| carcinogenic | /kɑːsɪnəˈdʒenɪk/ | 致癌的 | Ch. 2 |
| carcinoma | /ˌkɑːsɪˈnəʊmə/ | 癌 | Ch. 8 |
| cardiomegaly | /ˌkɑːdɪəʊˈmegəlɪ/ | 心脏肥大 | Ch. 2 |
| cardioplegia | /ˌkɑːdɪəʊˈpliːdʒɪə/ | 心麻痹 | Ch. 2 |
| cardium | /ˈkɑːdɪəm/ | 心脏 | Ch. 2 |
| carpectomy | /kɑːˈpektəmɪ/ | 腕骨切除术 | Ch. 13 |
| carpokyphosis | /ˌkɑːpəʊkaɪˈfəʊsɪs/ | 腕后弯 | Ch. 13 |
| carpoptosis | /ˌkɑːpəʊˌptəʊsɪs/ | 腕下垂 | Ch. 13 |
| catabolism | /kəˈtæbəlɪzəm/ | 分解代谢 | Ch. 3 |
| catalyst | /ˈkætəlɪst/ | 催化剂 | Ch. 3 |
| caudad | /ˈkɔːdæd/ | 尾的;向尾侧的 | Ch. 2 |
| caudal | /ˈkɔːdl/ | 近尾部的 | Ch. 4 |
| cecocolostomy | /ˌsɪkəkəˈlɒstəmɪ/ | 结肠盲肠吻合术 | Ch. 6 |

| | | | |
|---|---|---|---|
| cecoptosis | /ˌsɪkɒˈptəʊsɪs/ | 盲肠下垂 | Ch. 6 |
| celiac | /ˈsiːlɪˌæk/ | 腹腔的 | Ch. 6 |
| celiotomy | /ˌsiːlɪˈɒtəmɪ/ | 剖腹手术 | Ch. 6 |
| centesis | /senˈtiːsɪs/ | 穿刺术 | Ch. 2 |
| centimeter | /ˈsentɪˌmiːtə/ | 厘米 | Ch. 3 |
| centrifugal | /ˌsentrɪˈfjuːgl/ | 离心的 | Ch. 10 |
| centriole | /ˈsentrɪəʊl/ | （细胞）中心粒 | Ch. 11 |
| centripetal | /senˈtrɪpɪtl/ | 向心的 | Ch. 10 |
| cephalad | /ˈsefəˌlæd/ | 头的；头侧的 | Ch. 2 |
| cephalalgia | /ˌsefəˈlældʒɪə/ | 头痛 | Ch. 4 |
| cephalic | /sɪˈfælɪk/ | 头部的 | Ch. 4 |
| cerebellopontine | /ˌserɪbeləˈpɒntaɪn/ | 小脑脑桥的 | Ch. 9 |
| cerebrospinal | /ˌserɪbrəʊˈspaɪnəl/ | 脑脊髓的 | Ch. 9 |
| cerebrotomy | /ˌserɪˈbrɒtəmɪ/ | 脑切开术 | Ch. 9 |
| cerebrovascular | /ˌserɪbrəʊˈvæskjələ/ | 脑血管的 | Ch. 9 |
| cervical | /ˈsɜːvɪkl/ | 颈的；宫颈的 | Ch. 4 |
| cervicectomy | /ˌsɜːvɪˈsektəmɪ/ | 宫颈切除术 | Ch. 12 |
| cervicitis | /ˌsɜːvɪˈsaɪtɪs/ | 宫颈炎 | Ch. 12 |
| cervicodorsal | /ˌsɜːvɪkəʊˈdɔːsl/ | 颈背的 | Ch. 13 |
| cervicodynia | /ˌsɜːvɪˈkəʊdɪnɪə/ | 颈痛 | Ch. 4 |
| cervicofacial | /ˌsɜːvɪkəʊˈfeɪʃl/ | 颈颜面的 | Ch. 13 |
| cheiloplasty | /ˌkaɪləˈplæstɪ/ | 唇成形术 | Ch. 6 |
| cheilosis | /kaɪˈləʊsɪs/ | 唇干裂 | Ch. 6 |
| chemolysis | /kɪˈmɒləsɪs/ | 化学溶蚀 | Ch. 8 |
| chemotherapy | /ˌkiːməʊˈθerəpɪ/ | 化学疗法 | Ch. 8 |
| chiroplasty | /ˌkaɪrəʊˈplæstɪ/ | 手成形术 | Ch. 13 |
| chiropodist | /kaɪrəˈpəʊdɪst/ | 手足病医生 | Ch. 13 |
| chirospasm | /ˌkaɪrəʊˈspæzəm/ | 手痉挛 | Ch. 13 |
| chloroma | /klɔːˈrəʊmə/ | 绿色瘤 | Ch. 14 |
| chlorophyll | /ˈklɒrəfɪl/ | 叶绿素 | Ch. 14 |
| cholangiocarcinoma | /kəʊlændʒɪəˌkɑːsɪˈnəʊmə/ | 胆管癌 | Ch. 6 |
| cholangiography | /kəʊˌlændʒɪˈɒgrəfɪ/ | 胆管造影术 | Ch. 6 |
| cholecystitis | /ˌkəʊləsɪsˈtaɪtɪs/ | 胆囊炎 | Ch. 6 |

| | | | |
|---|---|---|---|
| choledocholithiasis | /ˌkəʊlədɒkəʊlɪˈθaɪəsɪs/ | 胆总管结石 | Ch. 6 |
| choledochotomy | /ˌkəʊlədɒˈkɒtəmɪ/ | 总胆管切除术 | Ch. 6 |
| cholelith | /ˈkɒləlɪθ/ | 胆石 | Ch. 6 |
| cholemesis | /kəˈleməsɪs/ | 呕胆 | Ch. 6 |
| choleperitonitis | /ˌkəʊləˌpærɪtəʊˈnaɪtɪs/ | 胆汁性腹膜炎 | Ch. 6 |
| cholestasis | /ˌkəʊləˈsteɪsɪs/ | 胆汁阻塞 | Ch. 7 |
| chondroclast | /ˈkɒndrəʊklæst/ | 破软骨细胞 | Ch. 13 |
| chondrosarcoma | /ˌkɒndrəʊsɑːˈkəʊmə/ | 软骨肉瘤 | Ch. 13 |
| chorioretinal | /ˌkɒrɪəˈrætɪnəl/ | 脉络膜视网膜的 | Ch. 15 |
| choroidopathy | /ˌkɒrɔɪˈdɔːpəθɪ/ | 脉络膜病 | Ch. 15 |
| chromophil | /ˈkrəʊməfɪl/ | 易染色的, 嗜色的 | Ch. 7 |
| chromosome | /ˈkrəʊməsəʊm/ | 染色体 | Ch. 2, 4 |
| circumcorneal | /ˌsɜːkəmˈkɔːnɪəl/ | 角膜周(围)的 | Ch. 15 |
| circumflex | /ˈsɜːkəmfleks/ | 旋绕的 | Ch. 3 |
| circumoral | /ˌsɜːkəmˈɔːrəl/ | 口周的 | Ch. 3 |
| cirrhosis | /səˈrəʊsɪs/ | 肝硬化 | Ch. 14 |
| clitorectomy | /ˌklɪtəˈrektəmɪ/ | 阴蒂切除术 | Ch. 12 |
| clitoriditis | /ˌklɪtərɪˈdɪtɪs/ | 阴蒂炎 | Ch. 12 |
| coccygalgia | /ˌkɒksɪˈgældʒɪə/ | 尾骨痛 | Ch. 13 |
| coccygectomy | /ˌkɒksɪˈdʒektəmɪ/ | 尾骨切除术 | Ch. 13 |
| cochleitis | /ˌkɒklɪˈaɪtɪs/ | 耳蜗炎 | Ch. 15 |
| coitophobia | /ˌkɔɪtəˈfəʊbɪə/ | 性交恐怖 | Ch. 12 |
| colectomy | /kəˈlektəmɪ/ | 结肠切除术 | Ch. 6 |
| colitis | /kəˈlaɪtɪs/ | 结肠炎 | Ch. 6 |
| collagen | /ˈkɒlədʒən/ | 胶原 | Ch. 14 |
| colloid | /ˈkɒlɔɪd/ | 胶体 | Ch. 14 |
| colonalgia | /ˌkɒləʊˈnældʒə/ | 结肠痛 | Ch. 6 |
| colonic | /kəˈlɒnɪk/ | 结肠的 | Ch. 6 |
| colorectum | /ˌkɒləˈrektəm/ | 结肠直肠 | Ch. 6 |
| colpoplasty | /ˈkɒlpəʊplæstaɪ/ | 阴道成形术 | Ch. 12 |
| colposcope | /ˈkɒlpəskəʊp/ | 阴道镜 | Ch. 12 |
| commissure | /ˈkɒmɪsjʊə/ | 接合 | Ch. 3 |
| coniometer | /ˌkəʊnɪˈɒmɪtə/ | 计尘器 | Ch. 5 |

# Appendix 1  Glossary

| | | | |
|---|---|---|---|
| conjunctivoplasty | /kəndʒʌŋktɪvəˈplæstɪ/ | 结膜成形术 | Ch. 15 |
| contraception | /ˌkɒntrəˈsepʃən/ | 避孕 | Ch. 3 |
| contraction | /kənˈtrækʃən/ | 收缩 | Ch. 3 |
| contralateral | /ˌkɒntrəˈlætərəl/ | 对侧的 | Ch. 3 |
| coprolith | /ˈkɒprəlɪθ/ | 粪石 | Ch. 6 |
| coprophagia | /ˌkɒprəˈfeɪdʒɪə/ | 食粪癖 | Ch. 6 |
| corectasis | /kəˈrektəsɪs/ | 瞳孔扩大 | Ch. 15 |
| coreometer | /kɔːrɪˈɒmɪtə/ | 瞳孔计 | Ch. 15 |
| corneosclera | /kɔːnɪəʊskˈlerə/ | 角巩膜 | Ch. 15 |
| corticectomy | /kɔːtɪˈsektəmɪ/ | 皮质切除术 | Ch. 10 |
| corticofugal | /ˈkɔːtɪkəʊfjuːgl/ | 离皮质的 | Ch. 10 |
| corticopetal | /ˈkɔːtɪkəʊpetl/ | 向皮质的 | Ch. 10 |
| corticorenal | /ˌkɔːtɪkəˈriːnl/ | 肾脏皮质的 | Ch. 10 |
| corticospinal | /ˌkɔːtɪkəʊˈspaɪnl/ | 皮质脊髓的 | Ch. 9 |
| costochondral | /ˌkɒstəʊˈkɒndrəl/ | 肋骨软骨的 | Ch. 13 |
| counteract | /ˌkaʊntəˈækt/ | 抵制,抵抗 | Ch. 3 |
| counterclockwise | /ˌkaʊntəˈklɒkwaɪz/ | 反时针方向的 | Ch. 3 |
| counterextension | /ˌkaʊntəˌɪksˈtenʃn/ | 对抗牵伸术 | Ch. 3 |
| counterirritant | /ˌkaʊntəˈɪrɪtənt/ | 抗刺激剂 | Ch. 3 |
| craniodidymus | /ˌkreɪnɪəˈdɪdɪməs/ | 双头畸胎 | Ch. 12 |
| craniomalacia | /ˌkreɪnɪɒməˈleɪʃɪə/ | 颅骨软化 | Ch. 13 |
| craniometry | /ˌkreɪnɪˈɒmɪtrɪ/ | 颅骨测量 | Ch. 2 |
| cranioschisis | /ˌkreɪnɪəʊˈskɪːsɪs/ | 颅裂(畸形) | Ch. 13 |
| craniosclerosis | /ˌkreɪnɪəʊskləˈrəʊsɪs/ | 颅骨硬化 | Ch. 13 |
| craniotomy | /ˌkreɪnɪˈɒtəmɪ/ | 颅骨切开术 | Ch. 4 |
| cryosurgery | /ˌkraɪəʊˈsɜːdʒərɪ/ | 冷冻手术 | Ch. 14 |
| cryotherapy | /ˌkraɪəʊˈθerəpɪ/ | 冷冻疗法 | Ch. 14 |
| cryptomnesia | /ˌkrɪptɒmˈniːzɪə/ | 潜在记忆 | Ch. 12 |
| cryptorchism | /krɪpˈtɔːkɪzəm/ | 隐睾病 | Ch. 12 |
| cupremia | /kjʊˈpriːmɪə/ | 铜血 | Ch. 10 |
| cupriuria | /ˌkjʊprɪˈjuːrɪə/ | 铜尿 | Ch. 10 |
| cyanopathy | /saɪəˈnɒpəθɪ/ | 绀病 | Ch. 5 |
| cyanosis | /ˌsaɪəˈnəʊsɪs/ | 发绀 | Ch. 5, 14 |

| | | | |
|---|---|---|---|
| cycloplegia | /ˌsaɪkləˈpliːdʒɪə/ | 睫状肌 | Ch. 15 |
| cyclospasm | /ˈsaɪkləsˌpæzəm/ | 睫状体痉挛 | Ch. 15 |
| cystography | /sɪsˈtɒgrəfɪ/ | 膀胱造影术 | Ch. 11 |
| cystorrhexia | /sɪstəʊˈreksɪə/ | 膀胱破裂 | Ch. 11 |
| cystostomy | /sɪsˈtɒstəmɪ/ | 膀胱造口术 | Ch. 11 |
| cytoclasis | /saɪˈtɒkləsɪs/ | 细胞破裂 | Ch. 13 |
| cytokalipenia | /saɪtʊkælɪˈpiːnɪə/ | (血)细胞钾缺乏 | Ch. 10 |
| cytology | /saɪˈtɒlədʒɪ/ | 细胞学 | Ch. 4 |
| cytometer | /saɪˈtɒmɪtə/ | 细胞计数器 | Ch. 2 |
| cytoplasm | /ˈsaɪtəʊplæzəm/ | 细胞质 | Ch. 8 |
| cytosome | /ˈsaɪtəsəʊm/ | 胞质体 | Ch. 2 |

## D

| | | | |
|---|---|---|---|
| dacryocystitis | /ˌdækrɪəˈsɪstaɪtɪs/ | 泪囊炎 | Ch. 15 |
| dacryocystorhinostomy | /ˈdækrɪəʊsɪstəʊraɪˈnɒstəmɪ/ | 泪囊鼻腔造瘘术 | Ch. 15 |
| dacryolith | /ˈdeɪkriːəlɪθ/ | 泪石 | Ch. 15 |
| dacryorrhea | /ˌdeɪkriːəˈrɪə/ | 溢泪 | Ch. 15 |
| dactylogram | /dækˈtɪləgræm/ | 指纹 | Ch. 13 |
| decade | /ˈdekeɪd/ | 十年 | Ch. 3 |
| decapoda | /dəˈkæpədə/ | 十足目 | Ch. 3 |
| decerebellation | /dɪserɪbəˈleɪʃn/ | 小脑切除术 | Ch. 9 |
| deciliter | /ˈdesɪˌliːtə/ | 1/10升(分升) | Ch. 3 |
| decimeter | /ˈdesɪˌmiːtə/ | 1/10米(分米) | Ch. 3 |
| decompose | /ˌdiːkəmˈpəʊz/ | 分解 | Ch. 3 |
| defecation | /ˌdefəˈkeɪʃn/ | 排便 | Ch. 6 |
| dehydration | /ˌdiːhaɪˈdreɪʃn/ | 脱水 | Ch. 3 |
| denticle | /ˈdentɪkl/ | 小齿 | Ch. 11 |
| dentist | /ˈdentɪst/ | 口腔医生 | Ch. 2 |
| dentistry | /ˈdentɪstrɪ/ | 口腔科 | Ch. 6 |
| dermatology | /ˌdɜːməˈtɒlədʒi/ | 皮肤(病)学 | Ch. 14 |
| dermatomycosis | /dɜːmətəʊmaɪˈkəʊsɪs/ | 皮真菌病 | Ch. 14 |
| dermitis | /dɜːˈmaɪtɪs/ | 皮炎 | Ch. 14 |
| dextrocardia | /ˌdekstrəʊˈkɑːdɪə/ | 右位心 | Ch. 15 |
| dextrocular | /ˈdekstrɒkjʊlə/ | 惯用右耳的 | Ch. 15 |

# Appendix 1　Glossary

| | | | |
|---|---|---|---|
| diagnosis | /ˌdaɪəɡˈnəʊsɪs/ | 诊断 | Ch. 3, 6 |
| diagonal | /daɪˈæɡənl/ | 对角线的 | Ch. 3 |
| dialysis | /daɪˈæləsɪs/ | 透析 | Ch. 3, 11 |
| diaphoresis | /ˌdaɪəfəˈriːsɪs/ | 发汗 | Ch. 14 |
| diaphragmatic | /ˌdaɪəfræɡˈmætɪk/ | 膈的 | Ch. 5 |
| diarrhea | /ˌdaɪəˈrɪə/ | 腹泻 | Ch. 3, 5, 6 |
| dicentric | /daɪˈsentrɪk/ | 双着丝(粒)的 | Ch. 3 |
| dioxide | /daɪˈɒksaɪd/ | 二氧化物 | Ch. 3 |
| diplacusis | /ˌdɪpləˈkjuːsɪs/ | 复听 | Ch. 15 |
| diplegia | /daɪˈpliːdʒɪə/ | 双侧瘫痪 | Ch. 9 |
| diplopia | /dɪˈpləʊpɪə/ | 复视 | Ch. 15 |
| dipsosis | /dɪpˈsəʊsɪs/ | 烦渴 | Ch. 11 |
| disinfection | /ˌdɪsɪnˈfekʃn/ | 消毒 | Ch. 3 |
| diskette | /dɪsˈket/ | 小盘 | Ch. 11 |
| dislocation | /ˌdɪsləˈkeɪʃn/ | 脱白 | Ch. 3 |
| distal | /ˈdɪstl/ | 远端的；末梢的 | Ch. 4 |
| distolingual | /ˌdɪstəʊˈlɪŋwəl/ | 远中舌的 | Ch. 4 |
| dorsalgia | /dɔːˈsældʒɪə/ | 背痛 | Ch. 4, 13 |
| dorsolateral | /ˌdɔːsəʊˈlætərəl/ | 背外侧的 | Ch. 4, 13 |
| droplet | /ˈdrɒplət/ | 小滴 | Ch. 11 |
| duodenoscopy | /ˌdjuədɪˈnɒskəpɪ/ | 十二指肠镜检 | Ch. 6 |
| duodenostomy | /ˌdjuədɪˈnɒstəmɪ/ | 十二指肠切除术 | Ch. 6 |
| dyskinesia | /ˌdɪskɪˈniːsɪə/ | 运动障碍 | Ch. 13 |
| dyslexia | /dɪsˈleksɪə/ | 阅读障碍 | Ch. 9 |
| dysmenorrhea | /ˌdɪsmenəʊˈriːə/ | 痛经 | Ch. 12 |
| dyspareunia | /ˌdɪspərɪˈjuːnɪə/ | 性交困难 | Ch. 12 |
| dyspepsia | /dɪsˈpepsɪə/ | 消化不良 | Ch. 6 |
| dysphagia | /dɪsˈfeɪdʒɪə/ | 吞咽困难 | Ch. 6 |
| dysphonia | /dɪsˈfəʊnɪə/ | 发音障碍 | Ch. 5 |
| dysplasia | /dɪsˈpleɪʒə/ | 发育异常 | Ch. 3, 8 |
| dyspneic | /dɪspˈniːk/ | 呼吸困难的 | Ch. 5 |
| dystocia | /dɪsˈtəʊʃɪə/ | 难产 | Ch. 10 |
| dystonia | /dɪsˈtəʊnɪə/ | 肌张力障碍 | Ch. 9 |

| | | | |
|---|---|---|---|
| dystrophy | /ˈdɪstrəfɪ/ | 营养不良 | Ch. 3 |
| **E** | | | |
| echocardiograph | /ˌekəʊˈkɑːdɪəgræf/ | 超声心动描记仪 | Ch. 7 |
| echogram | /ˈekəʊgræm/ | 超声波回波图 | Ch. 7 |
| electrocardiogram | /ɪˌlektrəʊˈkɑːdɪəgræm/ | 心电图 | Ch. 7 |
| electrocardiograph | /ɪˌlektrəʊˈkɑːdɪəgræf/ | 心电描记器 | Ch. 2 |
| electrocardiography | /ɪˌlektrəʊkɑːdɪˈɒgrəfɪ/ | 心电描记术 | Ch. 7 |
| electroencephalogram | /ɪˌlektrəʊɪnˈsefələʊˌgræm/ | 脑电图 | Ch. 2, 9 |
| electromyograph | /ɪˈlektrəʊˈmaɪəʊgrɑːf/ | 肌电描记器 | Ch. 2 |
| electrosurgery | /ɪˈlektrəʊˈsɜːdʒərɪ/ | 电外科 | Ch. 7 |
| embolectomy | /ˌembəˈlektəmɪ/ | 栓子取出术 | Ch. 7 |
| embolic | /emˈbɒlɪk/ | 栓塞的 | Ch. 7 |
| embolism | /ˈembəlɪzəm/ | 栓塞 | Ch. 2 |
| embryogenesis | /ˌembrɪəʊˈdʒenəsɪs/ | 胚胎发育 | Ch. 12 |
| embryology | /ˌembrɪˈɒlədʒɪ/ | 胚胎学 | Ch. 12 |
| empyesis | /empaɪˈiːsɪs/ | 积脓 | Ch. 13 |
| encephalocele | /enˈsefələʊˌsiːl/ | 脑膨出 | Ch. 2 |
| encephalomalacia | /enˌsefələʊməˈleɪʃɪə/ | 脑软化 | Ch. 9 |
| encephalomyelitis | /enˌsefələʊmaɪəˈlaɪtɪs/ | 脑脊髓炎 | Ch. 13 |
| encephalon | /enˈsefəlɒn/ | 脑 | Ch. 3 |
| endarterectomy | /enˌdɑːtəˈrektəmɪ/ | 动脉内膜切除术 | Ch. 7 |
| endoarticular | /endəʊɑːˈtɪkjʊlə/ | 内关节的 | Ch. 13 |
| endocarditis | /ˌendəʊkɑːˈdaɪtɪs/ | 心内膜炎 | Ch. 7 |
| endocrine | /ˈendəʊkraɪn/ | 内分泌 | Ch. 3, 10 |
| endodontics | /ˌendəʊˈdɒntɪks/ | 牙髓学 | Ch. 6 |
| endoscope | /ˈendəskəʊp/ | 内镜 | Ch. 3 |
| endovascular | /endəʊˈvæskjʊlə/ | 血管内的 | Ch. 7 |
| enterectasis | /ˌentəˈrektəsɪs/ | 肠扩张 | Ch. 5 |
| enteropexy | /entərəʊˈpeksɪ/ | 肠固定术 | Ch. 11 |
| enteroptosis | /ˌentərəʊˈptəʊsɪs/ | 肠下垂 | Ch. 2 |
| enteroscope | /ˈentərəskəʊp/ | 肠镜 | Ch. 2 |
| enterospasm | /ˌentərəʊˈspæzəm/ | 肠痉挛 | Ch. 2, 6 |
| enuresis | /ˌenjuːˈriːsɪs/ | 遗尿 | Ch. 11 |

## Appendix 1  Glossary

| | | | |
|---|---|---|---|
| eosinopenia | /ˌiːəsɪnəˈpiːnɪə/ | 嗜酸性粒细胞减少 | Ch. 14 |
| eosinophil | /ˌiːəˈsɪnəfɪl/ | 嗜酸性粒细胞 | Ch. 14 |
| epidermis | /ˌepɪˈdɜːmɪs/ | 表皮 | Ch. 3 |
| epididymectomy | /epɪdɪdɪˈmektəmɪ/ | 附睾切除术 | Ch. 12 |
| epididymitis | /ˌepɪdɪdɪˈmaɪtɪs/ | 附睾炎 | Ch. 12 |
| epidural | /epɪˈdjʊərəl/ | 硬膜上的 | Ch. 9 |
| epigastric | /epɪˈɡæstrɪk/ | 上腹部的 | Ch. 3, 6 |
| epiglottitis | /epɪɡlɒˈtaɪtɪs/ | 会厌炎 | Ch. 5 |
| episiorrhaphy | /ˌepɪzɪˈɒrəfɪ/ | 外阴缝合术 | Ch. 12 |
| episiotomy | /ˌepɪzɪˈɒtəmi/ | 外阴切开术 | Ch. 12 |
| epispadias | /epɪˈspeɪdɪəs/ | 尿道上裂 | Ch. 12 |
| epithelial | /ˌepɪˈθiːlɪəl/ | 上皮的 | Ch. 4 |
| epithelioma | /ˌepɪˌθiːlɪˈəʊmə/ | 上皮瘤 | Ch. 4 |
| erythema | /ˌerɪˈθiːmə/ | 红斑 | Ch. 14 |
| erythrocyte | /ɪˈrɪθrəsaɪt/ | 红细胞 | Ch. 7, 14 |
| erythrocytosis | /ɪrɪˌθrəʊsaɪˈtəʊsɪs/ | 红细胞增多症 | Ch. 7 |
| erythropoiesis | /ɪˌrɪθrəpɔɪˈiːsɪs/ | 红细胞生成 | Ch. 7 |
| erythropoietin | /ɪrɪθrəˈpɔɪtɪn/ | (促)红细胞生成素 | Ch. 11 |
| esophagology | /ɪˌsɒfəˈɡɒlədʒɪ/ | 食管病学 | Ch. 6 |
| esotropia | /esəʊˈtrəʊpɪə/ | 内斜眼 | Ch. 15 |
| estrogen | /ˈestrədʒən/ | 雌激素 | Ch. 10 |
| eucapnia | /juːˈkæpnɪə/ | 血碳酸正常 | Ch. 5 |
| euosmia | /juːˈɒzmɪə/ | 嗅觉正常 | Ch. 5 |
| eupnea | /juːˈpniːə/ | 呼吸正常 | Ch. 5 |
| eupraxia | /juːˈpræksɪə/ | 协同动作正常 | Ch. 9 |
| eutocia | /jʊˈtəʊʃɪə/ | 安产 | Ch. 10, 12 |
| excision | /ɪkˈsɪʒn/ | 切除术 | Ch. 3 |
| exocrine | /ˈeksəʊkraɪn/ | 外分泌 | Ch. 10 |
| exogenous | /ekˈsɒdʒənəs/ | 外生的 | Ch. 3 |
| exotropia | /ˌeksəˈtrəʊpɪə/ | 外斜视 | Ch. 15 |
| expectorant | /ɪksˈpektərənt/ | 祛痰的 | Ch. 5 |
| extorsion | /ɪksˈtɔːʃn/ | 外旋 | Ch. 4 |
| extrabuccal | /ekstrəˈbʌkəl/ | (口)颊外的 | Ch. 6 |

| | | | |
|---|---|---|---|
| extracardiac | /ˌekstrəˈkɑːdɪæk/ | 心外的 | Ch. 3 |
| extracellular | /ˌekstrəˈseljʊlə/ | 细胞外的 | Ch. 3 |
| extramedullary | /ekstrəmɪˈdʌlərɪ/ | 髓外的 | Ch. 9 |
| extrathecal | /ekstrəˈθekəl/ | 鞘外的 | Ch. 9 |

## F

| | | | |
|---|---|---|---|
| fasciitis | /ˌfæʃɪˈaɪtɪs/ | 筋膜炎 | Ch. 13 |
| fasciodesis | /ˌfæʃiːəʊˈdiːsɪs/ | 筋膜固定术 | Ch. 13 |
| fecal | /ˈfiːkl/ | 排泄物的 | Ch. 6 |
| femoral | /ˈfemərəl/ | 大腿骨的 | Ch. 13 |
| femoro-articular | /ˈfemərəʊɑːˈtɪkjʊlə/ | 股关节的 | Ch. 13 |
| fibroid | /ˈfaɪbrɔɪd/ | 纤维样的 | Ch. 13 |
| fibromyxoma | /faɪbrəʊmɪksəmə/ | 纤维黏液瘤 | Ch. 13 |
| fibrosclerosis | /fɪbrɒskləˈrəʊsɪs/ | 纤维硬化 | Ch. 13 |
| fibular | /ˈfɪbjʊlə/ | 腓骨的 | Ch. 13 |
| folliculitis | /fəˌlɪkjʊˈlaɪtɪs/ | 毛囊炎 | Ch. 14 |
| footling | /ˈfuːtlɪŋ/ | 小足 | Ch. 11 |
| fungicide | /ˈfʌŋgɪsaɪd/ | 杀真菌剂 | Ch. 8 |
| fungistatic | /fʌndʒɪˈstætɪk/ | 抑制真菌的 | Ch. 8 |
| fungitoxic | /fʌndʒɪˈtɒksɪk/ | 对真菌有毒性的 | Ch. 8 |

## G

| | | | |
|---|---|---|---|
| galactophagous | /gəˈlæktəʊfeɪgəs/ | 乳食的 | Ch. 12 |
| galactorrhea | /gæˈlæktɒrɪə/ | 乳漏 | Ch. 12 |
| gametocide | /gəˈmiːtəsaɪd/ | 杀配子剂 | Ch. 12 |
| gametogenesis | /gæmətəˈdʒenəsɪs/ | 配子形成 | Ch. 12 |
| ganglionectomy | /gæŋglɪɒnˈektəmɪ/ | 神经节截除术 | Ch. 9 |
| gangliopathy | /gæŋglɪˈɒpəθɪ/ | 神经节病 | Ch. 9 |
| gastralgia | /gæsˈtrældʒɪə/ | 胃痛 | Ch. 2 |
| gastrocele | /ˈgæstrəʊˌsiːl/ | 胃膨出 | Ch. 6 |
| gastrojejunostomy | /ˈgæstrəʊdʒɪdʒuːˈnɒstəmɪ/ | 胃空肠吻合术 | Ch. 6 |
| gastroptosis | /ˌgæstrəʊˈptəʊsɪs/ | 胃下垂 | Ch. 2 |
| gastrorrhagia | /gæstrəˈreɪdʒɪə/ | 胃出血 | Ch. 7 |
| gastroscope | /ˈgæstrəskəʊp/ | 胃镜 | Ch. 2 |
| genesis | /ˈdʒenəsɪs/ | 起源 | Ch. 2 |

| | | | |
|---|---|---|---|
| genitoplasty | /ˌdʒenɪtəʊˈplæstɪ/ | 生殖器成形术 | Ch. 12 |
| genitourinary | /ˌdʒenɪtəʊjʊəˈrɪnərɪ/ | 泌尿生殖器的 | Ch. 12 |
| geriatrics | /ˌdʒerɪˈætrɪks/ | 老年病学 | Ch. 15 |
| gerontology | /ˌdʒerɒnˈtɒlədʒɪ/ | 老年学 | Ch. 15 |
| gingivitis | /ˌdʒɪndʒɪˈvaɪtɪs/ | 牙龈炎 | Ch. 6 |
| glaucoma | /glɔːˈkəʊmə/ | 青光眼 | Ch. 14 |
| glioma | /glaɪˈəʊmə/ | 神经胶质瘤 | Ch. 9 |
| gliotoxin | /glɪəˈtɒksɪn/ | 胶毒素 | Ch. 9 |
| glomerulonephritis | /glɒmeruːləʊneˈfraɪtɪs/ | 肾小球性肾炎 | Ch. 11 |
| glomerulopathy | /ˌglɒmeruːˈləʊpəθɪ/ | 肾小球病 | Ch. 11 |
| glucometer | /gluːˈkɒmɪtə/ | 血糖测量仪 | Ch. 6 |
| gluconeogenesis | /ˌgluːkəʊˌniːəʊˈdʒenəsɪs/ | 糖原异生 | Ch. 6 |
| gnathitis | /næˈθaɪtɪs/ | 颌炎 | Ch. 6 |
| gonadoblastoma | /ˌgɒnədəblæsˈtəʊmə/ | 性腺胚细胞瘤 | Ch. 10 |
| gonadogenesis | /ˌgɒnədəˈdʒenəsɪs/ | 性腺发生 | Ch. 10 |
| gonoblast | /ˈgɒnəblɑːst/ | 原生殖细胞 | Ch. 10 |
| gonocyte | /ˈgɒnəsaɪt/ | 生殖细胞 | Ch. 10 |
| granulocyte | /ˈgrænjʊləsaɪt/ | 粒细胞 | Ch. 7 |
| granulopenia | /ˌgrænjʊləʊˈpiːnɪə/ | 粒细胞减少症 | Ch. 7 |
| gynecology | /ˌgaɪnɪˈkɒlədʒɪ/ | 妇科 | Ch. 10 |
| gynecomastia | /ˌgaɪnɪkəʊˈmæstɪə/ | 男子女性型乳房 | Ch. 12 |
| gynecopathy | /ˌgaɪnəˈkɒpəθɪ/ | 妇科病 | Ch. 12 |
| gynecophobia | /ˌgaɪnɪkəˈfəʊbɪə/ | 女性恐怖 | Ch. 10 |

**H**

| | | | |
|---|---|---|---|
| hectometer | /ˈhektəʊˌmiːtə/ | 百米 | Ch. 3 |
| hematemesis | /ˌhiːməˈteməsɪs/ | 呕血 | Ch. 6 |
| hematochezia | /ˌheməˈkiːzɪə/ | 便血 | Ch. 6 |
| hematocyte | /ˈhemətəʊsaɪt/ | 血细胞 | Ch. 2 |
| hematoma | /ˌhiːməˈtəʊmə/ | 血肿 | Ch. 2, 7 |
| hematopoiesis | /ˌhemətəʊpɔɪˈiːsɪs/ | 造血作用 | Ch. 7 |
| hemiataxia | /ˌhemɪeɪˈtæksɪə/ | 偏身共济失调 | Ch. 9 |
| hemiglossectomy | /ˌhemɪglɒˈsektəmɪ/ | 半侧舌切除术 | Ch. 6 |
| hemihepatectomy | /ˌhemɪˌhepəˈtektəmɪ/ | 半肝切除术 | Ch. 3 |

| | | | |
|---|---|---|---|
| hemiparesis | /ˌhemɪpəˈriːsɪs/ | 轻偏瘫 | Ch. 9 |
| hemisphere | /ˈhemɪsfɪə/ | 半球 | Ch. 3 |
| hemolysis | /hɪˈmɒlɪsɪs/ | 溶血 | Ch. 2, 7 |
| hemopathy | /hɪˈmɒpəθɪ/ | 血液病 | Ch. 7 |
| hemopoiesis | /ˌhiːməpɔɪˈiːsɪs/ | 造血作用 | Ch. 11 |
| hemoptysis | /hɪˈmɒptɪsɪs/ | 咯血 | Ch. 5 |
| hemorrhage | /ˈhemərɪdʒ/ | 出血 | Ch. 7 |
| hemosiderosis | /ˌhiːməʊsɪdəˈrəʊsɪs/ | 血铁质 | Ch. 7 |
| hemostasis | /ˌhiːməˈsteɪsɪs/ | 止血法 | Ch. 7 |
| hemothorax | /ˌhiːməˈθɔːræks/ | 胸膜腔积血 | Ch. 5 |
| hepatectomy | /ˌhepəˈtektəmɪ/ | 肝切除术 | Ch. 2 |
| hepatitis | /ˌhepəˈtaɪtɪs/ | 肝炎 | Ch. 2, 6 |
| hepatocele | /hɪˈpætəʊˌsiːl/ | 肝膨出 | Ch. 2 |
| hepatogenic | /ˌhepətəˈdʒenɪk/ | 肝源性的 | Ch. 6 |
| hepatolienal | /hepətɒˈliːnl/ | 肝脾的 | Ch. 8 |
| hepatomegaly | /ˌhepətəʊˈmegəlɪ/ | 肝大 | Ch. 2 |
| heterogeneous | /ˌhetərəˈdʒiːnɪəs/ | 异种的 | Ch. 3 |
| heteropsia | /hetəˈrɒpsɪə/ | 双眼不等视 | Ch. 15 |
| heterosexuality | /ˌhetərəˌsekʃuˈælətɪ/ | 异性恋 | Ch. 3 |
| hidropoiesis | /hɪdrəʊpɔɪˈiːsɪs/ | 流汗 | Ch. 14 |
| histoclasia | /hɪstəʊˈkleɪzɪə/ | 组织破坏 | Ch. 13 |
| histology | /hɪsˈtɒlədʒɪ/ | 组织学 | Ch. 4 |
| histolysis | /hɪsˈtɒlɪsɪs/ | 组织溶解 | Ch. 4 |
| homeostasis | /ˌhəʊmɪəˈsteɪsɪs/ | 体内平衡 | Ch. 3 |
| homolateral | /həʊməˈlætərəl/ | 同侧的 | Ch. 3 |
| homosexuality | /ˌhɒməʊˌsekʃuˈælətɪ/ | 同性恋 | Ch. 3 |
| hormonagogue | /hɔːˈmɒnəɒg/ | 催激素的 | Ch. 10 |
| hormonogenic | /hɜːmɒnəʊˈdʒenɪk/ | 激素生成的 | Ch. 10 |
| hormonoprivia | /hɔːmɒnɒˈprɪvɪə/ | 激素缺乏 | Ch. 10 |
| hormonotherapy | /hɔːmɒnəʊˈθerəpɪ/ | 激素疗法 | Ch. 8, 10 |
| humeroradial | /hjuːmərəˈreɪdɪəl/ | 肱桡的 | Ch. 13 |
| humeroscapular | /hjuːmərəˈskæpjʊlə/ | 肱(骨)肩胛的 | Ch. 13 |
| humeroulnar | /hjuːmərəˈʌlnə/ | 肱尺的 | Ch. 13 |

| | | | |
|---|---|---|---|
| hyalosis | /haɪəˈləʊsɪs/ | 玻璃体退变 | Ch. 15 |
| hydronephrosis | /ˌhaɪdrəʊnɪˈfrəʊsɪs/ | 肾积水 | Ch. 11 |
| hydrophobia | /ˌhaɪdrəˈfəʊbɪə/ | 恐水症 | Ch. 9 |
| hydrosalpinx | /haɪdrəˈsælpɪŋks/ | 输卵管积水 | Ch. 12 |
| hydrotherapy | /ˌhaɪdrəˈθerəpɪ/ | 水疗法 | Ch. 8 |
| hydroureter | /haɪdrəjuːˈriːtə/ | 输尿管积水 | Ch. 11 |
| hyperacusis | /haɪpərəˈkjuːsɪs/ | 听觉过敏 | Ch. 15 |
| hyperalbuminemia | /haɪpəˌælbjuːmɪˈniːmɪə/ | 高白蛋白血症 | Ch. 11 |
| hyperazotemia | /haɪpərəzəʊˈtiːmɪə/ | 高氮血症 | Ch. 11 |
| hyperbilirubinemia | /ˌhaɪpəˌbɪlɪˌruːbɪˈniːmɪə/ | 高胆红素血症 | Ch. 6 |
| hypercapnia | /ˌhaɪpəˈkæpnɪə/ | 血碳酸过多症 | Ch. 5 |
| hyperemesis | /haɪpəˈremɪsɪs/ | 剧吐 | Ch. 6 |
| hyperesthesia | /ˌhaɪpəresˈθiːʒə/ | 感觉过敏 | Ch. 9 |
| hyperkalemia | /haɪpəkəˈliːmɪə/ | 高钾血症 | Ch. 10 |
| hyperkinesia | /ˌhaɪpəkɪˈniːsɪə/ | 运动功能亢奋 | Ch. 13 |
| hyperkinesis | /ˌhaɪpəkaɪˈniːsɪs/ | 运动功能亢奋 | Ch. 9 |
| hypernatremia | /haɪpənəˈtriːmɪə/ | 高钠血症 | Ch. 10 |
| hyperopia | /haɪpəˈrəʊpɪə/ | 远视 | Ch. 15 |
| hyperorexia | /haɪpərəˈreksɪə/ | 食欲过盛 | Ch. 6 |
| hyperphagia | /ˌhaɪpəˈfeɪdʒɪə/ | 摄食过量 | Ch. 6 |
| hyperpituitarism | /ˌhaɪpəpɪˈtjuːɪtərɪzəm/ | 垂体功能亢进 | Ch. 10 |
| hyperplasia | /ˌhaɪpəˈpleɪzɪə/ | 增生 | Ch. 3, 8 |
| hypersplenism | /haɪpəˈsplenɪzəm/ | 脾功能亢进 | Ch. 8 |
| hyperthyroidism | /ˌhaɪpəˈθaɪrɔɪdɪzəm/ | 甲状腺功能亢进 | Ch. 10 |
| hypertrophy | /haɪˈpɜːtrəfɪ/ | 肥大 | Ch. 3 |
| hypnosis | /hɪpˈnəʊsɪs/ | 催眠状态 | Ch. 9 |
| hypnotize | /ˈhɪpnətaɪz/ | 催眠 | Ch. 9 |
| hypobilirubinemia | /ˌhaɪpəʊbɪlɪˌruːbɪˈniːmɪə/ | 低胆红素血症 | Ch. 6 |
| hypochromic | /haɪpəʊˈkrəʊmɪk/ | 着色不足的 | Ch. 14 |
| hypoepiglottic | /ˌhaɪpəʊˌepɪˈɡlɒtɪk/ | 会厌下的 | Ch. 5 |
| hypoglycemia | /ˌhaɪpəɡlaɪˈsiːmɪə/ | 低血糖症 | Ch. 6 |
| hypoglycemic | /ˌhaɪpəɡlaɪˈsiːmɪk/ | 低血糖症的 | Ch. 6 |
| hyponatremia | /haɪpʊnəˈtremɪə/ | 低钠血症 | Ch. 10 |

| | | | |
|---|---|---|---|
| hypophysectomy | /ˌhaɪpɒfɪˈsektəmɪ/ | 垂体切除术 | Ch. 10 |
| hypophysopathy | /ˌhaɪpɒufɪˈzɒpəθɪ/ | 垂体病 | Ch. 10 |
| hypopituitarism | /ˌhaɪpɒpɪˈtjuːɪtərɪzəm/ | 垂体功能减退 | Ch. 10 |
| hypospadias | /haɪpəʊˈspeɪdɪəs/ | 尿道下裂 | Ch. 12 |
| hypotension | /ˌhaɪpəˈtenʃən/ | 低血压 | Ch. 3 |
| hypothalamic | /haɪpəʊθəˈlæmɪk/ | 下丘脑的 | Ch. 9 |
| hypothermic | /ˌhaɪpəʊˈθɜːmɪk/ | 低体温的 | Ch. 14 |
| hypoxia | /haɪˈpɒksɪə/ | 低氧 | Ch. 3, 5 |
| hysteralgia | /hɪstəˈrældʒɪə/ | 子宫痛 | Ch. 12 |
| hysteromyoma | /hɪstərəʊmaɪˈəʊmə/ | 子宫肌瘤 | Ch. 12 |

**I**

| | | | |
|---|---|---|---|
| iatrogenic | /aɪˌətrəʊˈdʒenɪk/ | 医源性的 | Ch. 2 |
| idiolysis | /ˌɪdɪˈɒlɪsɪs/ | 自发溶解 | Ch. 10 |
| idiopathy | /ˌɪdɪˈɒpəθɪ/ | 特发症 | Ch. 10 |
| ileectomy | /ɪlɪˈektəmɪ/ | 回肠切除术 | Ch. 6 |
| ileopexy | /ˌɪlɪəˈpeksɪ/ | 回肠固定术 | Ch. 6 |
| ileosigmoidostomy | /ɪlɪəʊsɪgmɔɪˈdɒstəmɪ/ | 回肠乙状结肠吻合术 | Ch. 6 |
| iliococcygeal | /ɪlɪəkɒkˈsɪdʒiːl/ | 髂尾骨的 | Ch. 13 |
| iliocostal | /ɪlɪəˈkɒstl/ | 髂肋的 | Ch. 13 |
| immobility | /ˌɪməʊˈbɪlətɪ/ | 不动状态 | Ch. 3 |
| immunologist | /ˌɪmjuˈnɒlədʒɪst/ | 免疫学家 | Ch. 8 |
| inferocostal | /ˌɪnfərəʊˈkɒstl/ | 肋下的 | Ch. 4 |
| inferonasal | /ˌɪnfərəʊˈneɪzl/ | 鼻下的 | Ch. 4 |
| infertile | /ɪnˈfɜːtaɪl/ | 不育的 | Ch. 3 |
| infracardiac | /ˌɪnfrəˈkɑːdɪæk/ | 心下的 | Ch. 3 |
| infraduction | /ˌɪnfrəˈdʌkʃn/ | 下转 | Ch. 3 |
| inguinoabdominal | /ˌɪŋɡuɪnəʊəbˈdɒmɪnl/ | 腹股沟腹的 | Ch. 4 |
| inguinodynia | /ˌɪŋɡuɪnəʊˈdɪnɪə/ | 腹股沟痛 | Ch. 4 |
| inoblast | /ˈɪnəblɑːst/ | 成纤维细胞 | Ch. 13 |
| inomyoma | /ˌɪnəmaɪˈəʊmə/ | 纤维肌瘤 | Ch. 13 |
| inseminate | /ɪnˈsemɪneɪt/ | 人工授精 | Ch. 12 |
| insomnia | /ɪnˈsɒmnɪə/ | 失眠症 | Ch. 3 |

## Appendix 1  Glossary

| | | | |
|---|---|---|---|
| insulinoma | /ɪnsjʊlɪˈnəʊmə/ | 胰岛瘤 | Ch. 10 |
| insulinopenia | /ɪnsjʊlɪˈnəʊpiːnɪə/ | 胰岛素不足 | Ch. 10 |
| interalveolar | /ˌɪntərælˈvɪələ/ | 牙槽间的;小泡间的 | Ch. 5 |
| interatrial | /ˌɪntəˈreɪtrɪəl/ | 心房间的 | Ch. 7 |
| interclavicular | /ˌɪntəkləˈvɪkjʊlə(r)/ | 锁骨间的 | Ch. 13 |
| intercostal | /ˌɪntəˈkɒstl/ | 肋间的 | Ch. 3, 13 |
| interdental | /ˌɪntəˈdentl/ | 齿间的 | Ch. 3 |
| interlabial | /ˌɪntɜːˈleɪbɪəl/ | 唇间的 | Ch. 6 |
| interpalpebral | /ˌɪntɜːˈpælpɪbrəl/ | 睑间的 | Ch. 15 |
| interpleural | /ˌɪntəˈplʊərəl/ | 胸膜间的 | Ch. 5 |
| interventricular | /ˌɪntəˈventrɪkjʊlə/ | 室间的 | Ch. 7 |
| intrabuccal | /ˌɪntrəˈbʌkəl/ | 颊内的;口内的 | Ch. 6 |
| intracardiac | /ˌɪntrəˈkɑːdɪæk/ | 心脏内的 | Ch. 3 |
| intracranial | /ˌɪntrəˈkreɪnɪəl/ | 颅内的 | Ch. 4 |
| intradermal | /ˌɪntrəˈdɜːməl/ | 皮内的 | Ch. 14 |
| intramedullary | /ˌɪntrəmɪˈdʌlərɪ/ | 髓内的 | Ch. 9 |
| intrapulmonary | /ˌɪntrəˈpʌlmənərɪ/ | 肺内的 | Ch. 5 |
| intrathecal | /ˌɪntrəˈθekəl/ | 鞘内的 | Ch. 9 |
| intravenous | /ˌɪntrəˈviːnəs/ | 静脉的 | Ch. 3, 7 |
| inversion | /ɪnˈvɜːʃn/ | 反向 | Ch. 4 |
| iodemia | /aɪəˈdiːmɪə/ | 碘血症 | Ch. 10 |
| iodimetry | /aɪəˈdɪmɪtrɪ/ | 碘量法 | Ch. 10 |
| iridectomy | /ˌaɪrɪˈdektəmɪ/ | 虹膜切除术 | Ch. 15 |
| iridomalacia | /ˌaɪrɪdəʊməˈleɪʃɪə/ | 虹膜软化 | Ch. 15 |
| iritis | /aɪˈraɪtɪs/ | 虹膜炎 | Ch. 15 |
| ischemia | /ɪsˈkiːmɪə/ | 局部缺血 | Ch. 7 |
| ischioanal | /ɪskɪəʊˈeɪnl/ | 坐骨肛门的 | Ch. 13 |
| ischioneuralgia | /ɪskɪəʊnjʊəˈrældʒɪə/ | 坐骨神经痛 | Ch. 13 |

**J**

| | | | |
|---|---|---|---|
| jaundice | /ˈdʒɔːndɪs/ | 黄疸 | Ch. 14 |
| jejunitis | /dʒiːdʒʊˈnaɪtɪs/ | 空肠炎 | Ch. 6 |

| | | | |
|---|---|---|---|
| jejunoplasty | /dʒəˌdʒuːnəuˈplæstɪ/ | 空肠成形术 | Ch. 6 |

**K**

| | | | |
|---|---|---|---|
| karyolysis | /ˌkærɪˈɒlɪsɪs/ | 核溶解 | Ch. 4 |
| karyomegaly | /ˌkærɪəˈmegəlɪ/ | 巨大核 | Ch. 4 |
| karyotype | /ˈkærɪəˌtaɪp/ | 核型 | Ch. 7 |
| keratin | /ˈkerətɪn/ | 角蛋白 | Ch. 14 |
| keratome | /ˈkerəˌtəum/ | 角膜刀 | Ch. 15 |
| keratoplasty | /ˈkerətəuˌplæstɪ/ | 角膜成形术 | Ch. 15 |
| keratosis | /ˌkerəˈtəusɪs/ | 角化病 | Ch. 14 |
| kilometer | /ˈkɪləˌmiːtə/ | 千米 | Ch. 3 |
| kinesiology | /ˌkɪniːsɪˈɒlədʒɪ/ | 运动功能学 | Ch. 9 |
| kleptomania | /ˌkleptəuˈmeɪnɪə/ | 盗窃癖 | Ch. 9 |
| kyphosis | /kaɪˈfəusɪs/ | 驼背 | Ch. 13 |

**L**

| | | | |
|---|---|---|---|
| labiodental | /ˌleɪbɪəuˈdentl/ | 唇齿的 | Ch. 6 |
| labyrinthine | /ˌlæbəˈrɪnθaɪn/ | （耳）迷路的 | Ch. 15 |
| labyrinthotomy | /ˌlæbərɪnˈθɒtəmɪ/ | （耳）迷路切开术 | Ch. 15 |
| lacrimation | /ˌlækrəˈmeɪʃən/ | 流泪 | Ch. 15 |
| lacrimotomy | /ˌlækrɪˈmɔːtəmɪ/ | 泪腺切开术 | Ch. 15 |
| lactagogue | /ˈlæktəgɒg/ | 催乳剂 | Ch. 10 |
| lactodensimeter | /ˌlæktəudənˈsɪmɪtə/ | 乳比重计 | Ch. 12 |
| lactogenesis | /ˌlæktəuˈdʒenəsɪs/ | 生乳 | Ch. 12 |
| lactorrhea | /ˌlæktəˈriːə/ | 乳溢 | Ch. 10 |
| lactotropin | /ˌlæktəuˈtrəupɪn/ | 泌乳激素 | Ch. 10 |
| laminectomy | /ˌlæmɪˈnektəmɪ/ | 椎板切除术 | Ch. 13 |
| laminoplasty | /ˌlæmɪnəuˈplæstɪ/ | 椎板成形术 | Ch. 13 |
| laparoscopy | /ˌlæpəˈrɒskəpɪ/ | 腹腔镜检查 | Ch. 6 |
| laparotome | /ˈlæpərəˌtəum/ | 剖腹刀 | Ch. 6 |
| laryngeal | /ləˈrɪndʒɪəl/ | 喉的 | Ch. 5 |
| laryngocentesis | /ləˌrɪŋgəusenˈtiːsɪs/ | 喉穿刺术 | Ch. 5 |
| laryngostenosis | /ləˌrɪŋgəustɪˈnəusɪs/ | 喉狭窄 | Ch. 5 |

## Appendix 1  Glossary

| | | | |
|---|---|---|---|
| laterotorsion | /ˌlætərəʊˈtɔːʃn/ | 侧扭转 | Ch. 4 |
| leiomyoma | /laɪəʊmaɪˈəʊmə/ | 平滑肌瘤 | Ch. 13 |
| leiomyosarcoma | /laɪəʊmaɪəʊsɑːˈkəʊmə/ | 平滑肌肉瘤 | Ch. 13 |
| leptomeningitis | /ˌleptəʊmenɪnˈdʒaɪtɪs/ | 软脑(脊)膜炎 | Ch. 9 |
| leptomeningopathy | /ˌleptəʊmenɪnˈgɒpəθɪ/ | 软脑(脊)膜病 | Ch. 9 |
| leukemia | /ljuːˈkiːmɪə/ | 白血病 | Ch. 7 |
| leukocyte | /ˈljuːkəˌsaɪt/ | 白细胞 | Ch. 7 |
| leukocytosis | /ˌljuːkəʊsaɪˈtəʊsɪs/ | 白细胞增多症 | Ch. 7 |
| leukoderma | /ˌljuːkəˈdɜːmə/ | 白斑病 | Ch. 14 |
| leukopoietin | /ljuːkəˈpɔɪtɪn/ | (促)白细胞生成素 | Ch. 11 |
| lienomalacia | /laɪˌənəʊməˈleɪʃɪə/ | 脾软化 | Ch. 8 |
| ligamentopexy | /lɪgəmentəʊˈpeksɪ/ | 韧带固定术 | Ch. 13 |
| ligamentotomy | /lɪgəmenˈtɔːtəmɪ/ | 韧带切开术 | Ch. 13 |
| lipoma | /lɪˈpəʊmə/ | 脂肪瘤 | Ch. 6, 14 |
| lipoprotein | /ˌlɪpəˈprəʊtiːn/ | 脂蛋白 | Ch. 6 |
| liposuction | /ˈlɪpəʊsʌkʃn/ | 吸脂术 | Ch. 14 |
| lithectomy | /lɪˈθektəmɪ/ | 切开取石术 | Ch. 6 |
| litholysis | /laɪˈtɒləsɪs/ | 结石溶解 | Ch. 6 |
| lithotripsy | /ˈlaɪθəʊtrɪpsɪ/ | 碎石术 | Ch. 11 |
| lobectomy | /ˌləʊˈbektəmɪ/ | 叶切除术 | Ch. 5 |
| lobule | /ˈlɒbjuːl/ | 小叶 | Ch. 5 |
| lordoscoliosis | /lɔːdəʊskɒlɪˈəʊsɪs/ | 脊柱前侧凸 | Ch. 13 |
| lordosis | /lɔːˈdəʊsɪs/ | 脊柱前凸 | Ch. 13 |
| lumbocostal | /ˌlʌmbəʊˈkɒstl/ | 腰肋的 | Ch. 4, 13 |
| lumbodorsal | /ˌlʌmbəʊˈdɔːsl/ | 腰背的 | Ch. 4, 13 |
| lymphadenectomy | /lɪmˌfædəˈnektəmɪ/ | 淋巴结切除术 | Ch. 8 |
| lymphadenopathy | /lɪmˌfædəˈnɒpəθɪ/ | 淋巴结病 | Ch. 8 |
| lymphangiitis | /lɪmˌfændʒɪˈaɪtɪs/ | 淋巴管炎 | Ch. 8 |
| lymphangiography | /lɪmˌfændʒɪˈɒgrəfɪ/ | 淋巴管造影术 | Ch. 8 |
| lymphectasia | /ˌlɪmfekˈteɪzɪə/ | 淋巴管扩张 | Ch. 5 |
| lymphedema | /lɪmfɪˈdiːmə/ | 淋巴水肿 | Ch. 8 |

| | | | |
|---|---|---|---|
| lymphoblast | /ˈlɪmfəblɑːst/ | 成淋巴细胞 | Ch. 8 |
| lymphocyte | /ˈlɪmfəsaɪt/ | 淋巴细胞 | Ch. 8 |
| lymphocytorrhexis | /ˌlɪmfəˌsaɪtəˈreksɪs/ | 淋巴细胞破裂 | Ch. 8 |
| lymphoid | /ˈlɪmfɔɪd/ | 淋巴样的 | Ch. 2 |

## M

| | | | |
|---|---|---|---|
| macrocyte | /ˈmækrəsaɪt/ | 巨红细胞 | Ch. 3 |
| macrodontia | /ˌmækrəˈdɒntɪə/ | 巨牙 | Ch. 3 |
| macrophage | /ˈmækrəfeɪdʒ/ | 巨噬细胞 | Ch. 8 |
| macrotia | /mæˈkrəʊtɪə/ | 巨耳 | Ch. 15 |
| malformation | /ˌmælfɔːˈmeɪʃn/ | 畸形 | Ch. 3 |
| malignant | /məˈlɪgnənt/ | 恶性的 | Ch. 3 |
| mammectomy | /məˈmektəmɪ/ | 乳房切除术 | Ch. 12 |
| mammoplasty | /ˈmæməʊplæstɪ/ | 乳房成形术 | Ch. 12 |
| mastitis | /mæsˈtaɪtɪs/ | 乳腺炎 | Ch. 12 |
| mastoid | /ˈmæstɔɪd/ | 乳头状的 | Ch. 12 |
| maxillodental | /mæksɪləʊˈdentl/ | 上颌牙的 | Ch. 13 |
| meatoscopy | /miːˈeɪtəskəpɪ/ | 尿道口镜检查 | Ch. 11 |
| meatotomy | /miːeɪˈtɒtəmɪ/ | 尿道口切开术 | Ch. 11 |
| medial | /ˈmiːdɪəl/ | 中间的 | Ch. 4 |
| mediastinoscopy | /ˌmiːdɪæstɪˈnɒskəpɪ/ | 纵隔镜检查 | Ch. 5 |
| mediofrontal | /ˌmiːdɪəˈfrʌntl/ | 中前部的 | Ch. 4 |
| megabyte | /ˈmegəbaɪt/ | 兆字节 | Ch. 3 |
| megacephaly | /megəˈsefəlɪ/ | 巨头 | Ch. 3 |
| megakaryocyte | /megəˈkærɪəʊsaɪt/ | 巨核细胞 | Ch. 7 |
| megalocardia | /ˌmegələʊˈkɑːdɪə/ | 心脏肥大 | Ch. 2 |
| megalogastria | /ˌmegələʊˈgæstrɪə/ | 巨胃 | Ch. 3 |
| megavolt | /ˈmegəvəʊlt/ | 百万伏特 | Ch. 3 |
| melanin | /ˈmelənɪn/ | 黑色素 | Ch. 14 |
| melanoderma | /melənəʊˈdɜːmə/ | 黑皮病 | Ch. 14 |
| menarche | /məˈnɑːkɪ/ | 初潮 | Ch. 12 |
| meningeal | /məˈnɪndʒɪəl/ | 脑膜的 | Ch. 9 |

## Appendix 1　Glossary

| | | | |
|---|---|---|---|
| meningioma | /mənɪndʒɪˈəʊmə/ | 脑膜瘤 | Ch. 9 |
| meningocele | /məˈnɪŋgəʊsiːl/ | 脑(脊)膜突出 | Ch. 9 |
| menorrhagia | /ˌmenəˈreɪdʒɪə/ | 月经过多 | Ch. 12 |
| mesiolingual | /ˈmiːsaɪəlɪŋgwəl/ | 近中舌侧的 | Ch. 6 |
| metabolism | /məˈtæbəlɪzəm/ | 新陈代谢 | Ch. 3 |
| metacarpectomy | /metəkɑːˈpektəmɪ/ | 掌骨切除术 | Ch. 13 |
| metacarpophalangeal | /ˌmetəkɑːpəʊfəˈlændʒiːl/ | 掌骨指骨的 | Ch. 13 |
| metachromia | /ˌmetəˈkrəʊmɪə/ | 异染性 | Ch. 3 |
| metamorphosis | /ˌmetəˈmɔːfəsɪs/ | 变形 | Ch. 4 |
| metastasis | /məˈtæstəsɪs/ | 转移 | Ch. 3 |
| metatarsalgia | /metətɑːˈsældʒɪə/ | 跖痛 | Ch. 13 |
| metatarsectomy | /metətɑːˈsektəmɪ/ | 跖骨切除术 | Ch. 13 |
| metrectasia | /miːtrekˈteɪsɪə/ | 子宫扩张 | Ch. 12 |
| metrocolpocele | /ˌmetrəʊˈkɒlpəʊsiːl/ | 子宫阴道突出 | Ch. 12 |
| microadenoma | /ˌmaɪkrəˌædəˈnəʊmə/ | 微腺瘤 | Ch. 3 |
| micrognathia | /maɪkrɒgˈnæθɪə/ | 小颌畸形 | Ch. 6 |
| microscope | /ˈmaɪkrəskəʊp/ | 显微镜 | Ch. 3 |
| microtia | /maɪˈkrəʊtɪə/ | 小耳 | Ch. 15 |
| milliliter | /ˈmɪlɪˌliːtə/ | 毫升 | Ch. 3 |
| monocellular | /ˌmɒnəʊˈseljʊlə/ | 单细胞的 | Ch. 3 |
| monocular | /mɒˈnɒkjʊlə/ | 单眼的 | Ch. 3 |
| monocyesis | /ˌmɒnəsaɪˈɪsɪs/ | 单胎妊娠 | Ch. 12 |
| mononuclear | /mɒnəʊˈnjuːklɪə/ | 单核的 | Ch. 7 |
| monophasia | /mɒnəˈfeɪzɪə/ | 单语症 | Ch. 9 |
| morphology | /mɔːˈfɒlədʒɪ/ | 形态学 | Ch. 4, 7 |
| muciform | /ˈmjuːsɪfɔːm/ | 黏液样的 | Ch. 2 |
| multicellular | /ˌmʌltɪˈseljʊlə/ | 多细胞的 | Ch. 3 |
| multiform | /ˈmʌltɪfɔːm/ | 多形的 | Ch. 3 |
| multigravida | /mʌltɪˈgrævɪdə/ | 经产孕妇 | Ch. 12 |
| multipara | /mʌlˈtɪpərə/ | 经产妇 | Ch. 12 |
| muscular | /ˈmʌskjʊlə/ | 肌肉的 | Ch. 13 |

| | | | |
|---|---|---|---|
| musculocutaneous | /mʌskjʊləʊkjʊˈteɪnɪəs/ | 肌皮的 | Ch. 13 |
| mutagenic | /ˌmjuːtəˈdʒenɪk/ | 基因变异的 | Ch. 8 |
| mutation | /mjuːˈteɪʃn/ | 突变 | Ch. 8 |
| mutism | /ˈmjuːtɪzəm/ | 哑 | Ch. 2 |
| myalgia | /maɪˈældʒɪə/ | 肌痛 | Ch. 2 |
| myasthenia | /ˌmaɪəsˈθiːnɪə/ | 肌无力 | Ch. 9 |
| mycology | /maɪˈkɒlədʒɪ/ | 真菌学 | Ch. 8 |
| mycosis | /maɪˈkəʊsɪs/ | 霉菌病 | Ch. 8 |
| myeloblast | /ˈmaɪələʊblɑːst/ | 成髓细胞 | Ch. 13 |
| myelography | /maɪˈlɒgrəfɪ/ | 脊髓造影术 | Ch. 9 |
| myeloma | /ˌmaɪəˈləʊmə/ | 骨髓瘤 | Ch. 8 |
| myeloschisis | /maɪələʊˈskiːsɪs/ | 脊髓裂 | Ch. 13 |
| myoma | /maɪˈəʊmə/ | 肌瘤 | Ch. 2, 8 |
| myomectomy | /maɪəˈmektəmɪ/ | 肌瘤切除术 | Ch. 13 |
| myoparesis | /maɪəpəˈriːsɪs/ | 肌麻痹 | Ch. 9 |
| myopia | /maɪˈəʊpɪə/ | 近视 | Ch. 15 |
| myoplegia | /ˌmaɪəʊˈpliːdʒɪə/ | 肌麻痹 | Ch. 2 |
| myosarcoma | /maɪəʊsɑːˈkəʊmə/ | 肌肉瘤 | Ch. 13 |
| myospasm | /ˌmaɪəʊˈspæzəm/ | 肌痉挛 | Ch. 2 |
| myotomy | /maɪˈɒtəmɪ/ | 肌切开术 | Ch. 2 |
| myringoplasty | /mɪˈrɪŋgəʊplæstɪ/ | 鼓膜成形术 | Ch. 15 |
| myringotomy | /mɪrɪŋˈgɒtəmɪ/ | 鼓膜切开术 | Ch. 15 |
| myxadenitis | /mɪkseɪdəˈnaɪtɪs/ | 黏液腺炎 | Ch. 13 |

## N

| | | | |
|---|---|---|---|
| narcosis | /nɑːˈkəʊsɪs/ | 麻醉 | Ch. 9 |
| nasopharynx | /ˌneɪzəʊˈfærɪŋks/ | 鼻咽部 | Ch. 5 |
| nasotracheal | /ˌneɪzəʊˈtrækɪəl/ | 鼻支气管的 | Ch. 5 |
| natality | /nəˈtælɪti/ | 出生率 | Ch. 12 |
| necropsy | /ˈnekrɒpsɪ/ | 尸体解剖 | Ch. 2 |
| neonatal | /ˌniːəʊˈneɪtl/ | 新生的 | Ch. 3, 12 |
| neonate | /ˈniːəneɪt/ | 新生儿 | Ch. 6 |

# Appendix 1  Glossary

| | | | |
|---|---|---|---|
| neophysis | /ˌniːəʊˈfeɪsɪs/ | 新生物,赘生物 | Ch. 13 |
| neoplasm | /ˈniːəʊplæzəm/ | 新生物;瘤 | Ch. 3, 8 |
| neostomy | /nɪˈɒstəmɪ/ | 造口术 | Ch. 6 |
| nephromegaly | /nefrəʊˈmegəlɪ/ | 巨肾 | Ch. 11 |
| nephropexy | /nefrəˈpeksɪ/ | 肾固定术 | Ch. 11 |
| neuralgia | /njʊˈrældʒɪə/ | 神经痛 | Ch. 2 |
| neurasthenia | /ˌnjʊərəsˈθiːnɪə/ | 神经衰弱症 | Ch. 9 |
| neurectomy | /njʊˈrektəmɪ/ | 神经切除 | Ch. 2 |
| neurodynia | /ˌnjʊrəˈdɪnɪə/ | 神经痛 | Ch. 2 |
| neurolysis | /njʊəˈrɒlɪsɪs/ | 神经松解(术) | Ch. 9 |
| neuropathy | /njʊˈrɒpəθɪ/ | 神经病 | Ch. 2 |
| neurosis | /njʊˈrəʊsɪs/ | 神经官能症 | Ch. 2 |
| neutralization | /ˌnjuːtrəlaɪˈzeɪʃn/ | 中和作用 | Ch. 7 |
| neutropenia | /ˌnjuːtrəˈpiːnɪə/ | 嗜中性白细胞减少症 | Ch. 7 |
| neutrophil | /ˈnjuːtrəfɪl/ | 嗜中性粒细胞 | Ch. 7 |
| nocturia | /nɒkˈtjʊrɪə/ | 夜尿症 | Ch. 11 |
| nocturnal | /nɒkˈtɜːnl/ | 在夜间的 | Ch. 11 |
| nodule | /ˈnɒdjuːl/ | 小节 | Ch. 11 |
| non-infectious | /nɒnɪnfekʃəs/ | 非传染性的 | Ch. 3 |
| nonviable | /nɒnˈvaɪəbl/ | 不能成活的 | Ch. 3 |
| nosomania | /nɒsəʊˈmeɪnjə/ | 疾病妄想 | Ch. 9 |
| nuclear | /ˈnjuːklɪə/ | 核的 | Ch. 4 |
| nucleocytoplasmic | /ˌnjuːklɪəˌsaɪtəʊˈplæzmɪk/ | (细胞)核与质的 | Ch. 4 |
| nucleoid | /ˈnjuːklɪɔɪd/ | 类核的 | Ch. 7 |
| nulligravida | /nʌlɪˈgrævɪdə/ | 未孕妇 | Ch. 12 |
| nullipara | /nʌˈlɪpərə/ | 未生育者 | Ch. 12 |
| nyctalopia | /ˌnɪktəˈləʊpɪə/ | 夜盲症 | Ch. 15 |
| nyctophobia | /ˌnɪktəˈfəʊbɪə/ | 黑夜恐怖症 | Ch. 15 |

**O**

| | | | |
|---|---|---|---|
| obstetrician | /ˌɒbstəˈtrɪʃn/ | 产科医生 | Ch. 12 |
| obstetrics | /əbˈstetrɪks/ | 产科学 | Ch. 12 |

| | | | |
|---|---|---|---|
| oculodynia | /ˌɒkjuləʊˈdɪnɪə/ | 眼疼 | Ch. 15 |
| oligodipsia | /ˌɒlɪˈgəʊdɪpsɪə/ | 渴感过少 | Ch. 11 |
| oligospermia | /ˌɒlɪˈgəʊspɜːmɪə/ | 精子减少 | Ch. 12 |
| oliguria | /ˌɒlɪˈgjʊərɪə/ | 尿过少 | Ch. 11 |
| omphalotomy | /ˌɒmfəˈlɒtəmɪ/ | 断脐术 | Ch. 12 |
| oncogenesis | /ˌɒŋkəˈdʒenəsɪs/ | 瘤形成 | Ch. 8 |
| oncology | /ɒŋˈkɒlədʒɪ/ | 肿瘤学 | Ch. 8 |
| onycholysis | /ˌɒnɪˈkɒlɪsɪs/ | 甲松离 | Ch. 14 |
| onychomycosis | /ˌɒnɪkəʊmaɪˈkəʊsɪs/ | 甲真菌病 | Ch. 14 |
| ooblast | /ˈəʊəblɑːst/ | 成卵细胞 | Ch. 12 |
| oogenesis | /ˌəʊəˈdʒenɪsɪs/ | 卵子发生 | Ch. 12 |
| oophoroma | /ˌəʊəfəˈrəʊmə/ | 卵巢瘤 | Ch. 12 |
| oophorrhagia | /ˌəʊəfəˈreɪdʒɪə/ | 卵巢出血 | Ch. 12 |
| ophthalmology | /ˌɒfθælˈmɒlədʒɪ/ | 眼科学 | Ch. 15 |
| ophthalmoscopy | /ɒfˈθælməʊskəpɪ/ | 检眼镜检查 | Ch. 15 |
| optic | /ˈɒptɪk/ | 视觉的 | Ch. 15 |
| optician | /ɒpˈtɪʃn/ | 光学仪器技师 | Ch. 15 |
| optometrist | /ɒpˈtɒmətrɪst/ | 验光师 | Ch. 15 |
| orchidectomy | /ˌɔːkɪˈdektəmɪ/ | 睾丸切除术 | Ch. 12 |
| orchidopathy | /ˌɔːkɪˈdɔːpəθɪ/ | 睾丸病 | Ch. 12 |
| orolingual | /ˌɔːrəˈlɪŋgwəl/ | 口舌的 | Ch. 6 |
| orthodontics | /ˌɔːθəˈdɒntɪks/ | 畸齿矫正学 | Ch. 5 |
| orthodontist | /ˌɔːθəˈdɒntɪst/ | 牙齿矫正医师 | Ch. 6 |
| orthopnea | /ɔːˈθɒpnɪə/ | 端坐呼吸 | Ch. 5 |
| oscheocele | /ˈɒstʃɪəʊsiːl/ | 阴囊肿大 | Ch. 12 |
| oscheoma | /ˈɒstʃɪəʊmə/ | 阴囊瘤 | Ch. 12 |
| osseofibrous | /ˌɒsɪəˈfaɪbrəs/ | 骨(与)纤维组织的 | Ch. 13 |
| osseous | /ˈɒsɪəs/ | 骨的 | Ch. 13 |
| ossiculoplasty | /ɒˈsɪkjʊləplæstɪ/ | 听小骨成形术 | Ch. 15 |
| ossiculotomy | /ˌɒsɪkjʊˈləʊtəmɪ/ | 听小骨切开术 | Ch. 15 |
| osteoarthropathy | /ˌɒstɪəʊɑːˈθrɒpəθɪ/ | 骨关节病 | Ch. 13 |

## Appendix 1　Glossary

| | | | |
|---|---|---|---|
| osteoblast | /ˈɒstɪəblɑːst/ | 成骨细胞 | Ch. 8 |
| osteoclasis | /ˌɒstɪəʊˈkleɪsɪs/ | 骨破折 | Ch. 13 |
| osteoclast | /ˈɒstɪəklæst/ | 破骨细胞 | Ch. 13 |
| osteocyte | /ˈɒstɪəsaɪt/ | 骨细胞 | Ch. 2 |
| osteodynia | /ˌɒstɪəˈdɪnɪə/ | 骨痛 | Ch. 2 |
| osteogenesis | /ˌɒstɪəˈdʒenəsɪs/ | 骨生成 | Ch. 2 |
| osteoma | /ˌɒstɪˈəʊmə/ | 骨瘤 | Ch. 2, 13 |
| osteomalacia | /ˌɒstɪəʊməˈleɪʃɪə/ | 软骨病 | Ch. 13 |
| osteomyelitis | /ˌɒstɪəʊˌmaɪəˈlaɪtɪs/ | 骨髓炎 | Ch. 13 |
| osteopyesis | /ˌɒstɪəʊpaɪˈiːsɪs/ | 骨化脓 | Ch. 13 |
| osteosarcoma | /ˌɒstɪəʊsɑːˈkəʊmə/ | 骨肉瘤 | Ch. 8 |
| osteotome | /ˈɒstɪəʊtəʊm/ | 骨凿 | Ch. 2, 13 |
| osteotomy | /ˌɒstɪˈɒtəmɪ/ | 骨切开术 | Ch. 2 |
| osteum | /ˈɒstɪəm/ | 骨 | Ch. 2 |
| otorrhea | /ˌɔːtəˈriːə/ | 耳液溢 | Ch. 15 |
| otosclerosis | /ˌɔːtəsklɪˈrəʊsɪs/ | 耳硬化症 | Ch. 15 |
| ovariectomy | /əʊveriˈektəmɪ/ | 卵巢切除术 | Ch. 12 |
| ovariocentesis | /əʊˌværɪəʊsenˈtiːsɪs/ | 卵巢穿刺术 | Ch. 12 |
| ovicide | /ˈəʊvɪsaɪd/ | 杀卵剂 | Ch. 12 |
| oviform | /ˈəʊvɪfɔːm/ | 卵形的 | Ch. 12 |
| oximeter | /ɒkˈsɪmɪtə/ | 血氧计 | Ch. 5 |
| oxyhemoglobin | /ˌɒksɪˈhiːməˌgləʊbɪn/ | 氧基血红素 | Ch. 10 |
| oxyhemograph | /ˌɒksiːˈhiːməˌgrɑːf/ | 血氧测定器 | Ch. 10 |
| oxyopia | /ˌɒksɪˈəʊpɪə/ | 视觉锐敏 | Ch. 10 |
| oxyphonia | /ˌɒksɪˈfəʊnjə/ | 尖音 | Ch. 10 |
| oxytocia | /ˌɒksɪˈtəʊʃə/ | 分娩急速 | Ch. 10 |
| oxytocin | /ˌɒksɪˈtəʊsɪn/ | 催产素 | Ch. 10 |

**P**

| | | | |
|---|---|---|---|
| pachyderma | /pækɪˈdɜːmə/ | 厚皮 | Ch. 14 |
| pachyonychia | /pækɪɒˈnɪkɪə/ | 甲肥厚 | Ch. 14 |
| palatine | /ˈpælətaɪn/ | 上颚的 | Ch. 6, 13 |

| | | | |
|---|---|---|---|
| palatorrhaphy | /ˌpæleɪˈtɒrəfɪ/ | 腭裂缝合术 | Ch. 6 |
| palatoschisis | /ˌpæleɪtəʊˈskɪsɪs/ | 腭裂 | Ch. 13 |
| palpebral | /ˈpælpɪbrəl/ | 眼睑的 | Ch. 15 |
| panacea | /ˌpænəˈsiːə/ | 万能药 | Ch. 3 |
| pancreatolysis | /ˌpæŋkrɪəˈtɒləsɪs/ | 胰组织破坏 | Ch. 6 |
| pancytopenia | /ˌpænsaɪtəˈpiːnɪə/ | 全血细胞减少症 | Ch. 7 |
| pangastrectomy | /ˌpænˌɡæsˈtrektəmɪ/ | 全胃切除术 | Ch. 3 |
| papilliform | /pəˈpɪlɪfɔːm/ | 乳头状的 | Ch. 12 |
| papilloma | /ˌpæpɪˈləʊmə/ | 乳突状瘤 | Ch. 12 |
| parafunction | /ˌpærəˈfʌŋkʃən/ | 功能异常 | Ch. 3 |
| parakinesia | /ˌpærəkɪˈniːsɪə/ | 运动倒错 | Ch. 3 |
| paranasal | /ˌpærəˈneɪzl/ | 鼻侧的 | Ch. 5 |
| paraneural | /ˌpærəˈnjʊərəl/ | 神经旁的 | Ch. 10 |
| paraphasia | /ˌpærəˈfeɪzɪə/ | 语言错乱 | Ch. 10 |
| paraplegia | /ˌpærəˈpliːdʒɪə/ | 截瘫 | Ch. 9 |
| parasecretion | /ˌpærəsɪˈkriːʃən/ | 分泌紊乱 | Ch. 10 |
| parathyroid | /ˌpærəˈθaɪrɔɪd/ | 甲状旁腺的 | Ch. 3, 10 |
| parathyroidectomy | /ˌpærəθaɪrɔɪˈdektəmɪ/ | 甲状旁腺切除术 | Ch. 10 |
| parathyroidoma | /ˌpærəθaɪrɔɪˈdəʊmə/ | 甲状旁腺肿瘤 | Ch. 10 |
| parenteral | /pəˈrentərəl/ | 肠外的 | Ch. 6 |
| paronychia | /ˌpærəˈnɪkɪə/ | 甲沟炎 | Ch. 14 |
| particle | /ˈpɑːtɪkl/ | 颗粒 | Ch. 11 |
| patellectomy | /ˌpətɪˈlektəmɪ/ | 髌骨切除术 | Ch. 13 |
| patellopexy | /ˌpətɪləʊˈpeksɪ/ | 髌骨固定术 | Ch. 13 |
| pathogen | /ˈpæθədʒən/ | 病原体 | Ch. 8 |
| pathogenic | /ˌpæθəˈdʒenɪk/ | 致病的 | Ch. 2 |
| pectoral | /ˈpektərəl/ | 胸部的 | Ch. 5 |
| pedal | /ˈpedl/ | 踏板 | Ch. 13 |
| pediatrician | /ˌpiːdɪəˈtrɪʃn/ | 儿科医生 | Ch. 2 |
| pediatrics | /ˌpiːdɪˈætrɪks/ | 儿科 | Ch. 2 |
| pelvimeter | /pelˈvɪmɪtə/ | 骨盆测量仪 | Ch. 4 |

## Appendix 1  Glossary

| | | | |
|---|---|---|---|
| pelvimetry | /pelˈvɪmɪtrɪ/ | 骨盆测量术 | Ch. 2, 13 |
| pelvioscopy | /ˌpelvɪˈɔːskɒpɪ/ | 骨盆腔检查 | Ch. 13 |
| pelvitomy | /pelˈvɪtəmɪ/ | 骨盆切开术 | Ch. 4 |
| penile | /ˈpiːnaɪl/ | 阴茎的 | Ch. 12 |
| penitis | /piːˈnɪtɪs/ | 阴茎炎 | Ch. 12 |
| pepsin | /ˈpepsɪn/ | 胃蛋白酶 | Ch. 10 |
| percutaneous | /ˌpɜːkjuːˈteɪnɪəs/ | 经由皮肤的 | Ch. 14 |
| perianal | /perɪˈeɪnəl/ | 肛门周围的 | Ch. 6 |
| periarticular | /perɪɑːˈtɪkjʊlə/ | 关节周的 | Ch. 13 |
| peribronchial | /ˌperɪˈbrɒŋkɪəl/ | 支气管周的 | Ch. 5 |
| pericardiocentesis | /ˌperɪˌkɑːdɪəˌsenˈtiːsɪs/ | 心包穿刺术 | Ch. 7 |
| pericarditis | /ˌperɪkɑːˈdaɪtɪs/ | 心包炎 | Ch. 7 |
| perineorrhaphy | /ˌperɪniːˈɔːrəfɪ/ | 会阴缝合术 | Ch. 12 |
| perineoscrotal | /ˌperɪniːəʊˈskrɒtl/ | 会阴阴囊的 | Ch. 12 |
| periodontal | /ˌperɪəˈdɒntl/ | 牙周的 | Ch. 3 |
| periodontium | /ˌperɪəʊˈdɒnʃɪəm/ | 牙周组织 | Ch. 6 |
| perioral | /ˈpɪərɪərəl/ | 口周的 | Ch. 6 |
| periosteum | /ˌperɪˈɒstɪəm/ | 骨膜 | Ch. 3 |
| peripartum | /perɪˈpɑːtəm/ | 围产的 | Ch. 12 |
| perisinusitis | /ˌperɪˌsaɪnəˈsaɪtɪs/ | 窦周炎 | Ch. 5 |
| peritoneoclysis | /perɪtəʊniːəʊˈklɪsɪs/ | 膜透析 | Ch. 11 |
| peritonitis | /ˌperɪtəˈnaɪtɪs/ | 腹膜炎 | Ch. 6 |
| pernasal | /pɜːˈneɪzl/ | 经鼻的 | Ch. 3 |
| peroral | /pɜːˈɔːrəl/ | 经口的 | Ch. 3 |
| phacolysis | /fəˈkɒləsɪs/ | 晶状体溶解 | Ch. 15 |
| phagocyte | /ˈfæɡəsaɪt/ | 吞噬细胞 | Ch. 8 |
| phagocytosis | /ˌfæɡəsaɪˈtəʊsɪs/ | 吞噬作用 | Ch. 8 |
| phalangeal | /feɪˈlændʒɪəl/ | 指骨的 | Ch. 13 |
| phalangectomy | /fælænˈdʒektəmɪ/ | 指骨切除术 | Ch. 13 |
| phallocampsis | /ˈfæləkæmpsɪs/ | 阴茎弯曲 | Ch. 12 |
| phalloplasty | /ˈfæləʊplæstɪ/ | 阴茎成形术 | Ch. 12 |

| | | | |
|---|---|---|---|
| pharmacist | /ˈfɑːməsɪst/ | 药剂师 | Ch. 2 |
| pharyngitis | /ˌfærɪnˈdʒaɪtɪs/ | 咽炎 | Ch. 5 |
| pharyngospasm | /færɪŋˈɡɒspæzəm/ | 咽痉挛 | Ch. 5 |
| pharyngotomy | /ˌfærɪŋˈɡɒtəmɪ/ | 咽切开术 | Ch. 5 |
| phlebectasia | /flɪbekˈteɪʒə/ | 静脉扩张 | Ch. 7 |
| phlebotomy | /fləˈbɒtəmɪ/ | 静脉切开术 | Ch. 7 |
| phonology | /fəˈnɒlədʒɪ/ | 语音学 | Ch. 5 |
| phosphopenia | /fɒsfəʊˈpiːnɪə/ | 磷质减少 | Ch. 10 |
| phosphorolysis | /fɒsfəˈrɒlɪsɪs/ | 磷酸解（作用） | Ch. 10 |
| phosphoruria | /fɒsfəˈrjʊərɪə/ | 磷尿 | Ch. 10 |
| photocoagulation | /ˌfəʊtəʊkəʊægjʊˈleɪʃən/ | （激）光焊接 | Ch. 15 |
| photophobia | /ˌfəʊtəˈfəʊbɪə/ | 恐光症，畏光 | Ch. 9, 15 |
| phrenalgia | /frɪˈnældʒɪə/ | 精神性痛 | Ch. 5 |
| phrenoptosis | /ˌfrenɒpˈtəʊsɪs/ | 膈下垂 | Ch. 5 |
| physician | /fɪˈzɪʃn/ | 内科医生 | Ch. 2 |
| phytogenesis | /faɪtəˈdʒenəsɪs/ | 植物发生论 | Ch. 8 |
| phytotoxin | /faɪtəˈtɒksɪn/ | 植物毒素 | Ch. 8 |
| piliform | /ˈpɪlɪfɔːm/ | 毛样的 | Ch. 14 |
| pilosebaceous | /paɪləʊsɪˈbeɪʃəs/ | 毛囊（腺）皮脂腺的 | Ch. 14 |
| pipette | /pɪˈpet/ | 移液管 | Ch. 11 |
| placentoma | /plæsenˈtəʊmə/ | 胎盘瘤 | Ch. 12 |
| placentopathy | /plæsənˈtɒpəθɪ/ | 胎盘病 | Ch. 12 |
| plasmapheresis | /ˌplæzməˈferɪsɪs/ | 血浆去除法 | Ch. 7 |
| platelet | /ˈpleɪtlət/ | 血小板 | Ch. 11 |
| plateletpheresis | /ˌplætəlɪtˈferɪsɪs/ | 血小板去除法 | Ch. 7 |
| pleuritis | /plʊəˈraɪtɪs/ | 胸膜炎 | Ch. 5 |
| pleurodesis | /plʊərəʊˈdiːsɪs/ | 胸膜固定术 | Ch. 13 |
| pneumatocardia | /ˌnjuːmətəʊˈkɑːdɪə/ | 心腔积气 | Ch. 5 |
| pneumatometry | /ˌnjuːməˈtɒmɪtrɪ/ | 呼吸气量测定法 | Ch. 5 |
| pneumectomy | /njuːˈmektəmɪ/ | 肺切除术 | Ch. 5 |
| pneumococcus | /ˌnjuːməˈkɒkəs/ | 肺炎球菌 | Ch. 5 |

## Appendix 1　Glossary

| | | | |
|---|---|---|---|
| pneumoconiosis | /ˌnjuːməˌkəʊniˈəʊsɪs/ | 肺尘埃沉着病 | Ch. 5 |
| pneumonia | /njuːˈməʊnɪə/ | 肺炎 | Ch. 5 |
| pneumothorax | /ˌnjuːməˈθɔːræks/ | 气胸 | Ch. 5 |
| pododynia | /ˌpɒdəˈdɪnjə/ | 足痛 | Ch. 13 |
| poikilocyte | /ˈpɔɪkɪləʊsaɪt/ | 异形红细胞 | Ch. 7 |
| poikilothrombocyte | /ˌpɔɪkɪləˈθrɒmbəsaɪt/ | 异形血小板 | Ch. 7 |
| poliomyelitis | /ˌpɒliəʊˌmaɪəˈlaɪtɪs/ | 脊髓灰质炎 | Ch. 9, 14 |
| polyarteritis | /ˌpɒliɑːtəˈraɪtɪs/ | 多发性动脉炎 | Ch. 7 |
| polyarthritis | /ˌpɒliɑːˈθraɪtɪs/ | 多发性关节炎 | Ch. 3 |
| polycyesis | /ˌpɒlisaɪˈiːsɪs/ | 多胎妊娠 | Ch. 12 |
| polycyte | /ˈpɒlisaɪt/ | 多形核细胞 | Ch. 3 |
| polydipsia | /ˌpɒlɪˈdɪpsɪə/ | 烦渴 | Ch. 11 |
| polymorphonuclear | /ˌpɒlɪˌmɔːfəˈnjuːklɪə/ | 多形核的 | Ch. 7 |
| polyneuritis | /ˌpɒlinjʊˈraɪtɪs/ | 多神经炎 | Ch. 9 |
| polyradiculitis | /ˌpɒlirədɪkjʊˈlaɪtɪs/ | 多神经根炎 | Ch. 9 |
| polysomnograph | /ˌpɒliˈsɒmnəʊɡræf/ | 多睡眠描计器 | Ch. 9 |
| polytrichia | /ˌpɒlɪˈtrɪkɪə/ | 多毛 | Ch. 14 |
| polyuresis | /ˌpɒlijʊˈrɪsɪs/ | 多尿 | Ch. 11 |
| polyuria | /ˌpɒlɪˈjuːrɪə/ | 多尿 | Ch. 11 |
| pontomedullary | /ˌpɒntəʊmɪˈdʌləri/ | 脑桥延髓的 | Ch. 9 |
| postauricular | /ˌpəʊstɔːˈrɪkjʊlə/ | 耳廓后的 | Ch. 15 |
| postcoital | /ˌpəʊstˈkɔɪtl/ | 性交后的 | Ch. 12 |
| posterior | /pəʊˈstɪərɪə/ | 后部的 | Ch. 4 |
| posteromedial | /ˌpəʊstərəʊˈmiːdɪəl/ | 后中的 | Ch. 4 |
| postmediastinal | /ˌpəʊstˌmiːdɪəˈstaɪnl/ | 纵隔后的 | Ch. 5 |
| postnatal | /ˌpəʊstˈneɪtl/ | 产后的 | Ch. 3 |
| postoperative | /ˌpəʊstˈɒpərətɪv/ | 术后的 | Ch. 3 |
| postprandial | /ˌpəʊstˈprændɪəl/ | 餐后的 | Ch. 6 |
| prediction | /prɪˈdɪkʃn/ | 预言 | Ch. 3 |
| premature | /ˈpremətʃər/ | 早产的 | Ch. 3 |
| presbyacusis | /ˌprezbɪəˈkjuːsɪs/ | 老年性聋 | Ch. 15 |

| | | | |
|---|---|---|---|
| presbyopia | /ˌprezbiˈəʊpɪə/ | 老花眼 | Ch. 15 |
| prespondylolisthesis | /prɪspɒndɪləʊlɪsˈθiːsɪs/ | 脊椎前移 | Ch. 13 |
| primigravida | /prɪmɪˈɡrævɪdə/ | 初孕妇 | Ch. 12 |
| primipara | /prɪˈmɪpərə/ | 初产妇 | Ch. 12 |
| proctology | /prɒkˈtɒlədʒɪ/ | 肛肠病学 | Ch. 6 |
| proctoscope | /ˈprɒktəskəʊp/ | 直肠镜 | Ch. 6 |
| prognosis | /prɒɡˈnəʊsɪs/ | 预后 | Ch. 3 |
| prolactin | /prəʊˈlæktɪn/ | 泌乳刺激素 | Ch. 10 |
| prophylaxis | /ˌprɒfɪˈlæksɪs/ | 预防 | Ch. 3 |
| prostatodynia | /prɒstətəʊˈdɪnjə/ | 前列腺痛 | Ch. 12 |
| prostatomegaly | /prɒsteɪtəʊˈmeɡəlɪ/ | 前列腺肥大 | Ch. 12 |
| protease | /ˈprəʊtɪeɪz/ | 蛋白酶 | Ch. 6 |
| proteolytic | /prəʊtɪəˈlɪtɪk/ | 水解蛋白的 | Ch. 6 |
| proteopepsis | /prəʊtɪəˈpepsɪs/ | 蛋白消化 | Ch. 6 |
| proximolabial | /ˌprɒksɪməˈleɪbɪəl/ | 邻唇的 | Ch. 4 |
| proximolingual | /ˌprɒksɪməʊˈlɪŋɡwəl/ | 邻舌的 | Ch. 4 |
| pseudocyesis | /ˌsjuːdəʊsaɪˈiːsɪs/ | 假妊娠 | Ch. 12 |
| pseudomyopia | /sjuːdəʊmaɪˈəʊpɪə/ | 假性近视 | Ch. 12 |
| pseudosmia | /ˈsjuːdəʊzmɪə/ | 嗅幻觉 | Ch. 5 |
| psychiatrist | /saɪˈkaɪətrɪst/ | 精神料医生 | Ch. 9 |
| psychiatry | /saɪˈkaɪətrɪ/ | 精神病学 | Ch. 2 |
| psychologist | /saɪˈkɒlədʒɪst/ | 心理学家 | Ch. 9 |
| psychology | /saɪˈkɒlədʒɪ/ | 心理学 | Ch. 2 |
| psychosis | /saɪˈkəʊsɪs/ | 精神病 | Ch. 2 |
| psychosomatic | /ˌsaɪkəʊsəˈmætɪk/ | 身心的 | Ch. 9 |
| pubarche | /ˈpjʊbɑːkɪ/ | 阴毛初生 | Ch. 12 |
| pulmonology | /ˌpʌlməˈnɒlədʒɪ/ | 肺(病)学 | Ch. 5 |
| pupillography | /pjuːpɪˈlɒɡrəfɪ/ | 瞳孔测定术 | Ch. 15 |
| pupillotonia | /pjuːpɪləˈtəʊnjə/ | 瞳孔紧张症 | Ch. 15 |
| purpura | /ˈpɜːpjʊrə/ | 紫癜 | Ch. 14 |
| purpuriferous | /pɜːpjʊˈrɪfərəs/ | 生视紫素的 | Ch. 14 |

Appendix 1  Glossary

| | | | |
|---|---|---|---|
| pyelonephritis | /paɪələʊnɪˈfraɪtɪs/ | 肾盂肾炎 | Ch. 11 |
| pyelotomy | /paɪəˈləʊtəmɪ/ | 肾盂切开术 | Ch. 11 |
| pyloroplasty | /paɪˈlɔːrəˌplæstɪ/ | 幽门成形术 | Ch. 6 |
| pylorostenosis | /paɪˌlɒrəʊstɪˈnəʊsɪs/ | 幽门狭窄 | Ch. 6 |
| pyoderma | /paɪəʊˈdɜːmə/ | 脓皮病 | Ch. 14 |
| pyogenic | /paɪəʊˈdʒenɪk/ | 化脓的 | Ch. 5 |
| pyoptysis | /ˌpaɪˈɒptɪsɪs/ | 咯脓 | Ch. 5 |
| pyosalpinx | /paɪəʊˈsælpɪŋks/ | 输卵管积脓 | Ch. 12 |
| pyothorax | /paɪəʊˈθɔːræks/ | 脓胸 | Ch. 5 |

Q

| | | | |
|---|---|---|---|
| quadrant | /ˈkwɒdrənt/ | 象限 | Ch. 3 |
| quadriceps | /ˈkwɒdrɪseps/ | 四头肌 | Ch. 3 |

R

| | | | |
|---|---|---|---|
| rachiocentesis | /rækɪəʊsenˈtiːsɪs/ | 椎管穿刺 | Ch. 13 |
| rachiodynia | /rækɪəʊˈdɪnɪə/ | 脊柱痛 | Ch. 13 |
| radial | /ˈreɪdɪəl/ | 桡骨的 | Ch. 13 |
| radiculalgia | /rædɪkjʊˈlældʒɪə/ | 神经根痛 | Ch. 9 |
| radiographer | /ˌreɪdɪˈɒgrəfə/ | 放射线技师 | Ch. 2 |
| radiologist | /ˌreɪdɪˈɒlədʒɪst/ | 放射学专家 | Ch. 8 |
| radiotherapy | /ˌreɪdɪəʊˈθerəpɪ/ | 放射疗法 | Ch. 8 |
| rectocele | /ˈrektəˌsiːl/ | 脱肛 | Ch. 6 |
| researcher | /rɪˈsɜːtʃə/ | 研究人员 | Ch. 2 |
| respiration | /ˌrespəˈreɪʃn/ | 呼吸 | Ch. 5 |
| retinopathy | /retɪˈnɒpəθɪ/ | 视网膜病 | Ch. 15 |
| retinoschisis | /ˈretɪnɒskɪsɪs/ | 视网膜剥离 | Ch. 15 |
| retrocochlear | /retrəʊˈkɒklɪər/ | 耳蜗后的 | Ch. 15 |
| retroesophageal | /retrəʊɪˈsɒfədʒiːəl/ | 食管后的 | Ch. 6 |
| retroperitoneal | /retrəʊperɪtəʊˈniːəl/ | 腹膜后的 | Ch. 11 |
| retrovesical | /retrəʊˈvesɪkəl/ | 膀胱后的 | Ch. 11 |
| reversion | /rɪˈvɜːʃn/ | 逆转 | Ch. 4 |
| rhinalgia | /ˌraɪˈnældʒɪə/ | 鼻痛 | Ch. 5 |

| | | | |
|---|---|---|---|
| rhinolithiasis | /ˌraɪnəlɪˈθaɪəsɪs/ | 鼻石病 | Ch. 11 |
| rhinopathy | /raɪˈnɒpəθɪ/ | 鼻病 | Ch. 5 |
| rhinoplasty | /ˈraɪnəʊˌplæstɪ/ | 鼻成形术 | Ch. 2 |
| rhinorrhagia | /ˌraɪnəˈreɪdʒɪə/ | 鼻出血 | Ch. 7 |
| rhinorrhea | /ˌraɪnərɪə/ | 鼻液溢 | Ch. 5 |
| rubella | /ruːˈbelə/ | 风疹 | Ch. 14 |

**S**

| | | | |
|---|---|---|---|
| saccharase | /ˈsækəreɪs/ | 蔗糖酶 | Ch. 10 |
| sacchariferous | /ˌsækəˈrɪfərəs/ | 产生糖的 | Ch. 10 |
| sacrolisthesis | /ˌseɪkrəˈlɪsθəsɪs/ | 骶骨滑脱 | Ch. 13 |
| sacrolumbar | /ˌseɪkrəˈlʌmbər/ | 腰骶的 | Ch. 13 |
| salpingo-ovaritis | /ˌsælpɪŋɡəʊəʊvæˈrɪtɪs/ | 输卵管卵巢炎 | Ch. 12 |
| salpingopexy | /sælˈpɪŋɡəʊpeksɪ/ | 输卵管固定术 | Ch. 12 |
| salpingopharyngeal | /sælpɪŋɡəfæˈrɪndʒiːəl/ | 咽鼓管咽的 | Ch. 15 |
| salpingoscope | /ˈsælpɪŋɡəʊskəʊp/ | 咽鼓管镜 | Ch. 15 |
| sarcoma | /sɑːˈkəʊmə/ | 肉瘤 | Ch. 8, 13 |
| sarcotome | /ˈsɑːkətəʊm/ | 肌刀 | Ch. 13 |
| scapulodynia | /ˌskæpjʊləˈdɪnɪə/ | 肩胛痛 | Ch. 13 |
| scapulopexy | /ˌskæpjʊləˈpeksɪ/ | 肩胛固定术 | Ch. 13 |
| schizophasia | /ˌskɪzəʊˈfeɪzɪə/ | 杂语症 | Ch. 9 |
| schizophrenia | /ˌskɪzəʊˈfriːnɪə/ | 精神分裂症 | Ch. 9 |
| scleroderma | /ˌsklɪərəˈdɜːmə/ | 硬皮病 | Ch. 14 |
| scleroiritis | /sklɪərəʊaɪˈraɪtɪs/ | 巩膜虹膜炎 | Ch. 15 |
| scleromalacia | /sklɪərəʊməˈleɪʃɪə/ | 巩膜软化 | Ch. 15 |
| scoliosis | /ˌskəʊlɪˈəʊsɪs/ | 脊柱侧凸 | Ch. 13 |
| scrotal | /ˈskrəʊtəl/ | 阴囊的 | Ch. 12 |
| sebaceous | /sɪˈbeɪʃəs/ | 脂肪的 | Ch. 14 |
| seborrhea | /ˌsɪbəˈriːə/ | 皮脂溢 | Ch. 14 |
| semilunar | /ˌsemɪˈluːnə/ | 半月形的 | Ch. 3 |
| seminiferous | /ˌsemɪˈnɪfərəs/ | 输精的 | Ch. 12 |
| septostomy | /sepˈtɒstəmɪ/ | 房间隔造口术 | Ch. 7 |

## Appendix 1  Glossary

| | | | |
|---|---|---|---|
| sialoadenectomy | /ˌsləudˈnektəmɪ/ | 涎腺切除术 | Ch. 6 |
| sialoadenotomy | /sˈləudenəutəmɪ/ | 涎腺切开术 | Ch. 6 |
| sialoangiitis | /sɪəˌləuændʒɪaɪtɪz/ | 涎管炎 | Ch. 6 |
| sialoangiography | /sɪələuændʒɪˈəugrəfɪ/ | 涎管造影术 | Ch. 6 |
| sialography | /saɪəˈlɒgrəfɪ/ | 涎管造影术 | Ch. 6 |
| sialolith | /saɪˈæləlɪθ/ | 涎石 | Ch. 6 |
| sialorrhea | /sɪəlɒˈrɪə/ | 流涎 | Ch. 6 |
| sibling | /ˈsɪblɪŋ/ | 兄弟姐妹 | Ch. 11 |
| siderogenous | /ˌsaɪdərədʒənəs/ | 生成铁的 | Ch. 10 |
| sideropenia | /ˌsaɪdərəuˈpiːnɪə/ | 铁缺乏 | Ch. 10 |
| siderophil | /ˈsɪdərəfɪl/ | 嗜铁的 | Ch. 7 |
| sigmoidopexy | /sɪgmɔɪdəuˈpeksɪ/ | 乙状结肠固定术 | Ch. 6 |
| sinistrocerebral | /sɪnɪstrəuˈserɪbrəl/ | 左脑的 | Ch. 15 |
| sinistrocular | /sɪnɪsˈtrɒkjulə/ | 惯用左眼的 | Ch. 15 |
| sinusitis | /ˌsaɪnəˈsaɪtɪs/ | 鼻窦炎 | Ch. 5 |
| somatocyte | /ˈsəumətəˌsaɪt/ | 体细胞 | Ch. 4, 10 |
| somatopathy | /ˌsəuməˈtɒpəθɪ/ | 躯体病 | Ch. 10 |
| somatotropin | /ˌsəumətəuˈtrəupɪn/ | 生长激素 | Ch. 10 |
| somatotype | /ˈsəumətəutaɪp/ | 体型(体式) | Ch. 9 |
| somnambulism | /sɒmˈnæmbjulɪzəm/ | 梦游病 | Ch. 9 |
| somnolence | /ˈsɒmnələns/ | 嗜睡 | Ch. 9 |
| spermatogenic | /ˌspɜːmətəˈdʒenɪk/ | 精子发生的 | Ch. 12 |
| spermatopathy | /spɜːməˈtɔːpəθɪ/ | 精液病 | Ch. 12 |
| spermolysis | /spɜːˈmɒlɪsɪs/ | 精子溶解 | Ch. 12 |
| sphygmology | /sfɪgˈmɒlədʒɪ/ | 脉搏学 | Ch. 7 |
| sphygmomanometer | /ˌsfɪgməuməˈnɒmɪtə/ | 血压计 | Ch. 7 |
| spinitis | /ˈspaɪnaɪtɪs/ | 脊髓炎 | Ch. 4 |
| spinogram | /ˈspaɪnəugræm/ | 脊髓造影片 | Ch. 4 |
| spirometer | /ˌspaɪˈrɒmɪtə/ | 肺量计 | Ch. 5 |
| splenomalacia | /ˌsplenəuməˈleɪʃɪə/ | 脾软化 | Ch. 8 |
| spondyloarthropathy | /ˌspɒndɪləuɑːˈθrɒpəθɪ/ | 脊椎关节病 | Ch. 13 |

| | | | |
|---|---|---|---|
| spondylodesis | /ˌspɒndɪləʊˈdiːsɪs/ | 脊柱制动术 | Ch. 13 |
| spondylolisthesis | /ˌspɒndɪləʊlɪsˈθiːsɪs/ | 脊椎滑脱 | Ch. 13 |
| spondylolysis | /ˌspɒndɪˈlɒlɪsɪs/ | 椎骨脱离 | Ch. 13 |
| spondyloschisis | /ˌspɒndɪləʊˈskiːsɪs/ | 椎裂 | Ch. 13 |
| spongiform | /ˈspʌndʒɪfɔːm/ | 海绵状的 | Ch. 2 |
| squamatization | /ˌskwəmətaɪˈzeɪʃn/ | 鳞状化 | Ch. 14 |
| squamous | /ˈskweɪməs/ | 有鳞的 | Ch. 14 |
| stapedectomy | /ˌstæpɪˈdektəmɪ/ | 镫骨切除术 | Ch. 15 |
| stapedolysis | /ˌstæpiːˈdɒlɪsɪs/ | 镫骨松解术 | Ch. 15 |
| staphylectomy | /ˌstæfɪˈlektəmɪ/ | 悬雍垂切除术 | Ch. 5 |
| staphyledema | /ˌstæfɪlɪˈdiːmə/ | 悬雍垂水肿 | Ch. 5 |
| staphylococcus | /ˌstæfɪləˈkɒkəs/ | 葡萄球菌 | Ch. 8 |
| steatolysis | /ˌstiːəˈtɒləsɪs/ | 脂肪分解 | Ch. 6 |
| steatoma | /ˌstiːəˈtəʊmə/ | 皮脂囊肿 | Ch. 14 |
| steatorrhea | /ˌstɪətəˈrɪə/ | 皮脂溢 | Ch. 6,14 |
| sternopericardia | /ˌstɜːnəˌperɪˈkɑːdɪə/ | 胸骨心包 | Ch. 13 |
| sternovertebral | /ˌstɜːnəˈvɜːtəbrəl/ | 胸骨椎骨的 | Ch. 13 |
| stethalgia | /ˌsteˈθældʒɪə/ | 胸痛 | Ch. 5 |
| stethoscope | /ˈsteθəuskəup/ | 听诊器 | Ch. 5 |
| stomatitis | /ˌstəʊməˈtaɪtɪs/ | 口腔炎 | Ch. 6 |
| stomatoglossitis | /stəˌmætəuglɒˈsaɪtɪs/ | 口舌炎 | Ch. 6 |
| stomatopathy | /stəˈmætəpəθɪ/ | 口腔病 | Ch. 6 |
| streptococcus | /ˌstreptəˈkɒkəs/ | 链球菌 | Ch. 8 |
| subconjunctival | /sʌbkənˈdʒʌŋktaɪvl/ | 结膜下的 | Ch. 15 |
| subcortical | /ˌsʌbˈkɔːtɪkəl/ | 皮质下的 | Ch. 9 |
| subcutaneous | /ˌsʌbkjuˈteɪnɪəs/ | 皮下的 | Ch. 14 |
| subdiaphragmatic | /sʌbˌdaɪəfrægˈmætɪk/ | 膈下的 | Ch. 5 |
| subdural | /sʌbˈdjʊərəl/ | 硬膜下的 | Ch. 9 |
| subhepatic | /sʌbhɪˈpætɪk/ | 肝下的 | Ch. 3 |
| sublingual | /sʌbˈlɪŋgwəl/ | 舌下的;舌下腺的 | Ch. 3, 6 |
| submandibular | /sʌbmænˈdɪbjʊlə/ | 下颚下的 | Ch. 13 |

# Appendix 1  Glossary

| | | | |
|---|---|---|---|
| subumbilical | /ˌsjuːˈbʌmbɪlaɪkl/ | 脐下的 | Ch. 4 |
| subungual | /səˈbʌgwəl/ | 甲下的 | Ch. 14 |
| sudoriferous | /ˌsjuːdəˈrɪfərəs/ | 分泌汗的 | Ch. 14 |
| sudorific | /ˌsjuːdəˈrɪfɪk/ | 使发汗的 | Ch. 14 |
| supracerebellar | /ˌsjuːprəˌserɪˈbelə/ | 小脑上的 | Ch. 9 |
| supraclavicular | /ˌsjuːprəkləˈvɪkjʊlə/ | 锁骨上的 | Ch. 13 |
| supraduction | /ˌsjuːprəˈdʌkʃn/ | 上转 | Ch. 3 |
| supragingival | /ˌsjuːprədʒɪnˈdʒaɪvəl/ | 牙龈缘上的 | Ch. 6 |
| supranasal | /ˌsjuːprəˈneɪzl/ | 鼻上的 | Ch. 3 |
| suprarenal | /ˌsuːprəˈriːnl/ | 肾上的 | Ch. 11 |
| supraspinal | /ˌsjuːprəˈspaɪnəl/ | 脊椎上的 | Ch. 9 |
| supraventricular | /ˌsjʊprəvenˈtrɪkjʊlə/ | 室上的 | Ch. 9 |
| symbiosis | /ˌsɪmbaɪˈəʊsɪs/ | 共生 | Ch. 3 |
| symphysis | /ˈsɪmfəsɪs/ | （骨）联合 | Ch. 13 |
| synchronous | /ˈsɪŋkrənəs/ | 同步的 | Ch. 3 |
| syndactyly | /sɪnˈdæktɪlɪ/ | 并指 | Ch. 13 |
| syndesmectomy | /ˌsɪndɪzˈmektəmɪ/ | 韧带切除术 | Ch. 13 |
| syndesmoma | /ˌsɪndzˈməʊmə/ | 韧带瘤,结缔组织瘤 | Ch. 13 |
| syndrome | /ˈsɪndrəʊm/ | 综合征 | Ch. 3 |
| synergy | /ˈsɪnədʒɪ/ | 协同作用 | Ch. 3 |
| synovioblast | /sɪˈnəʊvɪəblæst/ | 成滑膜细胞 | Ch. 13 |
| synoviotomy | /ˌsɪnəʊvɪˈɒtəmɪ/ | 滑膜切开 | Ch. 13 |
| synthermal | /sɪnˈθɜːml/ | 等温的 | Ch. 3 |

**T**

| | | | |
|---|---|---|---|
| tachyarrhythmia | /ˌtækɪəˈrɪθəmɪə/ | 快速性心律失常 | Ch. 7 |
| tachypnea | /ˌtækɪpˈniːə/ | 呼吸急促 | Ch. 7 |
| tarsomegaly | /ˌtɑːrsəˈmegəlɪ/ | 巨跟骨 | Ch. 13 |
| tarsoptosis | /ˌtɑːsəˈptəʊsɪs/ | 扁平足 | Ch. 13 |
| tendinitis | /ˌtendɪˈnaɪtɪs/ | 腱炎 | Ch. 13 |
| tendinoplasty | /ˈtendɪnɒˌplæstɪ/ | 腱成形术 | Ch. 13 |
| tenodynia | /ˌtenəˈdɪnɪə/ | 腱痛 | Ch. 13 |

| | | | |
|---|---|---|---|
| tenorrhaphy | /tɪˈnɔːrəfɪ/ | 腱缝合术 | Ch. 13 |
| teratoid | /ˈterətɔɪd/ | 畸胎样的 | Ch. 12 |
| teratoma | /ˌterəˈtəʊmə/ | 畸胎瘤 | Ch. 12 |
| testicular | /tesˈtɪkjʊlə(r)/ | 睾丸的 | Ch. 12 |
| tetradactyly | /ˌtetrəˈdæktɪlɪ/ | 四指(趾)畸形 | Ch. 3 |
| tetrahedron | /ˌtetrəˈhiːdrən/ | 四面体 | Ch. 3 |
| thalamotomy | /ˌθæləˈmɒtəmɪ/ | 丘脑切开术 | Ch. 9 |
| thermometer | /θɜːˈmɒmɪtə/ | 体温计 | Ch. 2 |
| thermoregulation | /ˌθɜːməʊˌregjʊˈleɪʃn/ | 温度调节 | Ch. 14 |
| thoracoabdominal | /ˌθɔːrəkəʊæbˈdɒmɪnəl/ | 胸腹的 | Ch. 4 |
| thoracocentesis | /ˌθɔːrəkəʊsenˈtiːsɪs/ | 胸腔穿刺术 | Ch. 2, 5 |
| thoracodidymus | /ˌθɔːrəkəʊˈdɪdɪməs/ | 胸部联胎 | Ch. 12 |
| thoracoscope | /θɒˈrækəskəʊp/ | 胸腔镜 | Ch. 5 |
| thoracotomy | /ˌθɔːrəˈkɒtəmɪ/ | 胸廓切开术 | Ch. 4 |
| thrombolytic | /θrɒmbəʊˈlɪtɪk/ | 溶解血栓的 | Ch. 7 |
| thrombosis | /θrɒmˈbəʊsɪs/ | 血栓栓塞 | Ch. 7 |
| thymoma | /θaɪˈməʊmə/ | 胸腺瘤 | Ch. 8 |
| thymotoxic | /ˌθaɪməʊˈtɒksɪk/ | 胸腺毒性的 | Ch. 8 |
| thyrocardiac | /ˌθaɪrəkɑːdɪæk/ | 甲状腺心脏的 | Ch. 10 |
| thyroidopathy | /ˌθaɪrɔɪˈdɒpəθɪ/ | 甲状腺病 | Ch. 10 |
| thyromegaly | /ˌθaɪrəˈmegəlɪ/ | 甲状腺巨大 | Ch. 10 |
| thyroprivia | /ˌθaɪrəˈprɪvɪə/ | 甲状腺缺乏症 | Ch. 10 |
| tibialgia | /tɪbɪˈældʒɪə/ | 胫骨痛 | Ch. 13 |
| tibiofemoral | /tɪbɪəˈfemərəl/ | 胫股的 | Ch. 13 |
| tocophobia | /təʊkəʊˈfəʊbɪə/ | 分娩恐怖 | Ch. 12 |
| tonometer | /təʊˈnɒmɪtə/ | 张力计 | Ch. 9 |
| tonsillectomy | /ˌtɒnsəˈlektəmɪ/ | 扁桃腺切除术 | Ch. 8 |
| tonsillitis | /ˌtɒnsəˈlaɪtɪs/ | 扁桃体炎 | Ch. 8 |
| torsiometer | /tɔːsɪˈɒmɪtə/ | 扭转测量器 | Ch. 4 |
| toxemia | /tɒksˈiːmɪə/ | 血毒症 | Ch. 10 |
| toxicodermatitis | /ˌtɒksɪkəʊdɜːməˈtaɪtɪs/ | 中毒性皮炎 | Ch. 10 |

# Appendix 1  Glossary

| | | | |
|---|---|---|---|
| toxicology | /ˌtɒksɪˈkɒlədʒi/ | 毒物学 | Ch. 10 |
| tracheostenosis | /trækiːəʊstɪˈnəʊsɪs/ | 气管狭窄 | Ch. 5 |
| tracheotome | /ˈtrækɪətəʊm/ | 气管刀 | Ch. 5 |
| transanal | /trænˈzeɪnl/ | 经肛的 | Ch. 6 |
| transdermal | /ˌtrænsˈdɜːməl/ | 经皮的 | Ch. 3 |
| transfer | /ˌtrænsˈfɜː/ | 迁移 | Ch. 3 |
| transnasal | /trænsˈneɪsəl/ | 经鼻的 | Ch. 11 |
| transurethral | /trænsjʊˈriːθrəl/ | 经尿道的 | Ch. 11 |
| triad | /ˈtraɪˌæd/ | 三联的 | Ch. 3 |
| triceps | /ˈtraɪseps/ | 三头肌 | Ch. 3 |
| trichosis | /trɪˈkəʊsɪs/ | （毛）发病 | Ch. 14 |
| trigonitis | /traɪɡəˈnaɪtɪs/ | 膀胱三角区炎 | Ch. 11 |
| tubular | /ˈtjuːbjələ/ | 管样的 | Ch. 11 |
| tubulopathy | /tjuːbjʊˈləʊpəθɪ/ | 肾小管病 | Ch. 11 |
| tympanocentesis | /tɪmpænəʊˈsentiːsɪs/ | 鼓膜穿刺术 | Ch. 15 |
| tympanometry | /tɪmpæˈnɒmɪtrɪ/ | 鼓室测压法 | Ch. 15 |
| **U** | | | |
| ulnocarpal | /ʌlnəˈkɑːpəl/ | 尺腕的 | Ch. 13 |
| ulnoradial | /ʌlnəˈreɪdɪəl/ | 尺桡的 | Ch. 13 |
| ultrasonic | /ˌʌltrəˈsɒnɪk/ | 超声波的 | Ch. 3 |
| ultrasonogram | /ˌʌltrəˈsɒnəɡræm/ | 超声记录图 | Ch. 3 |
| umbilical | /ʌmˈbɪlɪkl/ | 脐带的 | Ch. 4, 12 |
| unbalance | /ʌnˈbæləns/ | 失衡；精神紊乱 | Ch. 3 |
| unconscious | /ʌnˈkɒnʃəs/ | 失去知觉的 | Ch. 3 |
| ungual | /ˈʌŋɡwəl/ | 指（趾）甲的 | Ch. 14 |
| unilateral | /ˌjuːnɪˈlætərəl/ | 单侧的 | Ch. 3, 4 |
| ureteroplasty | /juːriːtərəˈplæstɪ/ | 输尿管成形术 | Ch. 11 |
| ureterorrhaphy | /juːriːtˈrɒrəfɪ/ | 输尿管缝术 | Ch. 11 |
| ureterostenosis | /juːriːtərəsteˈnəʊsɪs/ | 输尿管狭窄 | Ch. 11 |
| urethrocystitis | /juːreθrəsɪsˈtaɪtɪs/ | 尿道膀胱炎 | Ch. 11 |
| urethrodynia | /juːreθrəˈdɪnɪə/ | 尿道痛 | Ch. 11 |

| | | | |
|---|---|---|---|
| urethrorrhaphy | /juːrəˈθɒrəfɪ/ | 尿道缝术 | Ch. 11 |
| urethrorrhexia | /juːrəθɒˈrɪksɪə/ | 尿道破裂 | Ch. 11 |
| uroazotometer | /juːrəˌeɪˈzəʊtəʊmɪtə/ | 尿氮测量计 | Ch. 11 |
| urolithiasis | /juːrəʊlɪˈθaɪəsɪs/ | 尿石病 | Ch. 11 |
| urology | /juːˈrɒlədʒɪ/ | 泌尿学 | Ch. 11 |
| uropenia | /juːrəʊˈpiːnɪə/ | 尿过少 | Ch. 11 |
| uropoiesis | /juːrəˈpɔiːsɪs/ | 尿生成 | Ch. 11 |
| uterine | /ˈjuːtəraɪn/ | 子宫的 | Ch. 12 |
| uveitis | /ˌjuːvɪˈaɪtɪs/ | 眼色素层炎 | Ch. 15 |
| uveoscleritis | /juːvɪəʊsklɪəˈraɪtɪs/ | 眼色素层巩膜炎 | Ch. 15 |
| uvular | /ˈjuːvjʊlə/ | 悬雍垂的 | Ch. 5 |
| uvulitis | /ˌjuːvjʊˈlaɪtɪs/ | 悬雍垂炎 | Ch. 5 |

**V**

| | | | |
|---|---|---|---|
| vaginectomy | /vædʒɪˈnektəmɪ/ | 阴道切除术 | Ch. 12 |
| valvotomy | /ˈvælvəʊtəmɪ/ | 瓣膜切开术 | Ch. 7 |
| valvuloplasty | /ˌvælvjʊləˈplæstɪ/ | 瓣膜成形术 | Ch. 7 |
| varicocele | /ˈværɪkəʊsiːl/ | 精索静脉曲张 | Ch. 12 |
| varicocelectomy | /værɪkəʊsɪˈlektəmɪ/ | 精索曲张静脉切除术 | Ch. 12 |
| vasculopathy | /ˈvæskjʊləʊpəθɪ/ | 血管病变 | Ch. 7 |
| vasectomy | /vəˈsektəmɪ/ | 输精管切除 | Ch. 12 |
| vasoconstriction | /ˌveɪzəʊkənˈstrɪkʃn/ | 血管收缩 | Ch. 7 |
| vasospasm | /ˈveɪzəʊˌspæzəm/ | 血管痉挛 | Ch. 7 |
| vasovasostomy | /væsəʊvəˈsɒstəmɪ/ | 输精管吻合术 | Ch. 12 |
| venogram | /ˈvenəgræm/ | 静脉造影 | Ch. 7 |
| ventrad | /ˈventræd/ | 向腹部 | Ch. 4 |
| ventriculometry | /ventrɪkjʊˈlɒmɪtrɪ/ | 脑室压测量术 | Ch. 9 |
| ventriculoscopy | /venˌtrɪkjʊˈlɒskəpɪ/ | 心（脑）室镜检查 | Ch. 7 |
| ventroscopy | /venˈtrɒskəpɪ/ | 腹腔镜检查 | Ch. 4 |
| venular | /ˈvenjʊlə/ | 小静脉的 | Ch. 7 |
| venule | /ˈvenjuːl/ | 细静脉 | Ch. 11 |
| venulitis | /ˌvenjʊˈlaɪtɪs/ | 小静脉炎 | Ch. 7 |

| | | | |
|---|---|---|---|
| vertebrocostal | /vɜːtɪbrəʊˈkɒstəl/ | 椎肋的 | Ch. 13 |
| vertebrosternal | /vɜːtɪbrəʊˈstənl/ | 椎骨胸骨的 | Ch. 13 |
| vesicoclysis | /vesɪkəʊˈklɪsɪs/ | 膀胱灌洗术 | Ch. 11 |
| vesicorectal | /ˌvesɪkəʊˌrektl/ | 膀胱直肠的 | Ch. 11 |
| vesicostomy | /vesɪˈkɒstəmɪ/ | 膀胱造口术 | Ch. 11 |
| vesiculogram | /vəˈsɪkjʊləɡræm/ | 精囊造影照片 | Ch. 12 |
| vesiculotomy | /vəsɪkjʊˈlɔːtəmɪ/ | 精囊切开术 | Ch. 12 |
| vestibular | /vesˈtɪbjʊlə/ | 前庭的 | Ch. 15 |
| vestibulopathy | /vestɪbjʊˈləʊpəθɪ/ | 前庭病 | Ch. 15 |
| viremia | /vaɪˈriːmɪə/ | 病毒血症 | Ch. 8 |
| visceral | /ˈvɪsərəl/ | 内脏的 | Ch. 4 |
| visceroptosis | /ˌvɪsərəʊˈptəʊsɪs/ | 内脏下垂 | Ch. 4 |
| vitrectomy | /vɪˈtrektəmɪ/ | 玻璃体切除术 | Ch. 15 |
| vitreous | /ˈvɪtrɪəs/ | 玻璃的 | Ch. 15 |

**X**

| | | | |
|---|---|---|---|
| xanthoderma | /zænθəˈdɜːmə/ | 皮肤黄变 | Ch. 14 |
| xeroderma | /ˌzerəʊˈdɜːmə/ | 皮肤干燥症 | Ch. 14 |
| xerostomia | /ˌzerəʊˈstəʊmjə/ | 口腔干燥 | Ch. 14 |

**Z**

| | | | |
|---|---|---|---|
| zoosperm | /ˈzəʊəspɜːm/ | 游动精子 | Ch. 12 |

# Appendix 2  Medical Word Elements and Their Meanings

**A**

| | |
|---|---|
| a- | not, without /28 |
| ab- | away from /34 |
| abdomin/o | abdomen /50,84 |
| -ac | pertaining to /18 |
| acetabul/o | acetabulum, part of hipbone /213 |
| acous/o | sound; hearing /248 |
| acr/o | tip, top, extremitiy /52,160 |
| acromi/o | acromion, extension of the shoulder bone /211 |
| -acusia | hearing condition /250 |
| -acusis | hearing condition /250 |
| -ad | toward /19 |
| ad- | toward /34 |
| adenoid/o | adenoids /119 |
| adip/o | adipose, fat /52,233 |
| adren/o | adrenal glands /155 |
| adrenal/o | adrenal glands /155 |
| -agogue | inducing, leading /159 |
| -al | pertaining to /18 |
| albin/o | white /235 |
| albumin/o | albumin /177 |
| -algia | pain /11 |
| alveol/o | alveolus, tooth socket, air sac /65,81 |
| ambly/o | dull, dim /251 |
| ambul/o | walking /141 |
| amni/o | amnion /196 |
| amphi- | both, around /220 |
| amyl/o | starch /89 |
| an- | not, without /28 |
| an/o | anus /84 |
| ana- | up, back, again /38 |
| andr/o | androgen, male /157,191 |
| angi/o | vessel /104 |
| anis/o | unequal /251 |
| ankyl/o | stiff, adhesion /220 |
| ant(i)- | against /28 |
| ante- | before, forward /31 |
| anter/o | front /54 |
| aort/o | aorta /105 |
| -apheresis | removal /109 |
| append/o | appendix /84 |
| appendic/o | appendix /84 |
| -ar | pertaining to /18 |
| -arche | first /198 |
| arter/o | artery /105 |
| arteri/o | artery /105 |
| arteriol/o | arteriole, small artery /105 |
| arthr/o | joints /217 |
| articul/o | joints /217 |

## Appendix 2  Medical Word Elements and Their Meanings

| | | | |
|---|---|---|---|
| -ary | pertaining to /18 | **C** | |
| -ase | enzyme /90 | calc/i | calcium /161 |
| -asthenia | weakness, debility /143 | calc/o | calcium /161 |
| astr/o | stars haped /136 | calcane/o | calcaneus, heel bone /213 |
| atel/o | imperfect, defective /68 | cal/i | calyx, cup /171 |
| ather/o | fatty plaque /105 | calic/o | calyx, cup /171 |
| atri/o | atrium /102 | capn/o | carbon dioxide /68 |
| audi/o | hearing /248 | carb/o | carbon /161 |
| aur/o | ear, ear-like structure /249 | carcin/o | cancer /124 |
| auricul/o | ear, ear-like structure /249 | cardi/o | heart /102 |
| auto- | self /38 | carp/o | carpus, wrist /211 |
| azot/o | urea, nitrogen /177 | cata- | down /38 |
| **B** | | caud/o | cauda, tail /49 |
| bacill/i | bacillus (pl. bacilli), rod-shaped bacterium /122 | cec/o | cecum /84 |
| | | -cele | hernia, protrusion /11 |
| bacteri/o | bacterium (pl. bacteria) /122 | celi/o | abdomen /84 |
| balan/o | glans (head) penis /189 | centi- | hundred, one hundredth /36 |
| bas/o | base /107 | -centesis | surgical puncture /14 |
| ben(e)- | good /38 | cephal/o | head /49 |
| bi- | two, double /36 | cerebell/o | cerebellum /138 |
| bil/i | bile /89 | cerebr/o | cerebrum /138 |
| bilirubin/o | bilirubin, bile pigment /89 | cervic/o | uterine cervix, neck /50,193, 209 |
| -blast | embryonic cells /121 | | |
| blenn/o | mucus, pus /191 | cheil/o | lip /81 |
| blephar/o | eyelid /244 | chem/o | chemistry, drug /124 |
| brachi/o | arm /209 | -chezia | defecation, elimination of wastes /91 |
| brady- | slow /103 | | |
| bronch/o | bronchus, bronchial tube (pl. bronchi) /63 | chir/o | hand /209 |
| | | chlor/o | green /235 |
| bronchi/o | bronchus, bronchial tube (pl. bronchi) /63 | chol/e | bile /89 |
| | | cholangi/o | bile vessel /84 |
| bronchiol/o | bronchiole, small bronchus /63 | cholecyst/o | gallbladder /84 |
| bucc/o | cheek /81 | choledoch/o | common bile duct /85 |
| burs/o | bursa /217 | chondr/o | cartilage /209 |

| | | | |
|---|---|---|---|
| chori/o | choroids /244 | cost/o | rib /211 |
| choroid/o | choroids /244 | counter- | against, opposite /28 |
| chrom/o | color /53, 235 | crani/o | cranium, skull /50, 209 |
| -cian | specialist /17 | crin/o | secretion /157 |
| -cide | killing; an agent that kills or destroys /123 | cry/o | cold /233 |
| | | crypt/o | hidden /192 |
| circum- | around, about /32 | cupr/o | copper /162 |
| cirrh/o | yellow /235 | cutane/o | skin /230 |
| -clasia | breaking /220 | cyan/o | blue /68, 235 |
| -clasis | breaking /220 | cycl/o | ciliary body /245 |
| -clast | breaker /220 | -cyesis | pregnancy /198 |
| clavicul/o | clavicle, collar bone /211 | cyst/o | sac, bladder /171 |
| -cle | little one /179 | cyt/o | cell /52 |
| clitor/o | clitoris /193 | -cyte | cell /19 |
| clitorid/o | clitoris /193 | -cytosis | slight increace in cell numbers /109 |
| -clysis | washing, irrigation /174 | | |
| -coccus | round bacteria(pl. cocci) /123 | **D** | |
| coccyg/o | coccyx /213 | dacry/o | tear; lacrimal sac /245 |
| cochle/o | cochlea /249 | dactyl/o | phalanx, finger, toe /209 |
| coit/o | sexual intercourse, coitus /196 | dacryocyst/o | lacrimal sac /245 |
| col/o | colon /85 | de- | down, from, lack of /28 |
| coll/a | glue /233 | deca- | ten, one tenth /36 |
| coll/o | glue /233 | deci- | ten, one tenth /36 |
| colon/o | colon /85 | dent/i | tooth /81 |
| colp/o | vagina /193 | dent/o | tooth /81 |
| com- | together, with /39 | derm/o | skin /230 |
| con- | together, with /39 | -derma | skin condition /232 |
| coni/o | dust /68 | dermat/o | skin /230 |
| conjunctiv/o | conjunctiva /244 | -desis | binding together /215 |
| contra- | against, opposite /28 | dextro- | right side /252 |
| copr/o | feces /89 | di- | two, double /36 |
| core/o | pupil /244 | dia- | through, across, complete /34, 92 |
| corne/o | cornea /244 | | |
| cortic/o | cortex /138, 155 | diaphor/o | profuse sweating /231 |

## Appendix 2  Medical Word Elements and Their Meanings

| | | | |
|---|---|---|---|
| diaphragmat/o | diaphragm /65 | erythr/o | red, red blood cell /107, 236 |
| -didymus | joining up of fetuses /198 | esophag/o | esophagus /85 |
| dipl/o | double /251 | -esthesia | feeling, sensation /143 |
| dips/o | thirst /177 | estr/o | female, woman /158 |
| dis- | free from, absence, separation /28 | -ette | little one /179 |
| dist/o | far /54 | eu- | good, normal /71 |
| dors/o | back /50, 210 | ex- | out, outside /32 |
| duoden/o | duodenum /85 | exo- | out, outside /32 |
| dur/o | hard, dura mater /138 | extra- | out, outside /34 |
| -dynia | pain /11 | **F** | |
| dys- | bad, difficult /39 | fasci/o | fascia /218 |
| **E** | | fec/o | feces /89 |
| ech/o | sound reverberation /102 | femor/o | femur, thigh bone /213 |
| -ectasia | dilation /70 | fibr/o | fiber /218 |
| -ectasis | dilation /70 | fibul/o | fibula, smaller lower leg bone /213 |
| -ectomy | surgical removal /14 | follicul/o | follicle /231 |
| electr/o | electricity /102 | -form | in the form of, resembling /19 |
| embol/o | embolus (pl. emboli) /105 | -fugal | away from, flee /159 |
| embry/o | embryo /196 | fung/i | fungus (pl. fungi) /122 |
| -emesis | vomiting /91 | **G** | |
| -emia | abnormal blood condition /109 | galact/o | milk /196 |
| en- | inside /32 | gamet/o | gamete, mature reproductive cell /192 |
| encephal/o | brain /139 | | |
| endo- | inside /32 | gangli/o | ganglion (pl. ganglia) /136 |
| enter/o | small intestine /85 | ganglion/o | ganglion (pl. ganglia) /136 |
| eosin/o | rose-colored /236 | gastr/o | stomach /85 |
| epi- | on, above /32 | -gen | origin, producer /123 |
| epididym/o | epididymis /189 | -genesis | formation /19 |
| epiglott/o | epiglottis /63 | -genic | producing; produced by /19 |
| episi/o | vulva /193 | genit/o | genitalia, reproductive organs /192 |
| epitheli/o | epithelium /52 | | |
| -er | one who /16 | ger/o | old age /252 |
| erythem/o | red /236 | geront/o | old age /252 |

| | | | |
|---|---|---|---|
| gingiv/o | gingiva, gum /82 | hypn/o | sleep /141 |
| glauc/o | gray /236 | hypo- | below, deficiency /30 |
| gli/o | glue; neuroglia /136 | hypophys/o | pituitary gland, hypophysis /156 |
| glomerul/o | glomerulus (pl. glomeruli) /172 | hyster/o | uterus, womb /194 |
| gloss/o | tongue /82 | **I** | |
| gluc/o | glucose /89 | -ia | condition /16 |
| glyc/o | glucose /89 | -ian | specialist /17 |
| gnath/o | jaw /82 | -iatrics | treatment /16 |
| gon/o | sex glands, genetalia /156 | -iatry | treatment /16 |
| gonad/o | sex glands (ovaries and testes) /155 | -ican | specialist /17 |
| | | idi/o | self, unknown /158 |
| -gram | record, image /14 | ile/o | ileum /87 |
| granul/o | granule /107 | ili/o | ilium, part of the hipbone /214 |
| -graph | instrument to record /14 | im- | not /29 |
| -graphy | process of recording /14 | immun/o | defense /119 |
| -gravida | pregnant woman /198 | in- | not /29 |
| gynec/o | female, woman /158,196 | -in | substance /160 |
| **H** | | in/o | fiber /218 |
| hecto- | hundred, one hundredth /36 | -ine | substance /160 |
| hem/o | blood /107 | infer/o | under /54 |
| hemat/o | blood /107 | infra- | downward, below /32 |
| hemi- | half, part /35 | inguin/o | inguina, groin /50 |
| hepat/o | liver /87 | insulin/o | insulin, pancreatic islets /158 |
| hetero- | different /30 | inter- | between /32 |
| hidr/o | sweat /231 | intra- | inside /35 |
| hist/o | tissue /52 | iod/(o) | iodine /162 |
| homeo- | same /30 | ir/o | iris /245 |
| homo- | same /30 | irid/o | iris /245 |
| hormon/o | hormone /158 | ischi/o | ischium, part of the hipbone /214 |
| humer/o | humerus /212 | -ism | condition of /17 |
| hyal/o | glassy, vitreous body /247 | -ist | specialist /17 |
| hydr/o | water, fluid /177 | -itis | inflammation /12 |
| hyper- | above, excessive, beyond /30 | | |

*Appendix 2  Medical Word Elements and Their Meanings*

**J**
| | |
|---|---|
| jaund/o | yellow /235 |
| jejun/o | jejunum /87 |

**K**
| | |
|---|---|
| kal/i | potassium /162 |
| kary/o | nucleus, kernel /53,108 |
| kerat/o | horny, cornea, horny layer of the skin /233,244 |
| kilo- | thousand, one thousandth /37 |
| -kinesia | movement /220 |
| kinesi/o | movement /141 |
| -kinesis | movement /141 |
| kyph/o | humped, curved /215 |

**L**
| | |
|---|---|
| labi/o | lip /81 |
| labyrinth/o | labyrinth /249 |
| lacrim/o | tear; lacrimal sac /245 |
| lact/o | milk /158,196 |
| lamino | lamina, the back of the vertebra /215 |
| lapar/o | abdomen /84 |
| laryng/o | larynx, voice box /63 |
| later/o | side /54 |
| leiomy/o | smooth muscle /218 |
| lept/o | thin, slender /139 |
| -let | little one /179 |
| leuk/o | white, white blood cell /108,235 |
| -lexia | word, phrase /143 |
| lien/o | spleen /120 |
| ligament/o | ligament /218 |
| -ling | young, small /179 |
| lingu/o | tongue /82 |
| lip/o | fat /90,233 |
| -listhesis | displacement, slipping /215 |
| -lith | calculus, stone /90 |
| lith/o | calculus, stone /90 |
| -lithiasis | formation of stones /174 |
| lob/o | lobe /65 |
| -logy | study of /17 |
| lord/o | bending inward /215 |
| lumb/o | lower back /50,210 |
| lymph/o | lymph /120 |
| lymphaden/o | lymph node /120 |
| lymphangi/o | lymphatic vessel /120 |
| -lysis | breaking down, separation /12,174 |

**M**
| | |
|---|---|
| macro- | big, huge /30 |
| mal- | bad /39 |
| -malacia | softening /220 |
| mamm/o | breast, mammary gland /194 |
| mandibul/o | mandible, lower jawbone /212 |
| -mania | obsession /143 |
| mast/o | breast, mammary gland /194 |
| maxill/o | maxilla, upper jaw bone /212 |
| meat/o | opening, meatus /172 |
| medi/o | middle, midline /54 |
| mediastin/o | mediastinum /66 |
| medull/o | medulla /136 |
| mega- | huge, great, million /30 |
| megal(o)- | huge, great, million /30 |
| -megaly | enlargement /12 |
| melan/o | black /236 |
| men/o | menstruation, menses /196 |
| mening/o | menginges /137 |
| meningi/o | meninges /137 |
| meta- | change, beyond /39 |
| metacarp/o | metacarpus, hand bones /212 |

| | | | |
|---|---|---|---|
| metatars/o | metatarsals, ankle /214 | obstetr/o | midwife, delivery /197 |
| -meter | instrument to measure /14 | ocul/o | eye /246 |
| -metry | process of measuring /14 | odont/o | tooth /81 |
| metr/(o) | uterus, womb /194 | -oid | resembling; derived from /19 |
| micro- | small /31 | -ole | little, small /179 |
| milli- | thousand, one thousandth /37 | oligo- | scanty, few /177 |
| mono- | one, only /36 | -oma | mass or swelling, tumor /12, 125 |
| morph/o | shape, form /52, 108 | omphal/o | navel, umbilicus /197 |
| multi- | many, plenty /37 | onc/o | tumor /124 |
| muscul/o | muscle /218 | onych/o | nail /231 |
| mut/a | change /124 | oophor/o | ovary /194 |
| my/o | muscle /218 | ophthalm/o | eye /246 |
| myc/o | fungus (pl. fungi) /122 | -opia | vision /247 |
| -mycosis | fungal infection /234 | -opsia | vision /247 |
| myel/o | spinal cord, bone marrow /137, 215 | -opsy | viewing /15 |
| | | opt/o | eye; vision /246 |
| myring/o | tympanic membrane /249 | optic/o | eye; vision /246 |
| myx/o | mucus /220 | or/o | mouth /82 |
| **N** | | -orexia | appetite /91 |
| narc/o | stupor; sleep; numbness /141 | orchi/o | testis, testicles /189 |
| nas/o | nose /63 | orchid/o | testis, testicles /189 |
| nat/o | birth /196 | orth/o | straight /68 |
| natr/o | sodium /162 | osche/o | scrotum /189 |
| neo- | new /32, 93 | -osis | abnormal condition /12 |
| nephr/o | kidney /172 | -osmia | smelling /70 |
| neur/o | nerve /137 | osse/o | bone /210 |
| neutr/o | neutral, neutrophil /108 | ossicul/o | ossicle, small bone /249 |
| noct/o | night /177 | oste/o | bone /210 |
| non- | not /29 | ot/o | ear, ear-like structure /249 |
| nucle/o | nucleus, kernel /53, 108 | -otia | ear condition /250 |
| nulli- | none, zero /199 | -ous | pertaining to /18 |
| nyct/o | night /251 | ov/i | egg, ovum /194 |
| **O** | | ovari/o | ovary /194 |
| o/o | egg, ovum /194 | ox/i | oxygen /69 |

## Appendix 2  Medical Word Elements and Their Meanings

| | | | |
|---|---|---|---|
| ox/o | oxygen /69 | phag/o | eating, swallowing /120 |
| oxy- | oxygen, quick, sharp, acid /160 | -phage | eating, swallowing /120 |
| **P** | | -phagia | condition of eating or swallowing /92 |
| pachy- | thick /234 | | |
| palat/o | palate roof of the mouth /82,212 | phak/o | lens /246 |
| palpebr/o | eyelid /244 | phalang/o | finger, toe, phalanx /209 |
| pan- | all /37 | phall/o | penis /189 |
| pancreat/o | pancreas /87 | pharyng/o | pharynx /64 |
| papill/o | nipple, nipple-like structure /194 | -phasia | speech /144 |
| para- | beside, near, abnormal /39,160 | -phil | one having affinity for something /110 |
| -para | woman who has given birth /199 | | |
| | | phleb/o | vein /106 |
| parathyroid/o | parathyroid gland /156 | -phobia | fear /144 |
| -paresis | slight paralysis /144 | phon/o | sound; voice /69 |
| -pareunia | sexual intercourse /199 | phosph/o | phosphorus /162 |
| -partum | birth /199 | phosphor/o | phosphorus /162 |
| patell/o | patella, kneecap /214 | phot/o | light /251 |
| -pathy | disease /12 | phren/o | diaphragm, mind /65 |
| pector/o | chest /66 | -physis | a growing /220 |
| ped/o | foot /210 | phyt/o | plant /122 |
| pelv/i | pelvis /50,210 | pil/o | hair /231 |
| pelv/o | pelvis /50,210 | pituitar/i | pituitary gland /156 |
| pen/o | penis /189 | placent/o | placenta /197 |
| -penia | deficiency /109 | -plasia | formation /125 |
| -pepsia | digestion /92 | -plasm | anything formed or molded /125 |
| per- | through /35 | -plasty | surgical repair /15,92 |
| peri- | around, about /32 | -plegia | paralysis /12,144 |
| pericardi/o | pericardium /102 | pleur/o | pleura /66 |
| perine/o | perineum /190 | -pnea | breathing /70 |
| peritone/o | peritoneum /87 | -pneic | breathing /70 |
| periton/o | peritoneum /87 | pneumat/o | air; lung /66 |
| -petal | toward, seek /160 | pneum/o | lung /66 |
| -pexy | surgical fixation /174 | pneumon/o | air; lung /66 |
| phac/o | lens /246 | pod/o | foot /210 |

| | | | |
|---|---|---|---|
| -poiesis | formation, production /174 | rachi/o | vertebral column, spine /216 |
| -poietin | substance to produce /174 | radi/o | radius, outer bone of the forearm; rays, X-rays /124,212 |
| poikil/o | varied, irregular /108 | | |
| poli/o | gray /236 | radicul/o | root of the spinal nerve /137 |
| poly- | many, plenty /37 | rect/o | rectum /88 |
| pont/o | pons /139 | ren/o | kidney /172 |
| post- | after, behind /33 | retin/o | retina /247 |
| poster/o | back, behind /54 | retro- | behind, backward /177 |
| -prandial | meal /92 | rhin/o | nose /63 |
| -praxia | action /144 | -rrhage | excessive discharge of blood /110 |
| pre- | before /33 | -rrhagia | excessive discharge of blood /110 |
| presby/ | old age /252 | -rrhaphy | surgical suture /175 |
| primi- | first, early /199 | -rrhea | flow, discharge /70 |
| -privia | deprivation, without /160 | -rrhexia | rupture /175 |
| pro- | before, in front /33 | -rrhexis | rupture /121,175 |
| proct/o | anus and rectum /87 | rub/o | red /236 |
| prostat/o | prostate gland /190 | **S** | |
| prote/o | protein /90 | sacchar/(o) | sugar /162 |
| proxim/o | near /54 | sacr/o | sacrum /214 |
| pseudo- | false /199 | salping/o | fallopian tube, oviduct; Eustachhian tube /194,249 |
| psych/o | mind /141 | | |
| -ptosis | dropping, downward displacement /12 | -salpinx | condition of fallopian tube /199 |
| | | sarc/o | flesh, connective tissue /125, 218 |
| -ptysis | spitting /70 | | |
| pulmon/o | lung /66 | scapul/o | scapula, shoulder blade /212 |
| pupill/o | pupil /244 | -schisis | fissure, split /216 |
| purpur/o | purple /236 | schiz/o | a split or division /141 |
| py/o | pus /69 | scler/o | sclera /247 |
| pyel/o | renal pelvis /172 | -sclerosis | hardening /110 |
| -pyesis | suppuration, pus /221 | scoli/o | curved, crooked /216 |
| pylor/o | pylorus /87 | -scope | instrument to view /15 |
| **Q** | | -scopy | process of viewing /15 |
| quadr- | four /36 | scrot/o | scrotum /189 |
| **R** | | seb/o | sebum /231 |

## Appendix 2  Medical Word Elements and Their Meanings

| | | | |
|---|---|---|---|
| semi- | half, part /35 | stern/o | sternum /212 |
| semin/(o) | semen, seed /190 | steth/o | chest /66 |
| sept/o | septum /102 | stomat/o | mouth /82 |
| sial/o | saliva, salivary glands and ducts /83 | -stomy | surgical creation of an opening or a communication /92 |
| sialoaden/o | alivary gland /83 | sub- | under, below /33 |
| sialoangi/o | salivary ducts /83 | sudor/o | sweat /231 |
| sider/o | iron /108,162 | supra- | above /33 |
| sigmoid/o | sigmoid colon /88 | sym- | together, with, same /39 |
| sinistro- | left side /252 | syn- | together, with, same /39 |
| sinus/o | sinus, cavity /64 | syndesm/o | ligament /218 |
| -sis | condition /17 | synovi/o | synovial membrane /218 |
| somat/o | body /53,142,158 | **T** | |
| -some | body /20 | tachy- | fast /103 |
| somn/o | sleep /141 | tars/o | tarsals, foot bone /214 |
| -spadia | scutting, tearing /192 | -taxia | order, coordination /144 |
| -spasm | sudden, involuntary contraction /13,70 | ten/o | tendon /219 |
| | | tendin/o | tendon /219 |
| sperm/o | sperm, semen /190 | terat/o | monster /197 |
| spermat/o | sperm, semen /190 | test/o | testis, testicles /189 |
| sphygm/o | pulse /103 | tetra- | four /36 |
| spin/o | spine, the column of back bone, spinal cord /50,137 | thalam/o | thalamus /139 |
| | | thec/o | sheath, meninges /137 |
| spir/o | breathing /69 | -therapy | treatment /125 |
| splen/o | spleen /120 | therm/o | heat /234 |
| spondyl/o | vertebrae /216 | thorac/o | thorax, chest /50,66 |
| squam/o | scale-like /233 | -thorax | chest condition /71 |
| staped/o | stapes /250 | thromb/o | thrombus, blood clotting /106 |
| staphyl/o | uvula /64 | thym/o | thymus gland /121 |
| -stasis | control; stoppage /110 | thyr/o | thyroid gland /156 |
| -static | inhibiting; an agent that inhibits the growth of an organism /123 | thyroid/o | thyroid gland /156 |
| | | tibi/o | tibia, shin /214 |
| steat/o | fat /90,233 | -tic | pertaining to /18 |
| -stenosis | constriction, narrowing /71 | toc/o | labor /158,197 |

· 309 ·

| | | | |
|---|---|---|---|
| -tome | instrument to cut /20,221 | -uria | urine, urine condition /175 |
| -tomy | surgical incision /15 | uter/o | uterus, womb /194 |
| ton/o | tone; tension /142 | uve/o | uvea /247 |
| tonsill/o | tonsils /121 | uvul/o | uvula /64 |
| tors/i | twisting /55 | **V** | |
| tox/o | poison, toxin /158 | vagin/o | vagina /193 |
| toxic/o | poison, toxin /158 | valv/o | valve /103 |
| trache/o | trachea, windpipe /64 | valvul/o | valve /103 |
| trans- | across, through /35,177 | varic/o | varicose, swollen and twisted veins /192 |
| tri- | three /36 | | |
| trich/o | hair /231 | vas/o | vessel; vas deferens /104,190 |
| trigon/o | trigone /172 | vascul/o | vessel /104 |
| -tripsy | crushing /175 | ven/o | vein /106 |
| -tropia | turning /247 | ventr/o | abdomen /50 |
| -tropin | hormone to stimulate /160 | ventricul/o | ventricle /103,139 |
| tubul/o | small tube, tubule /172 | venul/o | venule, small vein /106 |
| tympan/o | tympanic membrane or cavity /250 | vers/o | turning /55 |
| | | vertebr/o | vertebrae /216 |
| **U** | | vesic/o | sac; bladder /171 |
| -ule | little, small /179 | vesicul/o | seminal vesicle /190 |
| uln/o | ulna, inner bone of the forearm /212 | vestibul/o | vestibule /250 |
| ultra- | beyond, excessive /31 | vir/o | virus /122 |
| -um | structure, tissue /17 | viscer/o | viscera, internal organs /53 |
| umbilic/o | navel, umbilicus /50,197 | vitre/o | glassy; vitreous body /247 |
| un- | not, without /29 | vulv/o | vulva /193 |
| ungu/o | nail /231 | **X** | |
| uni- | one, only /36 | xanth/o | yellow /235 |
| ur/o | urine, urinary system /172 | xer/o | dry /234 |
| -uresis | urination, urine /175 | **Z** | |
| ureter/o | ureter /172 | zo/o | animal, life /192 |
| urethr/o | urethra /172 | | |

# Appendix 3  Keys to Exercises in Integrated Practice

## Chapter 1
Exercise 4
1. a  2. c  3. b  4. c  5. a  6. a  7. a  8. c  9. d  10. b

## Chapter 2
Exercise 11
1. c  2. a  3. b  4. c  5. d  6. d  7. d  8. d  9. d  10. d

Excercise 12

1. study of the liver
2. a medical professional specialized in liver diseases
3. pain of the liver
4. pain of the liver
5. enlargement of the liver
6. tumor of the liver
7. diseased condition of the liver
8. any disease of the liver
9. incision into the liver
10. removal of the liver
11. formation of the liver
12. (x-ray) image of the liver
13. procedure to record the image of the liver
14. surgical repair of the liver
15. liver cell
16. surgical puncture into the liver
17. hernia of the liver
18. inflammation of the liver
19. destruction of the liver cells
20. pertaining the liver

## Chapter 3
Exercise 10
1. c  2. d  3. b  4. d  5. d  6. a  7. b  8. d  9. c  10. d

Excercise 11

1. having no cells
2. pertaining to two cells

3. inside cells
4. outside cells
5. pertaining to different cells
6. pertaining to the same cell
7. above the cell
8. below the cell
9. between cells
10. inside the cell
11. pertaining to a single cell
12. pertaining to many cells
13. pertaining to all cells
14. around the cell
15. pertaining to many cells
16. before the cell
17. below the cell
18. across the cell
19. pertaining to three cells
20. pertaing to one cell

## Chapter 4
Exercise 9
1. a  2. b  3. d  4. d  5. d  6. c  7. c  8. b  9. c  10. b
Exercise 10
1. saggital   2. frontal   3. anterior   4. posterior   5. medial
6. proximal   7. distal   8. superficial   9. ventral   10. dorsal

## Chapter 5
Exercise 10
1. a  2. c  3. a  4. c  5. b  6. a  7. a  8. b
9. c  10. b  11. a  12. b  13. d  14. c  15. a
Exercise 11
1. cyanosis   2. dyspnea   3. hemoptysis   4. pneumothorax   5. hyperpnea
6. thoracalgia/stethalgia   7. orthopnea   8. atelectasis   9. dysphonia
10. bronchiectasis

## Chapter 6
Exercise 12
1. jejunal   2. pancreatic   3. esophageal   4. palatine   5. biliary
6. ileal   7. duodenal   8. salivary   9. choledochal   10. colonic
Exercise 13
1. h  2. q  3. d  4. o  5. s  6. m  7. t  8. b  9. k  10. i
11. f  12. p  13. e  14. j  15. a  16. r  17. c  18. g  19. n  20. l

# Appendix 3  Keys to Exercises in Integrated Practice

## Chapter 7
Exercise 10

1. d  2. f  3. b  4. h  5. s  6. a  7. c  8. l  9. q  10. o
11. t  12. n  13. p  14. j  15. i  16. r  17. e  18. m  19. g  20. k

## Chapter 8
Exercise 9

1. b  2. b  3. c  4. b  5. c  6. b  7. a  8. b  9. c  10. a
11. b  12. c  13. a  14. a  15. b

## Chapter 9
Exercise 10

1. thalamic  2. pontine  3. comatose  4. meningeal  5. cortical  6. psychotic
7. syncopic  8. ganglia  9. plexus/plexuses  10. stimuli  11. sulci  12. gyri

Exercise 11

1. a  2. c  3. b  4. b  5. b  6. a  7. d  8. a  9. b  10. c
11. b  12. c  13. a  14. c  15. a  16. d  17. c  18. a  19. b  20. d

## Chapter 10
Exercise 11

1. c  2. e  3. f  4. a  5. d  6. o  7. b  8. k
9. i  10. m  11. l  12. j  13. g  14. h  15. n

Exersise 12

1. adenohypophysis  2. hypophysitis  3. endocrinology  4. antidiuretic hormone
5. epinephrine  6. hyperpituitarism  7. epinephrectomy
8. thyroidoparathyroidectomy  9. oxytocin  10. hypothyroidism

## Chapter 11
Exercise 11

1. c  2. c  3. d  4. b  5. d  6. c  7. d  8. d
9. b  10. a  11. c  12. c  13. c  14. c  15. c

Exercise 12

1. urethrostenosis, urethroplasty
2. nephroptosis, nephropexy
3. nephroureterectomy

4. nephropelvotomy

5. dysuria, urethritis

## Chapter 12
Exercise 13

1. c   2. k   3. o   4. a   5. m   6. f   7. b   8. n
9. l   10. g   11. d   12. h   13. i   14. e   15. j

## Chapter 13
Exercise 12

1. b   2. d   3. d   4. d   5. b   6. a   7. d   8. b
9. b   10. a   11. c   12. d   13. c   14. a   15. b

## Chapter 14
Exercise 8

1. c   2. l   3. m   4. i   5. o   6. a   7. k   8. b
9. g   10. e   11. h   12. j   13. f   14. d   15. n

## Chapter 15
Exercise 10

1. keratotomy   2. papillary   3. blepharoptosis   4. ophthalmic
5. vitreous   6. otopyorrhea   7. dacryoadenitis   8. iridic
9. binocular   10. corneoscleral   11. cerumen   12. macula

Exercise 11

1. a   2. d   3. a   4. b   5. b   6. a   7. d   8. c   9. b   10. d
11. c   12. a   13. b   14. d   15. a   16. b   17. b   18. b   19. a   20. c